POCKET
WORLD
ATLAS

IN ASSOCIATION WITH
THE ROYAL GEOGRAPHICAL SOCIETY
WITH THE INSTITUTE OF BRITISH GEOGRAPHERS

CONTENTS

4–5   Flight Paths

6–7   International Organizations

8–24   Gazetteer of Nations

WORLD MAPS

I   World Maps – general reference

2–3   The Land Hemisphere 1:133.3M

4–5   The Water Hemisphere 1:133.3M

EUROPE

6–7   Europe 1:26.7M

8–9   Scandinavia and the Baltic Lands
           1:13.3M

10–11 British Isles 1:6.7M

12–13 France 1:6.7M

14–15 Germany and Benelux 1:6.7M

16–17 Central Europe 1:6.7M

18–19 Spain and Portugal 1:6.7M

20–21 Italy and the Adriatic 1:6.7M

22–23 Greece and the Balkans 1:6.7M

24–25 Eastern Europe 1:13.3M

ASIA

26–27 Asia 1:67M

28–29 Western Russia and Central
           Asia 1:26.7M

30–31 Eastern Siberia 1:26.7M

32–33 Japan 1:8.5M

34–35 China 1:26.7M

36–37 Philippines and Eastern Indonesia
           1:16.7M

Published in Great Britain in 2016 by Philip's,
a division of Octopus Publishing Group Limited
(www.octopusbooks.co.uk)
Carmelite House, 50 Victoria Embankment,
London EC4Y 0DZ
An Hachette UK Company (www.hachette.co.uk)

Copyright © 2016 Philip's

Cartography by Philip's

ISBN 978-1-84907-408-7

A CIP catalogue record for this book is available from
the British Library.

Printed in Hong Kong

Details of other Philip's titles and services can be found
on our website at: **www.philips-maps.co.uk**

Philip's World Atlases are published in association
with The Royal Geographical Society (with The
Institute of British Geographers).
   The Society was founded in 1830 and given a
Royal Charter in 1859 for 'the advancement of
geographical science'. Today it is a leading world
centre for geographical learning – supporting
education, teaching, research and expeditions, and
promoting public understanding of the subject.
   Further information about the Society and how to
join may be found on its website at: **www.rgs.org**

38–39	South-east Asia 1:16.7M
40–41	Eastern India, Bangladesh and Burma 1:13.3M
42–43	Western India, Pakistan and Sri Lanka 1:13.3M
44–45	Persian Gulf, Iran and Afghanistan 1:13.3M
46–47	The Middle East and Turkey 1:13.3M
48–49	Arabia and the Horn of Africa 1:20M

AFRICA

50–51	Africa 1:56M
52–53	North-west Africa 1:20M
54–55	North-east Africa 1:20M
56–57	Central Africa 1:20M
58–59	Southern Africa 1:20M

AUSTRALASIA

60–61	Australia 1:26.7M
62–63	South-east Australia 1:10.7M
64–65	New Zealand 1:8M
	Central and South-west Pacific 1:72M

NORTH AMERICA

66–67	North America 1:46.7M
68–69	Western Canada 1:20M
	Alaska 1:38M

70–71	Eastern Canada 1:20M
72–73	North-west USA 1:8M
74–75	North-central USA 1:8M
76–77	North-east USA 1:8M
78–79	South-west USA 1:8M
80–81	Southern USA 1:8M
82–83	South-east USA 1:8M
84–85	Mexico 1:20M
86–87	Caribbean and Central America 1:20M

SOUTH AMERICA

88–89	South America 1:46.7M
90–91	South America – North-west 1:21.3M
92–93	South America – North-east 1:21.3M
94–95	South America – South 1:21.3M

POLAR REGIONS

96	Antarctica 1:46.7M

INDEX

97–120	Index to World Maps
121	Time Zones

FLIGHT PATHS

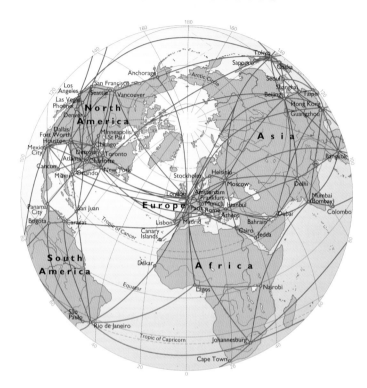

The flight paths shown on the maps above usually follow the shortest, most direct route from A to B, known as the *great-circle route*. A great circle is any circle that divides the globe into equal halves. Aircraft do not always fly along great-circle routes, however. Lack of search and rescue and emergency landing provisions, together with limits on fuel consumption and minimum flying altitudes, mean that commercial aircraft do not usually fly across Antarctica.

WORLD'S BUSIEST AIRPORTS

TOTAL NUMBER OF PASSENGERS IN MILLIONS (2013)

ATLANTA HARTSFIELD INTL. (ATL)	94.4
BEIJING CAPITAL INTL. (PEK)	83.7
LONDON HEATHROW (LHR)	72.4
TOKYO HANEDA (HND)	68.9
CHICAGO O'HARE INTL. (ORD)	66.9
LOS ANGELES INTL. (LAX)	66.7
DUBAI INTL. (DXB)	66.4
PARIS CHARLES DE GAULLE (CDG)	62.1
DALLAS FORT WORTH INTL. (DFW)	60.4

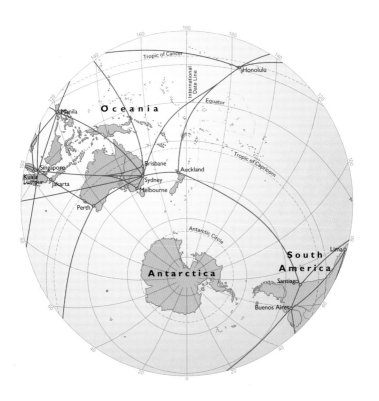

FLIGHT TIMES FROM LONDON

ATHENS	4hrs	05mins
AUCKLAND	24hrs	20mins
BANGKOK	14hrs	30mins
BUENOS AIRES	14hrs	20mins
HONG KONG	14hrs	10mins
LOS ANGELES	12hrs	00mins
MOSCOW	3hrs	50mins
MUMBAI (BOMBAY)	11hrs	15mins
NEW YORK	6hrs	50mins

FLIGHT TIMES FROM NEW YORK

FRANKFURT	8hrs	35mins
JOHANNESBURG	17hrs	45mins
MEXICO CITY	5hrs	45mins
PARIS	8hrs	15mins
ROME	9hrs	35mins
SANTIAGO	12hrs	55mins
SINGAPORE	23hrs	10mins
TOKYO	14hrs	35mins
VANCOUVER	7hrs	25mins

INTERNATIONAL ORGANIZATIONS

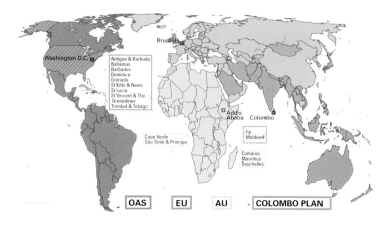

Brussels

Washington D.C.

Antigua & Barbuda
Bahamas
Barbados
Dominica
Grenada
St Kitts & Nevis
St Lucia
St Vincent & The
  Grenadines
Trinidad & Tobago

Addis Ababa

Colombo

Cape Verde
São Tomé & Príncipe

Fiji
Maldives

Comoros
Mauritius
Seychelles

OAS   **EU**   **AU**   **COLOMBO PLAN**

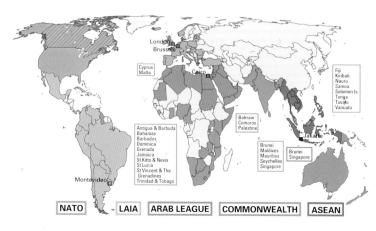

London
Brussels

Cyprus
Malta

Cairo

Fiji
Kiribati
Nauru
Samoa
Solomon Is.
Tonga
Tuvalu
Vanuatu

Antigua & Barbuda
Bahamas
Barbados
Dominica
Grenada
Jamaica
St Kitts & Nevis
St Lucia
St Vincent & The
  Grenadines
Trinidad & Tobago

Bahrain
Comoros
Palestine

Brunei
Maldives
Mauritius
Seychelles
Singapore

Brunei
Singapore

Jakarta

Montevideo

NATO   **LAIA**   **ARAB LEAGUE**   **COMMONWEALTH**   **ASEAN**

GLOSSARY OF ACRONYMS

ACP	African-Caribbean-Pacific	**LAIA**	Latin American Integration Association
APEC	Asia-Pacific Economic Co-operation	**NATO**	North Atlantic Treaty Organization
ASEAN	Association of South-east Asian Nations	**OAS**	Organization of American States
AU	African Union	**OECD**	Organization for Economic Co-operation and Development
EU	European Union	**OPEC**	Oganization for Petroleum Exporting Countries
G8	Group of 'Eight'		

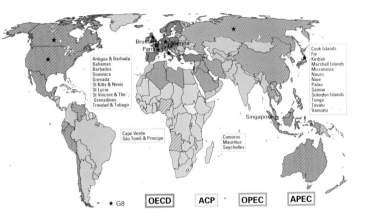

Antigua & Barbuda
Bahamas
Barbados
Dominica
Grenada
St Kitts & Nevis
St Lucia
St Vincent & The
Grenadines
Trinidad & Tobago

Brussels
Paris
Vienna

Cook Islands
Fiji
Kiribati
Marshall Islands
Micronesia
Nauru
Niue
Palau
Samoa
Solomon Islands
Tonga
Tuvalu
Vanuatu

Singapore

Cape Verde
São Tomé & Príncipe

Comoros
Mauritius
Seychelles

★ G8   OECD   ACP   OPEC   APEC

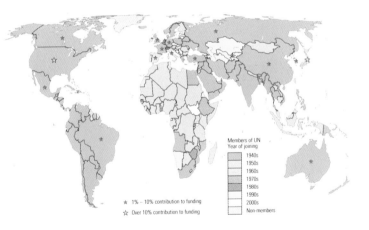

★ 1% – 10% contribution to funding
☆ Over 10% contribution to funding

Members of UN
Year of joining
1940s
1950s
1960s
1970s
1980s
1990s
2000s
Non-members

THE UNITED NATIONS

Created in 1945 to promote peace and co-operation and based in New York, the UN is the world's largest international organization. The UN budget for 2014–15 was around US$5.5 billion. Contributions are assessed by the members' ability to pay, with the maximum 22% of the total (the USA's share), and the minimum 0.001%. The 28-member European Union pays 35% of the budget. From the original 51, membership of the UN has now grown to 193. Recent additions include East Timor, Switzerland and South Sudan. There are only two independent states which are not members – Taiwan and the Vatican City.

GAZETTEER OF NATIONS

Listed below are the principal countries and territories of the world. The area figures give the total area of land, inland water and ice. The population figures are 2015 estimates

where available. The annual income is th Gross Domestic Product per capita in US dollar The figures are the latest available, usually 201 estimates.

AFGHANISTAN

AREA 652,090 sq km [251,772 sq mi]
POPULATION 32,564,000
CAPITAL Kabul
GOVERNMENT Islamic republic
ANNUAL INCOME US$1,900
CURRENCY Afghani = 100 puls

ALBANIA

AREA 28,748 sq km [11,100 sq mi]
POPULATION 3,029,000
CAPITAL Tirana
GOVERNMENT Multiparty republic
ANNUAL INCOME US$11,400
CURRENCY Lek = 100 qindars

ALGERIA

AREA 2,381,741 sq km [919,590 sq mi]
POPULATION 39,542,000
CAPITAL Algiers
GOVERNMENT Socialist republic
ANNUAL INCOME US$14,300
CURRENCY Algerian dinar = 100 centimes

ANDORRA

AREA 468 sq km [181 sq mi]
POPULATION 86,000
CAPITAL Andorra La Vella
GOVERNMENT Parliamentary co-princedom
ANNUAL INCOME US$37,200
CURRENCY Euro = 100 cents

ANGOLA

AREA 1,246,700 sq km [481,351 sq mi]
POPULATION 19,625,000
CAPITAL Luanda
GOVERNMENT Multiparty republic
ANNUAL INCOME US$7,200
CURRENCY Kwanza = 100 céntimos

ANTIGUA & BARBUDA

AREA 442 sq km [171 sq mi]
POPULATION 92,000
CAPITAL St John's
GOVERNMENT Constitutional monarchy
ANNUAL INCOME US$22,600
CURRENCY East Caribbean dollar = 100 cents

ARGENTINA

AREA 2,780,400 sq km [1,073,512 sq mi]
POPULATION 43,432,000
CAPITAL Buenos Aires
GOVERNMENT Federal republic
ANNUAL INCOME US$22,600
CURRENCY Argentine peso = 100 centavos

ARMENIA

AREA 29,800 sq km [11,506 sq mi]
POPULATION 3,056,000
CAPITAL Yerevan
GOVERNMENT Multiparty republic
ANNUAL INCOME US$7,400
CURRENCY Dram = 100 luma

AUSTRALIA

AREA 7,741,220 sq km [2,988,885 sq mi]
POPULATION 22,751,000
CAPITAL Canberra
GOVERNMENT Federal constitutional monarchy
ANNUAL INCOME US$46,400
CURRENCY Australian dollar = 100 cents

AUSTRIA

AREA 83,859 sq km [32,378 sq mi]
POPULATION 8,666,000
CAPITAL Vienna
GOVERNMENT Federal republic
ANNUAL INCOME US$46,400
CURRENCY Euro = 100 cents

AZERBAIJAN

AREA 86,600 sq km [33,436 sq mi]
POPULATION 9,781,000
CAPITAL Baku
GOVERNMENT Federal multiparty republic
ANNUAL INCOME US$17,600
CURRENCY Azerbaijani manat = 100 qapik

BAHAMAS

AREA 13,878 sq km [5,358 sq mi]
POPULATION 325,000 **CAPITAL** Nassau
GOVERNMENT Constitutional parliamentary
democracy
ANNUAL INCOME US$25,000
CURRENCY Bahamian dollar = 100 cents

BAHRAIN

AREA 694 sq km [268 sq mi]
POPULATION 1,347,000 **CAPITAL** Manama
GOVERNMENT Monarchy (emirate) with a
cabinet appointed by the Emir
ANNUAL INCOME US$51,700
CURRENCY Bahrain dinar = 1,000 fils

BANGLADESH

AREA 143,998 sq km [55,598 sq mi]
POPULATION 168,9581,000
CAPITAL Dhaka
GOVERNMENT Multiparty republic
ANNUAL INCOME US$3,400
CURRENCY Taka = 100 paisas

BARBADOS

AREA 430 sq km [166 sq mi]
POPULATION 291,000
CAPITAL Bridgetown
GOVERNMENT Parliamentary democracy
ANNUAL INCOME US$16,200
CURRENCY Barbados dollar = 100 cents

BELARUS

AREA 207,600 sq km [80,154 sq mi]
POPULATION 9,590,000
CAPITAL Minsk
GOVERNMENT Multiparty republic
ANNUAL INCOME US$18,200
CURRENCY Belarusian rouble = 100 kapyeyka

BELGIUM

AREA 30,528 sq km [11,787 sq mi]
POPULATION 11,324,000
CAPITAL Brussels
GOVERNMENT Federal constitutional monarchy
ANNUAL INCOME US$43,000
CURRENCY Euro = 100 cents

BELIZE

AREA 22,966 sq km [8,867 sq mi]
POPULATION 347,000
CAPITAL Belmopan
GOVERNMENT Constitutional monarchy
ANNUAL INCOME US$8,200
CURRENCY Belizean dollar = 100 cents

BENIN

AREA 112,622 sq km [43,483 sq mi]
POPULATION 10,449,000
CAPITAL Porto-Novo
GOVERNMENT Multiparty republic
ANNUAL INCOME US$1,900
CURRENCY CFA franc = 100 centimes

BHUTAN

AREA 47,000 sq km [18,147 sq mi]
POPULATION 742,000
CAPITAL Thimphu
GOVERNMENT Constitutional monarchy
ANNUAL INCOME US$7,600
CURRENCY Ngultrum = 100 chhertum

BOLIVIA

AREA 1,098,581 sq km [424,162 sq mi]
POPULATION 10,801,000 **CAPITAL** La Paz (seat of
govemment); Sucre (legal capital/seat of judiciary)
GOVERNMENT Multiparty republic
ANNUAL INCOME US$6,200
CURRENCY Boliviano = 100 centavos

BOSNIA-HERZEGOVINA

AREA 51,197 sq km [19,767 sq mi]
POPULATION 3,867,000
CAPITAL Sarajevo
GOVERNMENT Federal republic
ANNUAL INCOME US$9,800
CURRENCY Marka = 100 pfenniga

BOTSWANA

AREA 581,730 sq km [224,606 sq mi]
POPULATION 2,183,000
CAPITAL Gaborone
GOVERNMENT Multiparty republic
ANNUAL INCOME US$16,000
CURRENCY Pula = 100 thebe

BRAZIL

AREA 8,514,215 sq km [3,287,338 sq mi]
POPULATION 204,260,000
CAPITAL Brasília
GOVERNMENT Federal republic
ANNUAL INCOME US$16,100
CURRENCY Real = 100 centavos

BRUNEI

AREA 5,765 sq km [2,226 sq mi]
POPULATION 430,000
CAPITAL Bandar Seri Begawan
GOVERNMENT Constitutional sultanate
ANNUAL INCOME US$73,200
CURRENCY Bruneian dollar = 100 cents

BULGARIA

AREA 110,912 sq km [42,823 sq mi]
POPULATION 7,187,000
CAPITAL Sofia
GOVERNMENT Multiparty republic
ANNUAL INCOME US$17,900
CURRENCY Lev = 100 stotinki

BURKINA FASO

AREA 274,000 sq km [105,791 sq mi]
POPULATION 18,932,000
CAPITAL Ouagadougou
GOVERNMENT Multiparty republic
ANNUAL INCOME US$1,700
CURRENCY CFA franc = 100 centimes

BURMA (MYANMAR)

AREA 676,578 sq km [261,227 sq mi]
POPULATION 56,320,000 **CAPITAL** Yangôn
(Rangoon); Naypyidaw (administrative capital)
GOVERNMENT Parliamentary government
ANNUAL INCOME US$4,700
CURRENCY Kyat = 100 pyas

BURUNDI

AREA 27,834 sq km [10,747 sq mi]
POPULATION 10,742,000
CAPITAL Bujumbura
GOVERNMENT Republic
ANNUAL INCOME US$900
CURRENCY Burundi franc = 100 centimes

CABO VERDE

AREA 4,033 sq km [1,557 sq mi]
POPULATION 546,000
CAPITAL Praia
GOVERNMENT Multiparty republic
ANNUAL INCOME US$6,300
CURRENCY Cape Verde escudo = 100 centavos

CAMBODIA

AREA 181,035 sq km [69,898 sq mi]
POPULATION 15,709,000
CAPITAL Phnom Penh
GOVERNMENT Constitutional monarchy
ANNUAL INCOME US$3,300
CURRENCY Riel = 100 sen

CAMEROON

AREA 475,442 sq km [183,568 sq mi]
POPULATION 23,739,000
CAPITAL Yaoundé
GOVERNMENT Multiparty republic
ANNUAL INCOME US$3,000
CURRENCY CFA franc = 100 centimes

CANADA

AREA 9,970,610 sq km [3,849,653 sq mi]
POPULATION 35,100,000 **CAPITAL** Ottawa
GOVERNMENT Federal multiparty constitutional
monarchy
ANNUAL INCOME US$44,800
CURRENCY Canadian dollar = 100 cents

CENTRAL AFRICAN REPUBLIC

AREA 622,984 sq km [240,534 sq mi]
POPULATION 5,392,000
CAPITAL Bangui
GOVERNMENT Multiparty republic
ANNUAL INCOME US$600
CURRENCY CFA franc = 100 centimes

CHAD

AREA 1,284,000 sq km [495,752 sq mi]
POPULATION 11,631,000
CAPITAL Ndjamena
GOVERNMENT Multiparty republic
ANNUAL INCOME US$2,600
CURRENCY CFA franc = 100 centimes

CHILE

AREA 756,626 sq km [292,133 sq mi]
POPULATION 17,508,000
CAPITAL Santiago
GOVERNMENT Multiparty republic
ANNUAL INCOME US$23,000
CURRENCY Chilean peso = 100 centavos

CHINA

AREA 9,596,961 sq km [3,705,387 sq mi]
POPULATION 1,367,485,000
CAPITAL Beijing
GOVERNMENT Single-party Communist republic
ANNUAL INCOME US$12,900
CURRENCY Renminbi yuan = 10 jiao = 100 fen

COLOMBIA

AREA 1,138,914 sq km [439,735 sq mi]
POPULATION 46,737,000
CAPITAL Bogotá
GOVERNMENT Multiparty republic
ANNUAL INCOME US$13,400
CURRENCY Colombian peso = 100 centavos

COMOROS

AREA 2,235 sq km [863 sq mi]
POPULATION 781,000
CAPITAL Moroni
GOVERNMENT Multiparty republic
ANNUAL INCOME US$1,500
CURRENCY CFA franc = 100 centimes

CONGO

AREA 342,000 sq km [132,046 sq mi]
POPULATION 4,755,000
CAPITAL Brazzaville
GOVERNMENT Republic
ANNUAL INCOME US$6,600
CURRENCY CFA franc = 100 centimes

CONGO (DEM. REP. OF THE)

AREA 2,344,858 sq km [905,350 sq mi]
POPULATION 79,375,000
CAPITAL Kinshasa
GOVERNMENT Single-party republic
ANNUAL INCOME US$700
CURRENCY Congolese franc = 100 centimes

COSTA RICA

AREA 51,100 sq km [19,730 sq mi]
POPULATION 4,814,000
CAPITAL San José
GOVERNMENT Multiparty republic
ANNUAL INCOME US$14,900
CURRENCY Costa Rican colón = 100 céntimos

CROATIA

AREA 56,538 sq km [21,829 sq mi]
POPULATION 4,465,000
CAPITAL Zagreb
GOVERNMENT Multiparty republic
ANNUAL INCOME US$20,900
CURRENCY Kuna = 100 lipas

CUBA

AREA 110,861 sq km [42,803 sq mi]
POPULATION 11,031,000
CAPITAL Havana
GOVERNMENT Socialist republic
ANNUAL INCOME US$10,200
CURRENCY Cuban peso = 100 centavos

CYPRUS

AREA 9,251 sq km [3,572 sq mi]
POPULATION 1,189,000
CAPITAL Nicosia
GOVERNMENT Multiparty republic
ANNUAL INCOME US$30,800
CURRENCY Euro = 100 cents

CZECH REPUBLIC

AREA 78,866 sq km [30,450 sq mi]
POPULATION 10,645,000
CAPITAL Prague
GOVERNMENT Multiparty republic
ANNUAL INCOME US$29,900
CURRENCY Czech koruna = 100 haler

DENMARK

AREA 43,094 sq km [16,639 sq mi]
POPULATION 5,582,000
CAPITAL Copenhagen
GOVERNMENT Parliamentary monarchy
ANNUAL INCOME US$44,300
CURRENCY Danish krone = 100 øre

DJIBOUTI

AREA 23,200 sq km [8,958 sq mi]
POPULATION 828,000
CAPITAL Djibouti
GOVERNMENT Multiparty republic
ANNUAL INCOME US$3,100
CURRENCY Djiboutian franc = 100 centimes

DOMINICA

AREA 751 sq km [290 sq mi]
POPULATION 74,000
CAPITAL Roseau
GOVERNMENT Parliamentary democracy
ANNUAL INCOME US$10,800
CURRENCY East Caribbean dollar = 100 cents

DOMINICAN REPUBLIC

AREA 48,511 sq km [18,730 sq mi]
POPULATION 10,479,000
CAPITAL Santo Domingo
GOVERNMENT Multiparty republic
ANNUAL INCOME US$13,000
CURRENCY Dominican peso = 100 centavos

EAST TIMOR

AREA 14,874 sq km [5,743 sq mi]
POPULATION 1,231,000
CAPITAL Dili
GOVERNMENT Republic
ANNUAL INCOME US$4,900
CURRENCY US dollar = 100 cents

ECUADOR

AREA 283,561 sq km [109,483 sq mi]
POPULATION 15,868,000
CAPITAL Quito
GOVERNMENT Multiparty republic
ANNUAL INCOME US$11,200
CURRENCY US dollar = 100 cents

EGYPT

AREA 1,001,449 sq km [386,659 sq mi]
POPULATION 88,487,000
CAPITAL Cairo
GOVERNMENT Republic
ANNUAL INCOME US$10,900
CURRENCY Egyptian pound = 100 piastres

EL SALVADOR

AREA 21,041 sq km [8,124 sq mi]
POPULATION 6,141,000
CAPITAL San Salvador
GOVERNMENT Republic
ANNUAL INCOME US$8,000
CURRENCY US dollar = 100 cents

EQUATORIAL GUINEA

AREA 28,051 sq km [10,830 sq mi]
POPULATION 741,000
CAPITAL Malabo
GOVERNMENT Multiparty republic
ANNUAL INCOME US$32,300
CURRENCY CFA franc = 100 centimes

ERITREA

AREA 117,600 sq km [45,405 sq mi]
POPULATION 6,528,000
CAPITAL Asmara
GOVERNMENT Transitional government
ANNUAL INCOME US$1,200
CURRENCY Nakfa = 100 cents

ESTONIA

AREA 45,100 sq km [17,413 sq mi]
POPULATION 1,265,000
CAPITAL Tallinn
GOVERNMENT Multiparty republic
ANNUAL INCOME US$27,000
CURRENCY Euro = 100 cents

ETHIOPIA

AREA 1,104,300 sq km [426,370 sq mi]
POPULATION 99,466,000
CAPITAL Addis Ababa
GOVERNMENT Federation of nine provinces
ANNUAL INCOME US$1,600
CURRENCY Birr = 100 cents

FIJI

AREA 18,274 sq km [7,056 sq mi]
POPULATION 909,000
CAPITAL Suva
GOVERNMENT Republic
ANNUAL INCOME US$8,200
CURRENCY Fijian dollar = 100 cents

FINLAND

AREA 338,145 sq km [130,558 sq mi]
POPULATION 5,477,000
CAPITAL Helsinki
GOVERNMENT Multiparty republic
ANNUAL INCOME US$40,300
CURRENCY Euro = 100 cents

FRANCE

AREA 551,500 sq km [212,934 sq mi]
POPULATION 66,554,000
CAPITAL Paris
GOVERNMENT Multiparty republic
ANNUAL INCOME US$40,400
CURRENCY Euro = 100 cents

FRENCH GUIANA

AREA 90,000 sq km [34,749 sq mi]
POPULATION 250,000
CAPITAL Cayenne
GOVERNMENT Overseas department of France
ANNUAL INCOME US$8,300
CURRENCY Euro = 100 cents

FRENCH POLYNESIA

AREA 4,000 sq km [1,544 sq mi]
POPULATION 283,000
CAPITAL Papeete
GOVERNMENT French overseas territory
ANNUAL INCOME US$26,100
CURRENCY French Pacific franc = 100 cents

GABON

AREA 267,668 sq km [103,347 sq mi]
POPULATION 1,705,000
CAPITAL Libreville
GOVERNMENT Multiparty republic
ANNUAL INCOME US$22,900
CURRENCY CFA franc = 100 centimes

GAMBIA, THE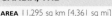

AREA 11,295 sq km [4,361 sq mi]
POPULATION 1,968,000
CAPITAL Banjul
GOVERNMENT Republic
ANNUAL INCOME US$1,600
CURRENCY Dalasi = 100 butut

GEORGIA

AREA 69,700 sq km [26,911 sq mi]
POPULATION 4,931,000
CAPITAL Tbilisi
GOVERNMENT Multiparty republic
ANNUAL INCOME US$7,700
CURRENCY Lari = 100 tetri

GERMANY

AREA 357,022 sq km [137,846 sq mi]
POPULATION 80,854,000
CAPITAL Berlin
GOVERNMENT Federal multiparty republic
ANNUAL INCOME US$45,900
CURRENCY Euro = 100 cents

GHANA

AREA 238,533 sq km [92,098 sq mi]
POPULATION 26,328,000
CAPITAL Accra
GOVERNMENT Republic
ANNUAL INCOME US$4,100
CURRENCY Cedi = 100 pesewas

GREECE

AREA 131,957 sq km [50,949 sq mi]
POPULATION 10,776,000
CAPITAL Athens
GOVERNMENT Multiparty republic
ANNUAL INCOME US$25,900
CURRENCY Euro = 100 cents

GREENLAND

AREA 2,175,600 sq km [838,999 sq mi]
POPULATION 58,000 **CAPITAL** Nuuk
GOVERNMENT Self-governing overseas
administrative division of Denmark
ANNUAL INCOME US$38,400
CURRENCY Danish krone = 100 øre

GRENADA

AREA 344 sq km [133 sq mi]
POPULATION 111,000
CAPITAL St George's
GOVERNMENT Constitutional monarchy
ANNUAL INCOME US$12,000
CURRENCY East Caribbean dollar = 100 cents

GUADELOUPE

AREA 1,705 sq km [658 sq mi]
POPULATION 449,000
CAPITAL Basse-Terre
GOVERNMENT French overseas territory
ANNUAL INCOME US$7,900
CURRENCY Euro = 100 cents

GUATEMALA

AREA 108,889 sq km [42,042 sq mi]
POPULATION 14,919,000
CAPITAL Guatemala City
GOVERNMENT Republic
ANNUAL INCOME US$7,500
CURRENCY US dollar; Quetzal = 100 centavos

GUINEA

AREA 245,857 sq km [94,925 sq mi]
POPULATION 11,780,000
CAPITAL Conakry
GOVERNMENT Multiparty republic
ANNUAL INCOME US$1,300
CURRENCY Guinean franc = 100 cauris

GUINEA-BISSAU

AREA 36,125 sq km [13,948 sq mi]
POPULATION 1,726,000
CAPITAL Bissau
GOVERNMENT Republic
ANNUAL INCOME US$1,400
CURRENCY CFA franc = 100 centimes

GUYANA

AREA 214,969 sq km [83,000 sq mi]
POPULATION 735,000
CAPITAL Georgetown
GOVERNMENT Multiparty republic
ANNUAL INCOME US$6,900
CURRENCY Guyanese dollar = 100 cents

HAITI

AREA 27,750 sq km [10,714 sq mi]
POPULATION 10,110,000
CAPITAL Port-au-Prince
GOVERNMENT Multiparty republic
ANNUAL INCOME US$1,800
CURRENCY Gourde = 100 centimes

HONDURAS

AREA 112,088 sq km [43,277 sq mi]
POPULATION 8,747,000
CAPITAL Tegucigalpa
GOVERNMENT Republic
ANNUAL INCOME US$4,700
CURRENCY Honduran lempira = 100 centavos

HUNGARY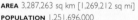

AREA 93,032 sq km [35,920 sq mi]
POPULATION 9,898,000
CAPITAL Budapest
GOVERNMENT Multiparty republic
ANNUAL INCOME US$24,900
CURRENCY Forint = 100 fillér

ICELAND

AREA 103,000 sq km [39,768 sq mi]
POPULATION 332,000
CAPITAL Reykjavik
GOVERNMENT Multiparty republic
ANNUAL INCOME US$43,600
CURRENCY Icelandic króna = 100 aurar

INDIA

AREA 3,287,263 sq km [1,269,212 sq mi]
POPULATION 1,251,696,000
CAPITAL New Delhi
GOVERNMENT Multiparty federal republic
ANNUAL INCOME US$5,900
CURRENCY Indian rupee = 100 paisa

INDONESIA

AREA 1,904,569 sq km [735,354 sq mi]
POPULATION 255,994,000
CAPITAL Jakarta
GOVERNMENT Multiparty republic
ANNUAL INCOME US$10,600
CURRENCY Indonesian rupiah = 100 sen

IRAN

AREA 1,648,195 sq km [636,368 sq mi]
POPULATION 81,824,000
CAPITAL Tehran
GOVERNMENT Islamic republic
ANNUAL INCOME US$17,100
CURRENCY Iranian rial = 100 dinars

IRAQ

AREA 438,317 sq km [169,235 sq mi]
POPULATION 37,056,000
CAPITAL Baghdad
GOVERNMENT Parliamentary democracy
ANNUAL INCOME US$14,600
CURRENCY Iraqi dinar

IRELAND

AREA 70,273 sq km [27,132 sq mi]
POPULATION 4,892,000
CAPITAL Dublin
GOVERNMENT Multiparty republic
ANNUAL INCOME US$49,200
CURRENCY Euro = 100 cents

ISRAEL

AREA 20,600 sq km [7,954 sq mi]
POPULATION 8,049,000
CAPITAL Jerusalem
GOVERNMENT Multiparty republic
ANNUAL INCOME US$32,700
CURRENCY New Israeli shekel = 100 agorat

ITALY

AREA 301,318 sq km [116,339 sq mi]
POPULATION 61,855,000
CAPITAL Rome
GOVERNMENT Multiparty republic
ANNUAL INCOME US$35,500
CURRENCY Euro = 100 cents

IVORY COAST (CÔTE D'IVOIRE)

AREA 322,463 sq km [124,503 sq mi]
POPULATION 23,295,000
CAPITAL Yamoussoukro
GOVERNMENT Multiparty republic
ANNUAL INCOME US$3,100
CURRENCY CFA franc = 100 centimes

JAMAICA

AREA 10,991 sq km [4,244 sq mi]
POPULATION 2,950,000
CAPITAL Kingston
GOVERNMENT Constitutional monarchy
ANNUAL INCOME US$8,600
CURRENCY Jamaican dollar = 100 cents

JAPAN

AREA 377,829 sq km [145,880 sq mi]
POPULATION 126,920,000
CAPITAL Tokyo
GOVERNMENT Constitutional monarchy
ANNUAL INCOME US$37,400
CURRENCY Yen = 100 sen

JORDAN

AREA 89,342 sq km [34,495 sq mi]
POPULATION 8,118,000
CAPITAL Amman
GOVERNMENT Constitutional monarchy
ANNUAL INCOME US$11,900
CURRENCY Jordanian dinar = 100 piastres

KAZAKHSTAN

AREA 2,724,900 sq km [1,052,084 sq mi]
POPULATION 18,157,000
CAPITAL Astana
GOVERNMENT Multiparty republic
ANNUAL INCOME US$24,000
CURRENCY Tenge = 100 tiyn

KENYA

AREA 580,367 sq km [224,080 sq mi]
POPULATION 45,925,000
CAPITAL Nairobi
GOVERNMENT Multiparty republic
ANNUAL INCOME US$3,100
CURRENCY Kenyan shilling = 100 cents

KIRIBATI

AREA 726 sq km [280 sq mi]
POPULATION 106,000
CAPITAL Tarawa
GOVERNMENT Republic
ANNUAL INCOME US$1,700
CURRENCY Australian dollar = 100 cents

KOREA, NORTH

AREA 120,538 sq km [46,540 sq mi]
POPULATION 24,983,000
CAPITAL Pyŏngyang
GOVERNMENT Single-party people's republic
ANNUAL INCOME US$1,800
CURRENCY North Korean won = 100 chon

KOREA, SOUTH

AREA 99,268 sq km [38,327 sq mi]
POPULATION 49,115,000
CAPITAL Seoul
GOVERNMENT Multiparty republic
ANNUAL INCOME US$35,300
CURRENCY South Korean won = 100 jeon

KOSOVO

AREA 10,887 sq km [4,203 sq mi]
POPULATION 1,871,000
CAPITAL Priština
GOVERNMENT Republic
ANNUAL INCOME US$8,000
CURRENCY Euro = 100 cents

KUWAIT

AREA 17,818 sq km [6,880 sq mi]
POPULATION 2,789,000
CAPITAL Kuwait City
GOVERNMENT Constitutional monarchy
ANNUAL INCOME US$71,000
CURRENCY Kuwaiti dinar = 1,000 fils

KYRGYZSTAN

AREA 199,900 sq km [77,181 sq mi]
POPULATION 5,665,000
CAPITAL Bishkek
GOVERNMENT Multiparty republic
ANNUAL INCOME US$3,400
CURRENCY Kyrgyzstani som = 100 tyiyn

LAOS

AREA 236,800 sq km [91,428 sq mi]
POPULATION 6,912,000
CAPITAL Vientiane
GOVERNMENT Single-party republic
ANNUAL INCOME US$5,000
CURRENCY Kip = 100 at

LATVIA

AREA 64,600 sq km [24,942 sq mi]
POPULATION 1,987,000
CAPITAL Riga
GOVERNMENT Multiparty republic
ANNUAL INCOME US$23,700
CURRENCY Euro = 100 cents

LEBANON

AREA 10,400 sq km [4,015 sq mi]
POPULATION 6,185,000
CAPITAL Beirut
GOVERNMENT Multiparty republic
ANNUAL INCOME US$18,000
CURRENCY Lebanese pound = 100 piastres

LESOTHO

AREA 30,355 sq km [11,720 sq mi]
POPULATION 1,948,000
CAPITAL Maseru
GOVERNMENT Constitutional monarchy
ANNUAL INCOME US$2,800
CURRENCY Loti = 100 lisente

LIBERIA

AREA 111,369 sq km [43,000 sq mi]
POPULATION 4,196,000
CAPITAL Monrovia
GOVERNMENT Multiparty republic
ANNUAL INCOME US$900
CURRENCY Liberian dollar = 100 cents

LIBYA

AREA 1,759,540 sq km [679,358 sq mi]
POPULATION 6,412,000
CAPITAL Tripoli
GOVERNMENT Transitional
ANNUAL INCOME US$15,700
CURRENCY Libyan dinar = 1,000 dirhams

LIECHTENSTEIN

AREA 160 sq km [62 sq mi]
POPULATION 38,000 **CAPITAL** Vaduz
GOVERNMENT Hereditary constitutional monarchy
ANNUAL INCOME US$89,400
CURRENCY Swiss franc = 100 centimes

LITHUANIA

AREA 65,200 sq km [25,174 sq mi]
POPULATION 2,884,000
CAPITAL Vilnius
GOVERNMENT Multiparty republic
ANNUAL INCOME US$27,100
CURRENCY Euro = 100 cents

LUXEMBOURG

AREA 2,586 sq km [998 sq mi]
POPULATION 570,000 **CAPITAL** Luxembourg
GOVERNMENT Constitutional monarchy
(Grand Duchy)
ANNUAL INCOME US$92,000
CURRENCY Euro = 100 cents

MACEDONIA (FYROM)

AREA 25,713 sq km [9,928 sq mi]
POPULATION 2,096,000
CAPITAL Skopje
GOVERNMENT Multiparty republic
ANNUAL INCOME US$13,300
CURRENCY Macedonian denar = 100 deni

MADAGASCAR

AREA 587,041 sq km [226,657 sq mi]
POPULATION 23,813,000
CAPITAL Antananarivo
GOVERNMENT Republic
ANNUAL INCOME US$1,400
CURRENCY Malagasy ariary = 5 iraimbilanja

MALAWI

AREA 118,484 sq km [45,747 sq mi]
POPULATION 17,965,000
CAPITAL Lilongwe
GOVERNMENT Multiparty republic
ANNUAL INCOME US$800
CURRENCY Malawian kwacha = 100 tambala

MALAYSIA

AREA 329,758 sq km [127,320 sq mi]
POPULATION 30,514,000 **CAPITAL** Kuala
Lumpur; Putrajaya (administrative capital)
GOVERNMENT Federal constitutional monarchy
ANNUAL INCOME US$24,700
CURRENCY Ringgit = 100 sen

MALDIVES

AREA 298 sq km [115 sq mi]
POPULATION 393,000
CAPITAL Malé
GOVERNMENT Republic
ANNUAL INCOME US$14,400
CURRENCY Rufiyaa = 100 laari

MALI

AREA 1,240,192 sq km [478,838 sq mi]
POPULATION 16,956,000
CAPITAL Bamako
GOVERNMENT Multiparty republic
ANNUAL INCOME US$1,700
CURRENCY CFA franc = 100 centimes

MALTA

AREA 316 sq km [122 sq mi]
POPULATION 414,000
CAPITAL Valletta
GOVERNMENT Multiparty republic
ANNUAL INCOME US$33,200
CURRENCY Euro = 100 cents

MARSHALL ISLANDS

AREA 181 sq km [70 sq mi]
POPULATION 72,000 **CAPITAL** Majuro
GOVERNMENT Constitutional government in
free association with the US
ANNUAL INCOME US$3,300
CURRENCY US dollar = 100 cents

MARTINIQUE

AREA 1,102 sq km [425 sq mi]
POPULATION 386,000
CAPITAL Fort-de-France
GOVERNMENT Overseas department of France
ANNUAL INCOME US$14,400
CURRENCY Euro = 100 cents

MAURITANIA

AREA 1,025,520 sq km [395,953 sq mi]
POPULATION 3,597,000
CAPITAL Nouakchott
GOVERNMENT Multiparty Islamic republic
ANNUAL INCOME US$4,300
CURRENCY Ouguiya = 5 khoums

MAURITIUS

AREA 2,040 sq km [788 sq mi]
POPULATION 1,340,000
CAPITAL Port Louis
GOVERNMENT Multiparty democracy
ANNUAL INCOME US$18,600
CURRENCY Mauritian rupee = 100 cents

MEXICO

AREA 1,958,201 sq km [756,061 sq mi]
POPULATION 121,737,000
CAPITAL Mexico City
GOVERNMENT Federal republic
ANNUAL INCOME US$17,900
CURRENCY Mexican peso = 100 centavos

MICRONESIA, FED. STATES OF

AREA 702 sq km [271 sq mi]
POPULATION 105,000 **CAPITAL** Palikir
GOVERNMENT Constitutional government in
free association with the US
ANNUAL INCOME US$3,000
CURRENCY US dollar = 100 cents

MOLDOVA

AREA 33,851 sq km [13,070 sq mi]
POPULATION 3,547,000
CAPITAL Chișinău
GOVERNMENT Multiparty republic
ANNUAL INCOME US$5,000
CURRENCY Moldovan leu = 100 bani

MONACO

AREA 1 sq km [0.4 sq mi]
POPULATION 31,000
CAPITAL Monaco
GOVERNMENT Constitutional monarchy
ANNUAL INCOME US$78,700
CURRENCY Euro = 100 cents

MONGOLIA

AREA 1,566,500 sq km [604,826 sq mi]
POPULATION 2,993,000
CAPITAL Ulan Bator
GOVERNMENT Multiparty republic
ANNUAL INCOME US$11,900
CURRENCY Tögrög = 100 möngös

MONTENEGRO

AREA 14,026 sq km [5,415 sq mi]
POPULATION 647,000
CAPITAL Podgorica
GOVERNMENT Republic
ANNUAL INCOME US$15,000
CURRENCY Euro = 100 cents

MOROCCO

AREA 446,550 sq km [172,413 sq mi]
POPULATION 33,323,000
CAPITAL Rabat
GOVERNMENT Constitutional monarchy
ANNUAL INCOME US$7,600
CURRENCY Moroccan dirham = 100 centimes

MOZAMBIQUE

AREA 801,590 sq km [309,494 sq mi]
POPULATION 25,303,000
CAPITAL Maputo
GOVERNMENT Multiparty republic
ANNUAL INCOME US$1,200
CURRENCY Metical = 100 centavos

NAMIBIA

AREA 824,292 sq km [318,259 sq mi]
POPULATION 2,212,000
CAPITAL Windhoek
GOVERNMENT Multiparty republic
ANNUAL INCOME US$10,800
CURRENCY Namibian dollar = 100 cents

NAURU

AREA 21 sq km [8 sq mi]
POPULATION 10,000
CAPITAL Yaren
GOVERNMENT Republic
ANNUAL INCOME US$5,000
CURRENCY Australian dollar = 100 cents

NEPAL

AREA 147,181 sq km [56,827 sq mi]
POPULATION 31,551,000
CAPITAL Katmandu
GOVERNMENT Multiparty republic
ANNUAL INCOME US$2,400
CURRENCY Nepalese rupee = 100 paisa

NETHERLANDS

AREA 41,526 sq km [16,033 sq mi]
POPULATION 16,948,000 **CAPITAL** Amsterdam;
The Hague (seat of government)
GOVERNMENT Constitutional monarchy
ANNUAL INCOME US$47,400
CURRENCY Euro = 100 cents

NEW CALEDONIA

AREA 18,575 sq km [7,172 sq mi]
POPULATION 272,000
CAPITAL Nouméa
GOVERNMENT French overseas territory
ANNUAL INCOME US$38,800
CURRENCY French Pacific franc = 100 cents

NEW ZEALAND

AREA 270,534 sq km [104,453 sq mi]
POPULATION 4,438,000
CAPITAL Wellington
GOVERNMENT Constitutional monarchy
ANNUAL INCOME US$36,200
CURRENCY New Zealand dollar = 100 cents

NICARAGUA

AREA 129,494 sq km [50,193 sq mi]
POPULATION 5,908,000 **CAPITAL** Managua
GOVERNMENT Multiparty republic
ANNUAL INCOME US$4,700
CURRENCY Córdoba oro (gold córdoba) =
100 centavos

NIGER

AREA 1,267,000 sq km [489,189 sq mi]
POPULATION 18,046,000
CAPITAL Niamey
GOVERNMENT Multiparty republic
ANNUAL INCOME US$1,000
CURRENCY CFA franc = 100 centimes

NIGERIA

AREA 923,768 sq km [356,667 sq mi]
POPULATION 181,562,000
CAPITAL Abuja
GOVERNMENT Federal multiparty republic
ANNUAL INCOME US$6,000
CURRENCY Naira = 100 kobo

NORWAY

AREA 323,877 sq km [125,049 sq mi]
POPULATION 5,208,000
CAPITAL Oslo
GOVERNMENT Constitutional monarchy
ANNUAL INCOME US$66,900
CURRENCY Norwegian krone = 100 ore

OMAN

AREA 309,500 sq km [119,498 sq mi]
POPULATION 3,287,000 **CAPITAL** Muscat
GOVERNMENT Monarchy with consultative
council
ANNUAL INCOME US$39,700
CURRENCY Omani rial = 100 baisas

PAKISTAN

AREA 796,095 sq km [307,372 sq mi]
POPULATION 199,086,000
CAPITAL Islamabad
GOVERNMENT Federal republic
ANNUAL INCOME US$4,700
CURRENCY Pakistani rupee = 100 paisa

PANAMA

AREA 75,517 sq km [29,157 sq mi]
POPULATION 3,657,000
CAPITAL Panamá
GOVERNMENT Multiparty republic
ANNUAL INCOME US$19,500
CURRENCY US dollar; Balboa = 100 centésimos

PAPUA NEW GUINEA

AREA 462,840 sq km [178,703 sq mi]
POPULATION 6,672,000
CAPITAL Port Moresby
GOVERNMENT Constitutional monarchy
ANNUAL INCOME US$2,400
CURRENCY Kina = 100 toea

PARAGUAY

AREA 406,752 sq km [157,047 sq mi]
POPULATION 6,783,000
CAPITAL Asunción
GOVERNMENT Multiparty republic
ANNUAL INCOME US$8,400
CURRENCY Guaraní = 100 céntimos

PERU

AREA 1,285,216 sq km [496,222 sq mi]
POPULATION 30,445,000
CAPITAL Lima
GOVERNMENT Constitutional republic
ANNUAL INCOME US$11,800
CURRENCY Nuevo sol = 100 centimos

PHILIPPINES

AREA 300,000 sq km [115,830 sq mi]
POPULATION 100,998,000
CAPITAL Manila
GOVERNMENT Multiparty republic
ANNUAL INCOME US$7,000
CURRENCY Philippine peso = 100 centavos

POLAND

AREA 323,250 sq km [124,807 sq mi]
POPULATION 38,562,000
CAPITAL Warsaw
GOVERNMENT Multiparty republic
ANNUAL INCOME US$25,100
CURRENCY Zloty = 100 groszy

PORTUGAL

AREA 88,797 sq km [34,285 sq mi]
POPULATION 10,825,000
CAPITAL Lisbon
GOVERNMENT Multiparty republic
ANNUAL INCOME US$27,000
CURRENCY Euro = 100 cents

PUERTO RICO

AREA 8,875 sq km [3,427 sq mi]
POPULATION 3,598,000
CAPITAL San Juan
GOVERNMENT Commonwealth of the US
ANNUAL INCOME US$28,500
CURRENCY US dollar = 100 cents

QATAR

AREA 11,000 sq km [4,247 sq mi]
POPULATION 2,195,000
CAPITAL Doha
GOVERNMENT Constitutional absolute monarchy
ANNUAL INCOME US$143,400
CURRENCY Qatari riyal = 100 dirhams

RÉUNION

AREA 2,510 sq km [969 sq mi]
POPULATION 841,000
CAPITAL St-Denis
GOVERNMENT Overseas department of France
ANNUAL INCOME US$6,200
CURRENCY Euro = 100 cents

ROMANIA

AREA 238,391 sq km [92,043 sq mi]
POPULATION 21,666,000
CAPITAL Bucharest
GOVERNMENT Multiparty republic
ANNUAL INCOME US$19,700
CURRENCY Leu = 100 bani

RUSSIA

AREA 17,075,400 sq km [6,592,812 sq mi]
POPULATION 142,424,000
CAPITAL Moscow
GOVERNMENT Federal multiparty republic
ANNUAL INCOME US$24,800
CURRENCY Russian ruble = 100 kopeks

RWANDA

AREA 26,338 sq km [10,169 sq mi]
POPULATION 12,662,000
CAPITAL Kigali
GOVERNMENT Republic
ANNUAL INCOME US$1,700
CURRENCY Rwandan franc = 100 centimes

ST KITTS & NEVIS

AREA 261 sq km [101 sq mi]
POPULATION 52,000
CAPITAL Basseterre
GOVERNMENT Constitutional monarchy
ANNUAL INCOME US$21,100
CURRENCY East Caribbean dollar = 100 cents

ST LUCIA

AREA 539 sq km [208 sq mi]
POPULATION 164,000
CAPITAL Castries
GOVERNMENT Parliamentary democracy
ANNUAL INCOME US$11,600
CURRENCY East Caribbean dollar = 100 cents

ST VINCENT & THE GRENADINES

AREA 388 sq km [150 sq mi]
POPULATION 103,000
CAPITAL Kingstown
GOVERNMENT Parliamentary democracy
ANNUAL INCOME US$10,800
CURRENCY East Caribbean dollar = 100 cents

SAMOA

AREA 2,831 sq km [1,093 sq mi]
POPULATION 198,000
CAPITAL Apia
GOVERNMENT Parliamentary democracy
ANNUAL INCOME US$5,200
CURRENCY Samoan dollar = 100 sene

SAN MARINO

AREA 61 sq km [24 sq mi]
POPULATION 33,000
CAPITAL San Marino
GOVERNMENT Independent republic
ANNUAL INCOME US$60,700
CURRENCY Euro = 100 cents

SÃO TOMÉ & PRÍNCIPE

AREA 964 sq km [372 sq mi]
POPULATION 194,000
CAPITAL São Tomé
GOVERNMENT Republic
ANNUAL INCOME US$3,200
CURRENCY Dobra = 100 cêntimos

SAUDI ARABIA

AREA 2,149,690 sq km [829,995 sq mi]
POPULATION 27,752,000 **CAPITAL** Riyadh
GOVERNMENT Absolute monarchy with
consultative assembly
ANNUAL INCOME US$52,200
CURRENCY Saudi riyal = 100 halalas

SENEGAL

AREA 196,722 sq km [75,954 sq mi]
POPULATION 13,976,000
CAPITAL Dakar
GOVERNMENT Multiparty republic
ANNUAL INCOME US$2,300
CURRENCY CFA franc = 100 centimes

SERBIA

AREA 77,474 sq km [29,913 sq mi]
POPULATION 7,177,000
CAPITAL Belgrade
GOVERNMENT Republic
ANNUAL INCOME US$13,300
CURRENCY New dinar = 100 paras

SEYCHELLES

AREA 455 sq km [176 sq mi]
POPULATION 92,000
CAPITAL Victoria
GOVERNMENT Multiparty republic
ANNUAL INCOME US$25,600
CURRENCY Seychelles rupee = 100 cents

SIERRA LEONE

AREA 71,740 sq km [27,699 sq mi]
POPULATION 5,879,000
CAPITAL Freetown
GOVERNMENT Single-party republic
ANNUAL INCOME US$2,000
CURRENCY Leone = 100 cents

SINGAPORE

AREA 683 sq km [264 sq mi]
POPULATION 5,674,000
CAPITAL Singapore City
GOVERNMENT Multiparty republic
ANNUAL INCOME US$82,800
CURRENCY Singapore dollar = 100 cents

SLOVAK REPUBLIC

AREA 49,012 sq km [18,924 sq mi]
POPULATION 5,445,000
CAPITAL Bratislava
GOVERNMENT Multiparty republic
ANNUAL INCOME US$28,200
CURRENCY Euro = 100 cents

SLOVENIA

AREA 20,256 sq km [7,821 sq mi]
POPULATION 1,983,000
CAPITAL Ljubljana
GOVERNMENT Multiparty republic
ANNUAL INCOME US$29,700
CURRENCY Euro = 100 cents

SOLOMON ISLANDS

AREA 28,896 sq km [11,157 sq mi]
POPULATION 622,000
CAPITAL Honiara
GOVERNMENT Parliamentary democracy
ANNUAL INCOME US$1,900
CURRENCY Solomon Islands dollar = 100 cents

SOMALIA

AREA 637,657 sq km [246,199 sq mi]
POPULATION 10,616,000 **CAPITAL** Mogadishu
GOVERNMENT Single-party republic, military dominated
ANNUAL INCOME US$600
CURRENCY Somali shilling = 100 cents

SOUTH AFRICA

AREA 1,221,037 sq km [471,442 sq mi]
POPULATION 53,676,000 **CAPITAL** Cape Town (legislative); Pretoria/Tshwane (administrative); Bloemfontein (judiciary) **GOVERNMENT** Multiparty republic **ANNUAL INCOME** US$13,000
CURRENCY Rand = 100 cents

SPAIN

AREA 497,548 sq km [192,103 sq mi]
POPULATION 48,146,000
CAPITAL Madrid
GOVERNMENT Constitutional monarchy
ANNUAL INCOME US$33,700
CURRENCY Euro = 100 cents

SRI LANKA

AREA 65,610 sq km [25,332 sq mi]
POPULATION 22,053,000
CAPITAL Colombo
GOVERNMENT Multiparty republic
ANNUAL INCOME US$10,400
CURRENCY Sri Lankan rupee = 100 cents

SUDAN

AREA 1,886,086 sq km [728,222 sq mi]
POPULATION 36,109,000 **CAPITAL** Khartoum
GOVERNMENT Federal presidential democratic republic
ANNUAL INCOME US$4,300
CURRENCY Sudanese pound = 100 piastres

SUDAN, SOUTH

AREA 619,745 sq km [239,285 sq mi]
POPULATION 12,043,000
CAPITAL Juba
GOVERNMENT Republic
ANNUAL INCOME US$2,300
CURRENCY South Sudanese pound = 100 piastres

SURINAME

AREA 163,265 sq km [63,037 sq mi]
POPULATION 580,000
CAPITAL Paramaribo
GOVERNMENT Multiparty republic
ANNUAL INCOME US$16,600
CURRENCY Surinamese dollar = 100 cents

SWAZILAND

AREA 17,364 sq km [6,704 sq mi]
POPULATION 1,436,000
CAPITAL Mbabane
GOVERNMENT Monarchy
ANNUAL INCOME US$7,800
CURRENCY Lilangeni = 100 cents

SWEDEN

AREA 449,964 sq km [173,731 sq mi]
POPULATION 9,802,000
CAPITAL Stockholm
GOVERNMENT Constitutional monarchy
ANNUAL INCOME US$46,000
CURRENCY Swedish krona = 100 öre

SWITZERLAND

AREA 41,284 sq km [15,940 sq mi]
POPULATION 8,122,000
CAPITAL Bern
GOVERNMENT Federal republic
ANNUAL INCOME US$58,100
CURRENCY Swiss franc = 100 centimes

SYRIA

AREA 185,180 sq km [71,498 sq mi]
POPULATION 17,065,000
CAPITAL Damascus
GOVERNMENT Multiparty republic
ANNUAL INCOME US$5,100
CURRENCY Syrian pound = 100 piastres

TAIWAN

AREA 36,000 sq km [13,900 sq mi]
POPULATION 23,415,000
CAPITAL Taipei
GOVERNMENT Unitary multiparty republic
ANNUAL INCOME US$45,900
CURRENCY New Taiwan dollar = 100 cents

TAJIKISTAN

AREA 143,100 sq km [55,521 sq mi]
POPULATION 8,192,000
CAPITAL Dushanbe
GOVERNMENT Republic
ANNUAL INCOME US$2,700
CURRENCY Somoni = 100 dirams

TANZANIA

AREA 945,090 sq km [364,899 sq mi]
POPULATION 51,046,000
CAPITAL Dodoma
GOVERNMENT Multiparty republic
ANNUAL INCOME US$2,700
CURRENCY Tanzanian shilling = 100 cents

THAILAND

AREA 513,115 sq km [198,114 sq mi]
POPULATION 67,976,000
CAPITAL Bangkok
GOVERNMENT Constitutional monarchy
ANNUAL INCOME US$14,400
CURRENCY Baht = 100 satang

TOGO

AREA 56,785 sq km [21,925 sq mi]
POPULATION 7,552,000
CAPITAL Lomé
GOVERNMENT Multiparty republic
ANNUAL INCOME US$14,000
CURRENCY CFA franc = 100 centimes

TONGA

AREA 650 sq km [251 sq mi]
POPULATION 107,000
CAPITAL Nuku'alofa
GOVERNMENT Hereditary constitutional monarchy
ANNUAL INCOME US$4,900
CURRENCY Pa'anga = 100 seniti

TRINIDAD & TOBAGO

AREA 5,130 sq km [1,981 sq mi]
POPULATION 1,222,000
CAPITAL Port of Spain
GOVERNMENT Parliamentary democracy
ANNUAL INCOME US$32,100
CURRENCY Trinidad & Tobago dollar = 100 cents

TUNISIA

AREA 163,610 sq km [63,170 sq mi]
POPULATION 11,037,000
CAPITAL Tunis
GOVERNMENT Multiparty republic
ANNUAL INCOME US$11,300
CURRENCY Tunisian dinar = 1,000 millimes

TURKEY

AREA 774,815 sq km [299,156 sq mi]
POPULATION 79,414,000
CAPITAL Ankara
GOVERNMENT Multiparty republic
ANNUAL INCOME US$19,600
CURRENCY New Turkish lira = 100 kurus

TURKMENISTAN

AREA 488,100 sq km [188,455 sq mi]
POPULATION 5,231,000
CAPITAL Ashkhabad
GOVERNMENT Single-party republic
ANNUAL INCOME US$14,200
CURRENCY Turkmen manat = 100 tenge

TUVALU

AREA 26 sq km [10 sq mi]
POPULATION 11,000 **CAPITAL** Fongafale
GOVERNMENT Constitutional monarchy with parliamentary democracy
ANNUAL INCOME US$3,300
CURRENCY Australian dollar; Tuvaluan dollar

UGANDA

AREA 241,038 sq km [93,065 sq mi]
POPULATION 37,102,000
CAPITAL Kampala
GOVERNMENT Republic
ANNUAL INCOME US$2,000
CURRENCY Ugandan shilling = 100 cents

UKRAINE

AREA 603,700 sq km [233,089 sq mi]
POPULATION 44,429,000
CAPITAL Kiev
GOVERNMENT Multiparty republic
ANNUAL INCOME US$8,700
CURRENCY Hryvnia = 100 kopiykas

UNITED ARAB EMIRATES

AREA 83,600 sq km [32,278 sq mi]
POPULATION 5,780,000 **CAPITAL** Abu Dhabi
GOVERNMENT Federation of seven emirates, each with its own government
ANNUAL INCOME US$64,500
CURRENCY Dirham = 100 fils

UNITED KINGDOM

AREA 241,857 sq km [93,381 sq mi]
POPULATION 64,088,000
CAPITAL London
GOVERNMENT Constitutional monarchy
ANNUAL INCOME US$39,500
CURRENCY Pound sterling = 100 pence

UNITED STATES OF AMERICA

AREA 9,629,091 sq km [3,717,792 sq mi]
POPULATION 321,369,000
CAPITAL Washington, DC
GOVERNMENT Federal republic
ANNUAL INCOME US$54,600
CURRENCY US dollar = 100 cents

URUGUAY

AREA 175,016 sq km [67,574 sq mi]
POPULATION 3,342,000
CAPITAL Montevideo
GOVERNMENT Multiparty republic
ANNUAL INCOME US$20,600
CURRENCY Uruguayan peso = 100 centésimos

UZBEKISTAN

AREA 447,400 sq km [172,741 sq mi]
POPULATION 29,200,000
CAPITAL Tashkent
GOVERNMENT Socialist republic
ANNUAL INCOME US$5,600
CURRENCY Uzbekistani sum = 100 tiyin

VANUATU

AREA 12,189 sq km [4,706 sq mi]
POPULATION 272,000
CAPITAL Port-Vila
GOVERNMENT Parliamentary republic
ANNUAL INCOME US$2,600
CURRENCY Vatu

VENEZUELA

AREA 912,050 sq km [352,143 sq mi]
POPULATION 29,275,000
CAPITAL Caracas
GOVERNMENT Federal republic
ANNUAL INCOME US$17,700
CURRENCY Bolívar = 100 céntimos

VIETNAM

AREA 331,689 sq km [128,065 sq mi]
POPULATION 94,349,000
CAPITAL Hanoi
GOVERNMENT Socialist republic
ANNUAL INCOME US$5,600
CURRENCY Dong = 10 hao = 100 xu

YEMEN

AREA 527,968 sq km [203,848 sq mi]
POPULATION 26,737,000
CAPITAL Sana'
GOVERNMENT Multiparty republic
ANNUAL INCOME US$3,800
CURRENCY Yemeni rial = 100 fils

ZAMBIA

AREA 752,618 sq km [290,586 sq mi]
POPULATION 15,066,000
CAPITAL Lusaka
GOVERNMENT Multiparty republic
ANNUAL INCOME US$4,100
CURRENCY Zambian kwacha = 100 ngwee

ZIMBABWE

AREA 390,757 sq km [150,871 sq mi]
POPULATION 14,230,000
CAPITAL Harare
GOVERNMENT Multiparty republic
ANNUAL INCOME US$2,000
CURRENCY multiple currencies

WORLD MAPS – GENERAL REFERENCE

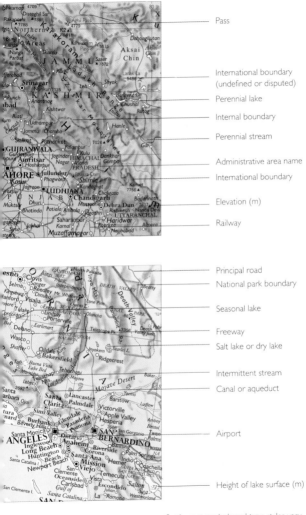

- Pass
- International boundary (undefined or disputed)
- Perennial lake
- Internal boundary
- Perennial stream
- Administrative area name
- International boundary
- Elevation (m)
- Railway

- Principal road
- National park boundary
- Seasonal lake
- Freeway
- Salt lake or dry lake
- Intermittent stream
- Canal or aqueduct
- Airport
- Height of lake surface (m)

Settlements ■ ● ◉ ◎ ○ ○

Capital cities have red infills

Settlement symbols and type styles vary according to the scale of each map and indicate the importance of towns rather than specific population figures.

3

Capital cities have red infills

The maps have been constructed on an Oblique Azimuthal Equidistant projection, on which all distances measured through the centre point are true to scale. The green lines are drawn at 5,000, 10,000 and 15,000 km from the central city.

PROJECTION CENTRED ON TOKYO

PROJECTION CENTRED ON MEXICO CITY

Projection: Oblique Azimuthal Equidistant

COPYRIGHT PHILIP'S

5

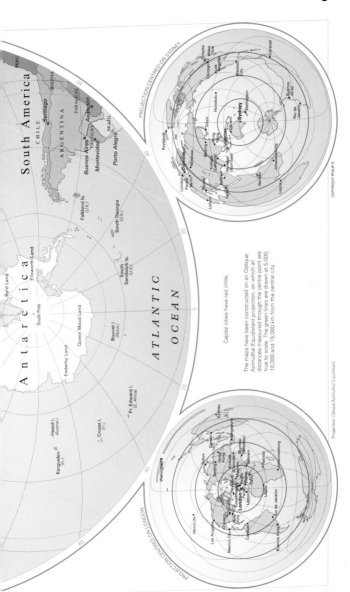

PROJECTION CENTRED ON SYDNEY

PROJECTION CENTRED ON LONDON

Capital cities have red infills

The maps have been constructed on an Oblique Azimuthal Equidistant projection, on which all distances measured through the centre point are true to scale. The green lines are drawn at 5,000, 10,000 and 15,000 km from the central city.

Projection: Oblique Azimuthal Equidistant

COPYRIGHT PHILIP'S

South America

CHILE
Santiago

ARGENTINA

PARAGUAY
Asunción

Buenos Aires *Montevideo*

Porto Alegre

BRAZIL

URUGUAY

BOLIVIA

PERU

Falkland Is. *(U.K.)*

South Georgia *(U.K.)*

South Sandwich Is. *(U.K.)*

Antarctica

Byrd Land

Ellsworth Land

South Pole

Queen Maud Land

Enderby Land

Bouvet I. *(Norw.)*

Pr. Edward I. *(S. African)*

Crozet I. *(Fr.)*

Heard I. *(Austral.)*

Kerguelen *(Fr.)*

ATLANTIC OCEAN

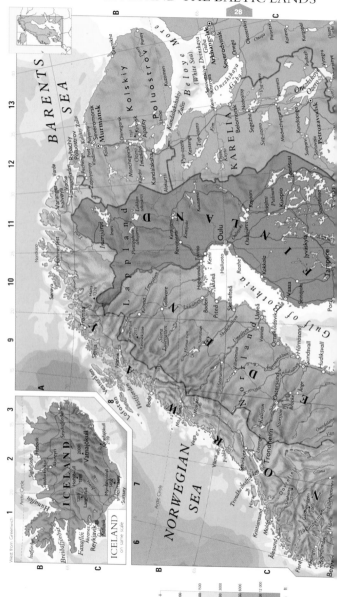

50 0 100 200 300 400 km
50 0 50 100 150 200 250 miles

Projection: Conical with two standard parallels

COPYRIGHT PHILIP'S

East from Greenwich

D E F

RUSSIA

Cherepovets
Rybinsk Res.
Rybinsk
Tver
Zelenograd
MOSKVA (Moscow)
Odintsovo
Kaluga
Orel
Oka
Don
Sumy
Okhtyrka
Poltava

Volochek
Borovichi
Vyshniy Volochek
Rzhev
Vyazma
Smolensk
Roslavl
Bryansk
Konotop
Nizhyn
Chernihiv
Pereyaslav-Khmelnytskyy
Bila Tserkva
Cherkasy

Tikhvin
Vologda
Bologoye
Staraya Russa
Valdayskaya Vozvyshennost
Velikiye Luki
Orsha
Mahilyow
Zhlobin
Homyel
Desna
Korosten
Zhytomyr
Berdychiv
KYYIV (Kiev)

U K R A I N E

Lake Ladoga
Kolpino
SANKT-PETERBURG (St. Petersburg)
Narva
Novgorod
Pskov
Gdov
Chudskoye
Dno
Velikaya
Lovat
Nevel
Lyepyel
Vitsyebsk
Polatsk
Barysaw
MINSK
Slutsk
Babruysk
Bar.
Mazyr
Pripet
Pinsk

Espoo Helsinki
Gulf of Finland
Tallinn
ESTONIA
Tartu
Pärnu
Värts
Võrtsjärv
LATVIA
Gulf of Riga
Rīga
Jelgava
Daugavpils
Daugava
Rēzekne
BELARUS
Baranavichy
Hrodna
Brest
Kovel
Lutsk
Rivne
Chervonohrad
Lviv

Hiiumaa (Dagö)
Saaremaa (Ösel)
Ventspils
Liepāja
Šiauliai
Panevėžys
LITHUANIA
Kaunas
Vilnius
Nemunas
Klaipėda
Kaliningrad (Russia)
Sovetsk
Suwałki
Bialystok
Łomża
Bug
Lublin
Rzeszów
Tarnów Przemyśl

Åland (Ahvenanmaa)
Hanko
BALTIC SEA
STOCKHOLM
Uppsala
Gotland
Visby
Öland
Kalmar
Karlskrona
Gdynia
Gdańsk
Elbląg
Olsztyn
Toruń
Wisła
POLAND
Płock
WARSZAWA (Warsaw)
Radom
Kielce
Częstochowa
Kraków
Tarnów
Żilina

Svealand
Västerås
Eskilstuna
Örebro
Norrköping
Linköping
Vättern
Vänern
Jönköping
Borås
Göta land
Göteborg (Gothenburg)
Trollhättan
Halmstad
Helsingborg
Lund
Malmö
Bornholm
Koszalin
Szczecin
Świnoujście
Odra
Bydgoszcz
Poznań
Warta
Kalisz
Łódź
Wrocław
Opole
Katowice
Chorzów
Tychy
Ostrava
CZECH REP.
PRAHA (Prague)
Plzeň

Frederikshavn
Ålborg
Randers
Aarhus
Kattegat
Sjælland
Store Bælt
Odense
Fyn
DENMARK
Esbjerg
Kolding
Flensburg
Kiel
Lübeck
Rostock
Stralsund
Rügen
Sassnitz
Greifswald
Frankfurt
BERLIN
Potsdam
Magdeburg
Elbe
Halle
Leipzig
Dresden
Chemnitz
Görlitz
Erfurt
Hradec Králové
Fichtelgeb.

Skien
Kristiansand
Mandal
Skagerrak
Holstebro
Helgoland
Emden
GERMANY
Bremen
Hamburg
Braunschweig
Hannover
Münster
Osnabrück
Dortmund
Kassel
Fulda
Frankfurt
Darmstadt
Würzburg
Heidelberg
Nürnberg

Stavanger
Egersund
Lista

7 8 9 10 11 12

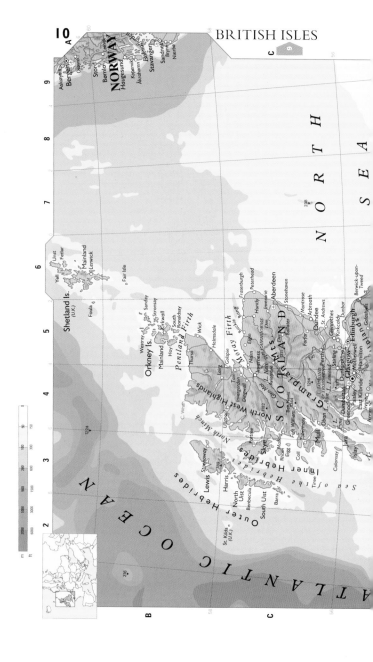

A

NORWAY

Askvoll
Bergen
Osøyro
Stord
Bømlo
Haugesund
Kopervik
Åkrehamn
Stavanger
Sandnes
Bryne
Nærbø

Shetland Is.
(U.K.)

Unst
Fetlar
Yell
Mainland
Lerwick
Fair Isle
Foula

Orkney Is.
Westray
Sanday
Stronsay
Kirkwall
Mainland
Hoy
South
Ronaldsay

Wick
Helmsdale
Thurso
Pentland Firth

N O R T H

S E A

Cape Wrath

North West Highlands

Golspie
Lairg
Dornoch
Tain
Invergordon
Dingwall
Inverness
Nairn
L. Ness
Loch
Ness
Aviemore

Moray Firth

Banff
Buckie
Elgin
Fraserburgh
Peterhead
Huntly
Inverurie

G R A M P I A N   M t s .
Ben Nevis
1344
Ben
Macdui

Aberdeen
Stonehaven

Grampian

Ballater
Forfar
Perth
T R O S S A C H S
Crieff
Stirling
Oban
Greenock
Dunbarton
Paisley
Glasgow
East Kilbride
Hamilton
Motherwell

Montrose
Arbroath
Dundee
St. Andrews
Glenrothes
Kirkcaldy
Dunfermline
Edinburgh
Dunbar
Coldstream
Berwick-upon-Tweed

S C O T L A N D

North Minch

Lewis
Stornoway
Harris

Outer Hebrides

North Uist
Benbecula
South Uist

Barra

St. Kilda
(U.K.)

Skye
Rum
Malaig
Eigg
Arisaig
Fort William
Loch Linnhe

Sea of the Hebrides

Inner Hebrides

Coll
Tiree
Mull
Tobermory
Loch Fyne
L. Lomond
Greenock

Colonsay
Jura
Islay

A T L A N T I C   O C E A N

336

1224

788

238

C

9

B

C

m
ft

2000
6000
1000
3000
500
1500
200
600
100
300
90
150
0
0

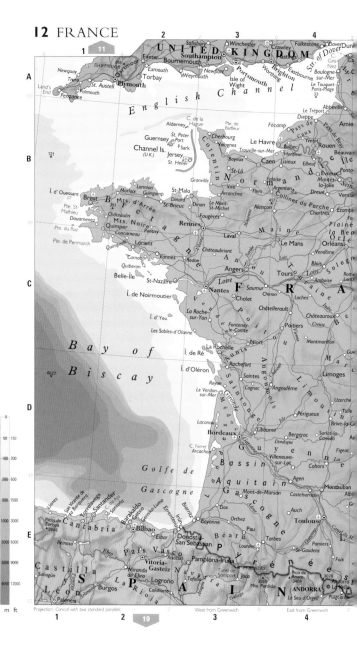

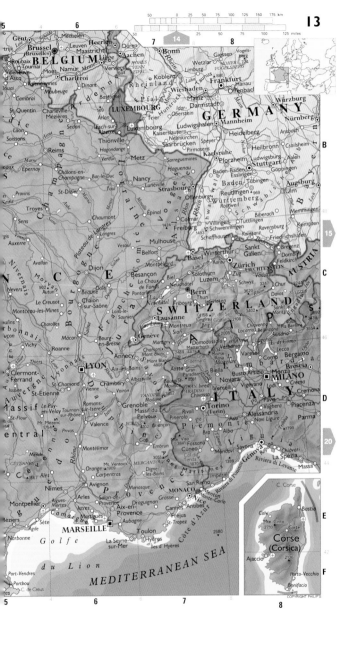

50 0 25 50 75 100 125 150 175 km
50 0 25 50 75 100 125 miles

7   8   9   10

BELARUS

MINSK

Lida Nyoman Dzyarzhynsk Hrodzyanka Bykhaw Slawharad

Hrodna Navahrudak Stowbtsy Nyasvizh Asipovichy Ragachow Zhlobin

Masty Dzyatlava Baranavichy Klyetsk Slutsk Bahruysk Homyel

Vawkavysk Slonim Lyakhavichy Hantsavichy Salihorsk Glusk Svyetlahorsk Rechytsa

Bialystok Svisloch Byaroza Tsyelyakhany Luninyets Pyetrikaw Vasilevichy Kalinkavichy Loyew

Bielsk Hajnówka Pruzhany Dragichyn Ivanava Pripyats Mazyr Khoyniki

Biała Zhabinka Kobryn Pinsk David Horodok Stolin Yelsk Chornobyl

Podlaska Brest Malaryta Prypeć PRIPYATSĆ Uhort Ovruch Kyivske Vdskh. Oster

Międzyrzec Kamin- Dubrovytsya Olevsk Belokovichi Korosten Dymer Irpin

Podlaski Kashyrskyy Narodychi

Włodawa Lyuboml Kovel Staryy Chortoriysk Kostopil Novohrad- Malyn Radomyshl **KYYIV (Kiev)**

Chełm Rozhyshche Kivertsi Korets Volynskyy Zhytomyr Korostyshev Fastiv Vasylkiv

Novovolynsk Volodymyr- Oleksandriya Rivne Zdolbuniv Slavuta Pershotravensk Berdychiv

Zamość Volynskyy Lutsk Dubno Ostroh Shepetivka Polonne **Bila Tserkva**

Sokal Horokhiv Chervonohrad Berestechko Kremenets Izyaslav Kozyatyn Skvyra Tarashcha

Rava- Radekhiv Brody Starokostyantyniv Khmelnik Tetiyev Zhashkiv

Ruska Kamyanka- Zolochiv Zbarazh Khmelnytskyy Vinnytsya Lipovets Uman

Nesterov Buzka Ternopil Skala **UKRAINE** Bar Zhmerynka Haysyn

Yavoriv Mostyska **Lviv (Lvov)** Khodoriv Berezhany Hrymayliv Horodok Tulchyn Vapnyarka Bershad

Horodok Drohobych Rogatyn Terebovlya Chortkiv Skala-Podilska Mohyliv- Kotovsk

Sambir Boryslav Stryy Buchach Zalishchyky Kamyanets-Podilskyy Podilskyy Ananyiv Balta

Truskavets Kalush Dnister Horodenka Novoselytsya Lipcani Ocnița Yampil Soroca

Skole Bolekhiv **Ivano-Frankivsk** Nadvirna Kolomyya Snyatyn Khotyn Drochia Florești **Transnistria**

Uzhhorod Volovets Pechenizhyn Yaremcha Tyasmyn Hlyboka Edineț Briceni **MOLDOVA** Rîbnița Dubăsari

Mukacheve Berehove Khust Tyachiv Rakhiv Rădăuți Dorohoi Bălți Fălești Dubăsari Vdskh. Tiraspol

Vynohradiv Satu Mare Sighetu Borșa Suceava Botoșani Fălticeni Cornești Orhei **Chișinău** Tighina

Carei Marmației Baia Mare Pietrosul Vatra-Dornei Pașcani Ungheni Leova Comrat Basarabeasca Bilhorod-

Zalău Dej Bistrița Piatra Iași Huși Cimișlia Dnistrovskyy

Oradea Cluj-Napoca Reghin Neamț Roman Vaslui Bîrlad Comrat Ciadîr-Lunga Artsyz

Turda Târgu Mureș Odorheiu Miercurea-Ciuc Bacău Bârlad Cahul Tatarbunary

Munții Bihor Secuiesc Tecuci Vulcănești Bolhrad Kiliya

Abrud Târnăveni Sighișoara Sfântu Focșani Reni Izmayil

Brad Alba-Iulia Aiud Mediaș Gheorghe Galați Sulina

ROMANIA Deva Sibiu Făgăraș Brașov Săcele Râmnicu Sărat Brăila Danube

Simeria Carpații Meridionali Vf. Moldoveanu Buzău Dunării

Hunedoara Petroșani Câmpulung Curtea de Argeș Câmpina

Vulcan Parângul Mare

6   7   East from Greenwich   8   COPYRIGHT PHILIP'S

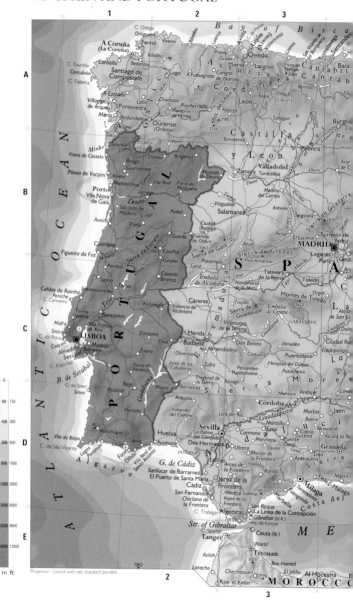

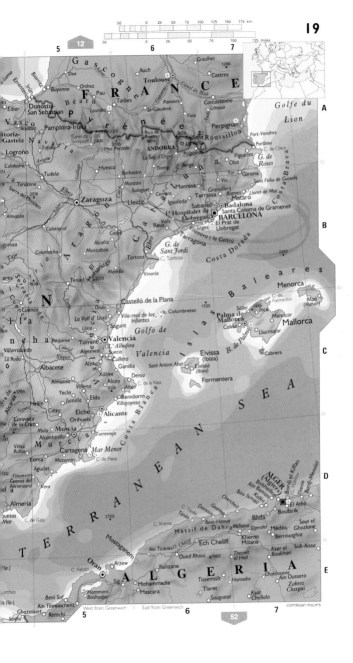

50 0 25 50 75 100 125 150 175 km

50 0 25 50 75 100 125 miles

FRANCE

Graulhet
Auch
Toulouse
Castres
Dax
Orthez
Béarn Pau Tarbes Canal du Midi 1266
Bayonne
Lourdes St-Gaudens Carcassonne
Biarritz Castres
Eibar Pamiers Limoux
Donostia- Pyrénées Foix Perpignan
San Sebastián Roussillon
Vasco Nico de Andorra Port-Vendres
Pamplona-Iruña Aneto 3404 La Vella Porthou
Vitoria- Navarra 3355 ANDORRA C. de Creus
Gasteiz Túnel de Mte. Perdido Figueres G. de
Logroño Jaca La Seu d'Urgell Roses
Aragón Puigcerdà Olot
Calahorra Huesca Berga Girona
Tudela Tremp Ter Sant Feliu de Guíxols
Sierra del Moncayo Barbastro Vic
Tarazona 2316 Balaguer Manresa Granollers Blanes
Zaragoza Lleida Cervera Terrassa Lloret de Mar
Almazán Calatayud Igualada Sabadell Mataró
Tajo Alcañiz Castellón L'Hospitalet de Badalona
Guenza Calamocha Montalbán Valls Llobregat Santa Coloma de Gramenet
Teruel Morella Reus BARCELONA
Ebro Tarragona El Prat de
Cuenca 2019 Vinaròs G. de Sitges Llobregat
ares 1839 Sant Jordi Vilanova i la Geltrú
C. Tortosa Costa Dorada
Tortosa 3410

N

Castelló de la Plana Baleares
La Roda Onda Is. Columbretes Menorca
Cuenca Vila-real de los 1700 C. de Maó
Villarrobledo La Vall d'Uixó Infantes Sóller 1445 Formentor (Mahón)
Requena Llíria Inca Menorca
Albacete Sagunt Palma de Manacor
Torrent L'Albufera Golfo de Mallorca Mallorca
Almansa Algemesí Valencia Calvià Llucmajor
Yecla Alzira Sueca B. de Palma
Villena Cullera Cabrera
Alcaraz 1798 Xàtiva Gandia
Segura Almansa Denia Sant Antoni Abat
Hellín Alcoy C. de la Nao Eivissa
Caravaca 1558 Benidorm (Ibiza) Eivissa
de la Cruz Jumilla Elda Altea Villajoyosa (Ibiza)
Cieza Alicante Formentera
Mula Orihuela
Murcia Elche
Alcantarilla Torrevieja
Vélez Cartagena Mar Menor
Rubio Lorca C. de Palos
Aguilas Mazarrón

MEDITERRANEAN SEA

Almanzora Cuevas del
Almanzora Vera
Almería C. de Gata 2700
quetas Mar

ALGERIA

Mostaganem ALGER Bordj el Kiffan
(Algiers) Thénia Bordj-Menaïel
C. Ténès Blikhadem Kaddous
Ténès Aïn Benian Kaddous
Cherchell Bou Ismaïl El Arba
Beni-Haoua Gouraya Boufarik
Massif de Dahra Miliana Blida Sour el
Aïn Tédelès Chlef Djendel Médéa Ghozlane
Oued Rhiou 1983 Khemis Berrouaghia
Arzew Miliana Ksar el Sidi-Aissa
Oran Relizane Boukhari
C. Falcon Theniet Chahbounia
El Had Aïn Oussera
Sig Tissemsilt Hamadia Zahrez
Mohammadia Ksar Chergui
Beni Saf Hammam Mascara Tiaret Chellala
Aïn Témouchent Bouhadjar Sougueur
Ghazaouet Remchi

COPYRIGHT PHILIP'S

A

B

C

D

E

50   0   25   50   75   100   125   150   175 km
50   0   25   50   75   100   125 miles

IONIAN SEA

Golfo di Taranto

IONIAN SEA

Brindisi
Francavilla
Fontana
Gallipoli
Nardò
Otranto
Lecce
Martina
Franca
Taranto
Matera
Potenza

Crotone
Catanzaro
Rossano
Cosenza
Castrovillari
POLLINO
Lametia
Nicotera
Vibo Valéntia
Palmi
Reggio di Calábria
Str. di Messina
Messina
Taormina
Acireale
Catania
Augusta
Siracusa
Ávola
Noto
C. Passero
Pachino
Módica
Ragusa
Vittória
Gela
Comiso
Caltagirone
Scicli
Niscemi
 Enna
Adrano
Monti Nebròdi
Barcellona Pozzo di Gotto
Milazzo
Isole Eólie
Strómboli
Salina
Lipari
Vulcano
Acireale

TYRRHENIAN SEA

Palermo
Partinico
Trápani
Érice
Marsala
Mazara del Vallo
Sciacca
Porto Empédocle
Castelvetrano
Caltanissetta
Agrigento
Favara
Licata
Gela
Isole Égadi
Favignana
Pantelleria (Italy)

MEDITERRANEAN SEA

Ústica (Italy)

Isole Pelágie (Italy)
Linosa
Lampione
Lampedusa

MALTA
Valletta
Gozo

Sardegna
(Sardinia)
Cágliari
G. di Cágliari
Quartu Sant'Élena
Sant'Antioco
San Pietro
G. di Oristano
G. di Palmas
C. Spartivento
C. Carbonara

TUNISIA

TUNIS
CARTHAGE
Golfe de Tunis
C. Blanc
Bizerte
Menzel-Bourguiba
Mateur
Menzel-Temime
Kélibia
Ra's at Tib (C. Bon)
Hammamet
Golfe de Hammamet
Soliman
Korba
Nabeul
Ben Arous
Zaghouan
Sousse
Monastir
M'saken
Mokmine
Mahdia
Kairouan
Béja
El Fahs
Medjez-el-Bab
Testour
Téboursouk
Le Kef
Sbikha
Sidi Bou Zid
Kasserine
Makthar
Thala
Foussana
El Kala
Jendouba
Bou Salem
Souk Ahras
Guelma
Sedrata
Ouenza
Tébessa
Aïn Beïda

ALGERIA
Annaba
C. Serrat

Projection: Conical with two standard parallels

m   4000 3000 2000 1000   500   200   100   0
ft 12000 9000 6000 3000 1500 600   300   0

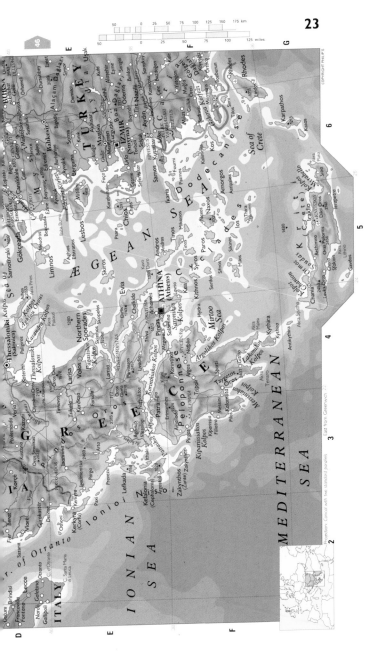

50 0 25 50 75 100 125 150 175 km
50 0 25 50 75 100 125 miles

COPYRIGHT PHILIP'S

Projection: Conical with two standard parallels

East from Greenwich

TURKEY

BURSA
Balıkesir
İZMİR (Smyrna)
Manisa
Aydın
Boz Dağları
Alaçam Dağları
Uşak
Denizli
Muğla
Rhodes
Karpathos
Kasos

Æ GEAN SEA

Lesbos
Chios
Samos
Ikaria
Patmos
Kos
D o d e c a n e s e
Astipalea
Amorgos
Naxos
Paros
Mikonos
Tinos
Andros
Skiros
Limnos
Samothraki
Gökçeada

Northern Sporades
Evia
ATHENS (Athina)
Pireás
Syros
Kithnos
Kea
Sérifos
Sifnos
Sikinos
Ios
Thira

Sea of Crete

K r i t i
C r e t e
Iráklio
Réthimno
Chaniá

Aegean

Kikládes
Kólpos

G R E E C E

P i n d o s
Thessaloníki (Salonica)
Thessaloníki Kólpos
Kómotini
Véroia
Lárisa
Vólos
Trikala
Kardhitsa
Lamía
Pátra
Korinthiakós Kólpos
Pírgos
Kalamáta
Trípoli
Árgos
Korinth
Mesolóngi
Agrínio

P e l o p o n n e s e

Saronikós Kólpos
Salamina
Hydra
Spétses
Kithira
Andikithira
Lakonikós Kólpos
Messiniakós Kólpos
Mirtóo Sea
AroTikós Kólpos

I o n i a n
Zákinthos (Zante)
Kefaloniá (Cephalonia)
Itháki
Lefkáda
Corfu (Kérkyra)
Paxoí
Othoni

Gulf of Otranto

ITALY

Brindisi
Lecce
Gallipoli
Nardò
Otranto
C. Santa Maria di Leuca
Francavilla
Fontana

IONIAN SEA

MEDITERRANEAN SEA

COPYRIGHT PHILIPS

Projection: Conical with two standard parallels

East from Greenwich

C A S P I A N   S E A

BAKI
(Baku)

A Z E R B A I J A N

Sumqayıt
Länkäran
Ardabil

Maḫachkala
Derbent

DAGESTAN

Kizlyar

IRAN

Naxçıvan

TABRIZ

ARMENIA

YEREVAN

Vanadzor

Gäncä
Rustavi

TBILISI

GEORGIA

Van Gölü

Van

Batumi
Rize

Kutaisi

Erzurum

Sokhumi

Trabzon

Kuzey Anadolu Daği

Gagra
Poti

Erzincan

Giresun

Ordu

Sochi

Tuapse

C a u c a s u s

M o u n t a i n s

Novorossiysk

Krasnodar

Maykop

Armavir

Labinsk

Krymsk

Anapa

Samsun

Bafra

Sinop

T U R K E Y

A n a t o l i a

Sivas

Tokat

Amasya

Çorum

Yozgat

ANKARA

Sea of Azov

Rostov

ROSTOV

Shakhty

Novocherkassk

Salsk

Tikhoretsk

Stavropol

Nevinnomyssk

Cherkessk

Georgiyevsk

Budennovsk

Grozny

CHECHENIA

B L A C K   S E A

Kerch

Feodosiya

Yalta

Sevastopol

Simferopol

CRIMEA

Yevpatoriya

Kherson

Melitopol

Nikopol

Mariupol

Berdyansk

Taganrog

Yeysk

Primorsko-Akhtarsk

DONETSK

Makiyivka

Horlivka

Artemovsk

Alchevsk

Zonguldak

Ereğli

Karabük

Bolu

Eskişehir

Kırıkkale

Kırşehir

Kayseri

Aksaray

ISTANBUL

İzmit

Gebze

BURSA

Balıkesir

Kütahya

Afyon

Uşak

İZMİR

Aydın

Manisa

Akhisar

Çanakkale

Bandırma

Edirne

Tekirdağ

BULGARIA

Varna

Burgas

Dobrich

Ruse

ROMANIA

BUCUREŞTI

(Bucharest)

Constanţa

Galaţi

Brăila

Ploieşti

Piteşti

Braşov

Iaşi

Bacău

MOLDOVA

Chişinău

Tiraspol

Tighina

ODESA

Bilhorod-
Dnistrovskyy

Mykolaïv

KALMYKIA

Elista

Astrakhan

Volgodonsk

Tsimlyansk

Shakhty

Krasny Luch

Krasnodon

Volga

Don

Dnipro

Dnipropetrovsk

Krvyy Rih

Kryvyy Rih

Zaporizhzhya

Pavlohrad

Dniprodzerzhynsk

SCALE

50   0   100   200   300   400 km

50   0   50   100   150   200   250 miles

Katmandu ◉ Capital Cities

27

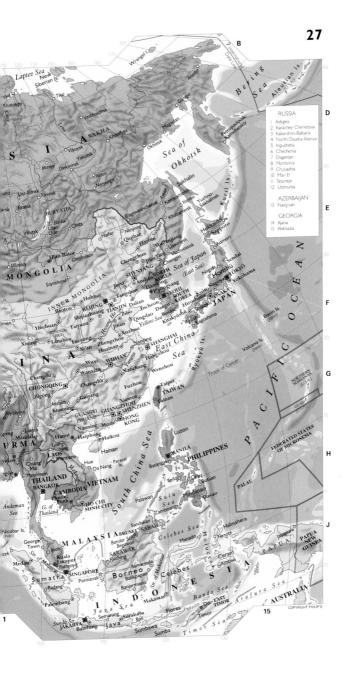

RUSSIA
1 Adygea
2 Karachey-Cherkessia
3 Kabardino-Balkaria
4 North Ossetia-Alania
5 Ingushetia
6 Chechenia
7 Dagestan
8 Mordvinia
9 Chuvashia
10 Mari El
11 Tatarstan
12 Udmurtia

AZERBAIJAN
13 Naxçivan

GEORGIA
14 Ajaria
15 Abkhazia

Laptev Sea
New Siberian Is.
Wrangel I.
International Date Line

Bering Sea
Aleutian Is.

Khatanga
Tiksi
dyk
Khatanga
Verkhoyansk

SIBERIA
SAKHA
Mirny
Olekminsk
Vilyuysk
Yakutsk
Aldan
Neryungri
Kirensk
Ust-Ilimsk
Bratsk
rsk
Irkutsk
BURYATIA
Ulan-Ude
Baikal
Chita

Ulan Bator
MONGOLIA
Ullastay
Saynshand
Choybalsan

Yinchuan
Lanzhou
Xining
I   N   A
Chengdu
Zigong
CHONGQING
Anshun
Kunming
Guiyang
Changsha
Wanxian
Nanchang
Wuzhou
Fuzhou
Wenzhou
Guangzhou
GUANGXI
ZHUANG
Nanning
Macau
Haikou
Hainan

Okhotsk
Sea of Okhotsk
Magadan

Petropavlovsk-
Kamchatskiy

Komsomolsk
Yuzhno-
Sakhalinsk
Sakhalin

Kuril Is.

Hokkaido
Sapporo

Aomori

Sendai
HONSHU
TOKYO
Yokohama

Bonin Is.
(Japan)

PACIFIC   OCEAN

Volcano Is.
(Japan)

NORTHERN
MARIANAS

GUAM
(USA)

FEDERATED STATES
OF MICRONESIA

PALAU

Manila
PHILIPPINES
Batangas
Luzon

Roxas
Cebu
Butuan
Davao
Mindanao
Zamboanga

Sandakan
BRUNEI SABAH
Bandar Seri
Begawan
SARAWAK
Kuching

Celebes Sea
Manado
Ternate
Halmahera
Jayapura
PAPUA

PAPUA
NEW
GUINEA

Ceram Sea
Ceram

INDONESIA

Blagoveshchensk
Khabarovsk
Vladivostok

Changchun
Jilin
Harbin
Qiqihar
Hailar
Nenjiang
SHENYANG
Anshan
Fushun
Dalian

Sea of Japan
(East Sea)

Niigata

Kyoto
NAGOYA
OSAKA
Hiroshima

KYUSHU
Nagasaki
Fukuoka

NORTH KOREA
P'yŏngyang
SEOUL
SOUTH KOREA
Incheon
Daegu
Busan
Kitakyūshū

INNER MONGOLIA
Hohhot
Baotou
BEIJING
TIANJIN
Tangshan
Shijiazhuang
Datong
Taiyuan
Yinchuan
Zibo
Jinan
Qingdao
Yellow Sea

Luoyang
Xi'an
Zhengzhou
Xuzhou
Huainan
Nanjing
SHANGHAI
WUHAN
Hangzhou
Nanchang

East China Sea

Ryukyu Is.

Tropic of Cancer

Taipei
TAIWAN

Kaohsiung

HONG KONG
SHENZHEN

South China Sea

Paracel Is.
Da Nang

Hue
VIETNAM
HO CHI
MINH CITY

Phnom
Penh
CAMBODIA

BANGKOK
THAILAND

Chiang
Mai
Mandalay
URMA
Luang
Prabang
LAOS
Vientiane

Haiphong
Hanoi

Palawan
Sulu
Sea
Sulu

Jolo

MALAYSIA
Kuala
Lumpur
Putrajaya
Ipoh
George
Town
SINGAPORE
Pontianak
Borneo
Balikpapan
Samarinda
Banjarmasin
Str. of Makassar
Makassar
Celebes

Java Sea
Semarang
Surabaya
JAKARTA
Bandung
Java
Bali
Sumbawa
Sumba

Flores
EAST
TIMOR
Timor
Timor Sea
Banda Sea
Arafura Sea

AUSTRALIA

COPYRIGHT PHILIP'S

Medan
ceh
Sumatra
Str. of Malacca
Padang
Palembang

Nicobar Is.
(India)
Andaman
Sea

Moulmein
ngon
G. of
Thailand

1   15

COPYRIGHT PHILIP'S

Projection: Conical Orthomorphic, with two standard parallels

East from Greenwich

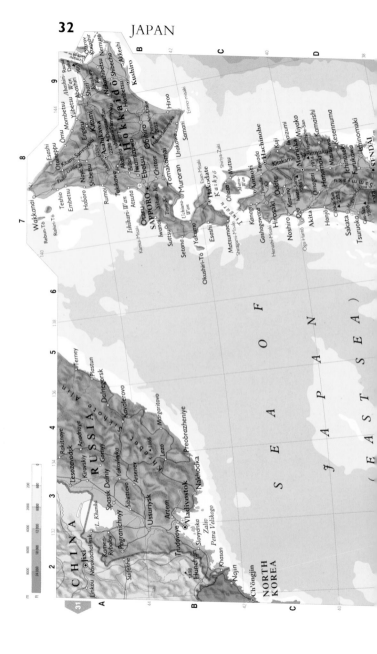

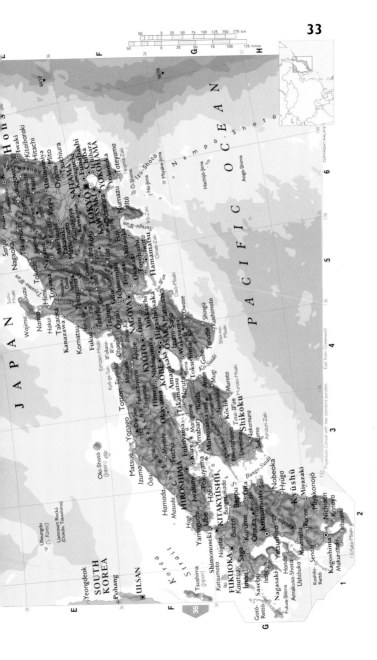

50 0 25 50 75 100 125 150 175 km
50 0 25 50 75 100 125 miles

PACIFIC OCEAN

JAPAN

HONSHŪ

Nampō-shotō

TŌKYŌ
KAWASAKI
YOKOHAMA
CHIBA
SAITAMA

Iwaki
Kitaibaraki
Hitachi
Mito
Utsunomiya
Koriyama
Iwakuni

Niigata
Nagaoka
Sanjo
Takada
Shibata
Takasaki

Toyama
Takaoka
Kanazawa
Himi
Hokui
Narao
Suzu

Wajima

NAGOYA
KYŌTO
ŌSAKA
KŌBE
Gifu
Fukui
Takefu
Tsuruga
Ōbama
Maizuru
Toyooka
Ayabe
Fukuchiyama
Nishinomiya
Higashiōsaka
Sakai
Nara
Wakayama
Amagasaki

HIROSHIMA
Okayama
Matsue
Yonago
Tottori
Izumo
Hamada
Masuda
Hagi
Miyoshi
Fuchū
Kure
Marugame
Imabari
Matsuyama
Uwajima
Kōchi
Nakamura
Sukumo

KITAKYŪSHŪ
FUKUOKA
Shimonoseki
Yamaguchi
Ube
Buzen
Beppu
Ōita
Kurume
Saga
Karatsu
Imari
Sasebo
Nagasaki
Isahaya
Ōmuta
Nōgata
Kagoshima
Miyakonojō
Miyazaki
Nichinan
Nobeoka
Hyūga
Kumamoto
Yatsushiro
Hondo
Minamata
Sendai
Makurazaki
Kanoya
Ibusuki
Yaku-Shima

KYŪSHŪ
SHIKOKU
Takamatsu
Tokushima
Naruto
Anan

Fuji
Numazu
Itō
Hamamatsu
Okazaki
Toyohashi
Iwata
Shizuoka
Atsugi
Odawara
Ōdate

SOUTH KOREA
Yeongdeok
Pohang
ULSAN

Tsushima (Japan)
Gotō-Rettō
Fukue-Shima
Amakusa-Shotō
Kaminokawa
Ushibuka

Oki-Shotō (Japan)
Ulleungdo (S. Korea)
Liancourt Rocks (Dokdo, Takeshima)

Korea Strait

Hachijō-jima
Aoga-Shima
Miyake-jima
Nii-jima
O-Shima

Izu-Shotō

Zampa

9076
8412

COPYRIGHT PHILIP'S

Projection Conical with two standard parallels

East from Greenwich

35

E F G H

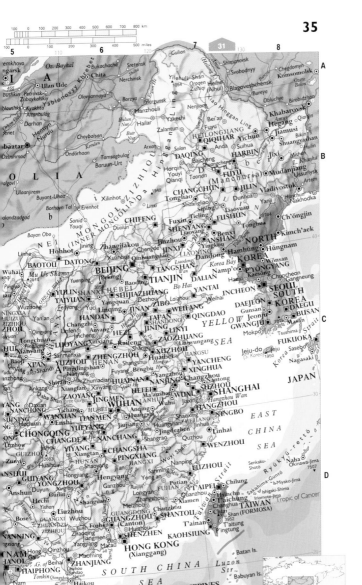

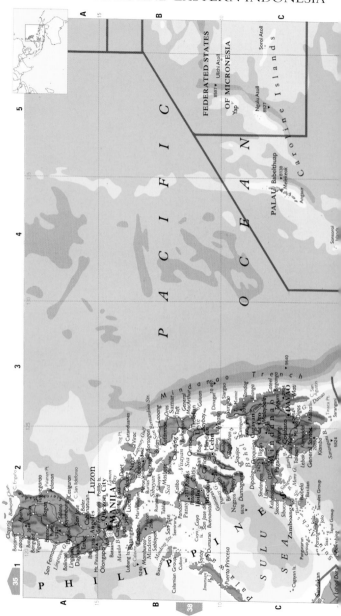

PAPUA NEW GUINEA

Projection: Mercator

East from Greenwich

100 0 100 200 300 400 500 km
100 0 50 100 150 200 250 300 350 miles

SEA

Kepulauan Sangihe

UTARA

Halmahera

M
(M) **a**
l **u**
k **u**

SERAM SEA

MALUKU

IRIAN
BARAT

Pegunungan Maoke

P A P U A

Van Res

Pegunungan Van Res

BANDA SEA

Kepulauan Banda

ARAFURA
SEA

A R A F U R A
S E A

GORONTALO
UTARA

Sulawesi (Celebes)

TENGAH

BARAT

SELATAN

MOLUCCA
SEA

FLORES SEA

Buton

I N D O N E S I A

B A N D A S E A

TENGGARA

NUSA TENGGARA TIMUR

Flores

Sumba

Savu Sea

EAST
TIMOR

MAKASSAR
(Ujung
Pandang)

F L O R E S
S E A

Sumbawa

L e s s e r   S u n d a   I s

S E A

Selat Makassar

m 8000 6000 4000 2000 1000 600 200
ft 24000 18000 12000 6000 3000 600

50 0 100 200 300 400 km
50 0 50 100 150 200 250 miles

8 34 **9** **10** **11** **12** **13**

B

C H I N A

Nagqu
Bagên
Nangqên
Gamtog
Qamdo
Baiyu
Garzê

H
Xinlong
Litang
Yajiang

Tangula Shan

Nu Jiang
Lhorong
Yidun
SICHUAN

34

Nam Co
4627
7080
Lhari
Zhaxizê
Niringjing
Muli Zangzu
Zizhixian

Lhinzub
Gongbo gyamda
Gogen
Namcha
7766
Barwa
Riga
Zhongdian

Lhasa
Yarlung Zangbo Jiang
Nang Xian
Mainkung
Weixi
Lijiang

Jido
Nizamghat
5881
Hkakabo Razi
(Thata La)
Zizhixian

Cona
Thunkar
Lhunze
Subansiri
Minutong
Hputao
Konglu

Tonga
Kangto
Mukkonselok
Daporijo
Along
Ghat
Chaukan Pass
3072
Jianchuan

Punakha
7554
North
Dibrugarh
Tinsukia
Pasai Bum
Hukawng
24114
Bumhpa Bum
Yunlong

BHUTAN
Tagg Dzong
Tongsa
Rupa
Lakhimpur
Joshat
Valley
Maingkwan
2424
Myitkyina
KACHIN
Baoshan

Tezpur
Mokokchung
Singkaling
Hkamti
Mogaung
YUNNAN

Kohima
NAGALAND
Tengchong
Longling
Changning

MEGHALAYA
Cherrapunji
1961
Barail Range
Hflong
Ukhrul
Homalin
Katha
Man Ne
Kunlong
Pang-Long

Shillong
Silchar
MANIPUR
Churachandpur
Tamu
Indaw
Shwegu
Hsenwi
Lashio
Kawng
Manpun

Guwahati
M
Barpeta
Maibari
Nagaon
Tamenglong
Imphal
Thaungdut
Tigyaing
Bhamo
2693

Jamalpur
Mymensingh
Laleghat
Kolasib
Sairang
Aizawl
Tiddim
Mawlaik
Bowdwin
Nantu
Mong Yang
Mong Hawk

DHAKA
Brahmanbaria
TRIPURA
Agartala
MIZORAM
Kyunhla
Mogok
Mong Mit
Lashio
Parig-Yang
Mong Hsu

Comilla
Belonia
Dhignala
2764
Mingin
Budalin
Mandalay
Gokteik
Peng-Yang

Narayanganj
Lungleh
Falam
Wuntho
Madaya
Monywa
Kyaukse
Mong Kung
Keng Tung
Mong Wa

KHULNA
Barisal
Maiju
CHIN
Gangaw
Yinmabin
Sagaing
SHAN

KATA
Patuakhali
Hatia
Dohazari
Paak
Myingyan
Taunggyi
Keng Tawng
Mong Nai
Mong Ton

Cox's Bazar
Paletwa
3053
Karpetlet
Pakokku
Meiktila
Heho
Inle L.
Mong Hsat
Muang
Chiang Rai

B U R M A

BAY
Sittwe
(Akyab)
RAKHINE
Kyaukpyu
MAGWE
Minbu
Thayetmyo
Yenangyaung
Thazi
Yamethin
Pyinmana
Naypyidaw
Bawlake
2620
KAYAH
Mawk Mai
Loi-kaw
2183
Mae Hong Son
2576
Chiang Mai
Muang Lamphun
Lampang

OF
Ramree I.
Letpan
Cheduba I.
Sandoway
Prome
Pyu
Taungdwingyi
Toungoo
Papun
Tak

BENGAL
Gwa
Lethadan
Myanaung
Henzada
Tharrawaddy
Madauk
THAILAND
Pa-an

Myungmya
Bassein
Maubin
Kyangin
Kyangpyaw
Hlegu
Thatôn
Martaban
Moulmein
MON
2080

IRRAWADDY
Eyabon
PEGU
YANGON
(Rangoon)
Pegu
Maudin Sun
G. of Martaban
Amherst

Mouths of the Irrawaddy
Kalegauk
Lamaing
Ye
Songkhla
Buri

OCEAN
Preparis North Channel
Natkyizin
Sangkhla

Pariparit Kyun
(Burma)
Preparis South Channel
Nam Tok
Yebyu
Toray

Koko Kyunzu
(Burma)
Moscos Is.
Maungmagan Is.
Launglon Bok

COPYRIGHT PHILIP'S

7 **8** **9** **10** **11** **12**

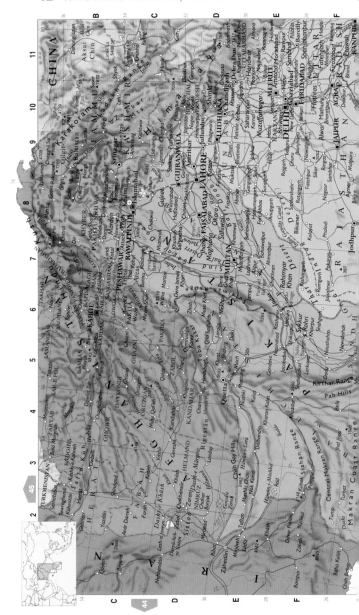

Projection: Conical Orthomorphic with two standard parallels   East from Greenwich

2 C. M. VA B. = CHAHĀR MAHĀLL VA BAKHTĪĀRĪ   3
K. VA B. A. = KOHKĪLŪYEH VA BŪYER AḤMADĪ

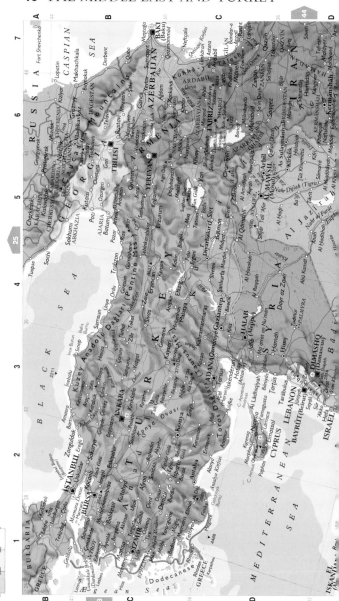

50 0 100 200 300 400 km
50 0 50 100 150 200 250 miles

44

48

54

54

E 32 E 28 F F G

7

6

5

4

3

East from Greenwich

Projection: Conical Orthomorphic with two standard parallels

F 24 F 24 G

P E R S I A N   G U L F

Bandar-e Deylam
Masjed
Soleymān
Āghā Jārī
Behbehān
Bandar-e
Moḩammad
KHŪZESTĀN
Ahvāz
Shaṭṭ al 'Arab
Khārk
Abū 'Alī
Al Juboyl
Al Qaṭīf
Az Zubayr
Al Khārj
Ad Dammām
Al Mubarraz
Al Hufūf
Al Jāfūrah
Al Khumm
Ḩaraḍ
'Uqaḍ Suqayr
As Saffānīyah
Al Manīfah
Ra's Mish'āb
Al Baṭḥā'
Wafrah
Burqān
Al Aḩmadī
Mīnā al Aḩmadī
Al Jahrah
AL KUWAYT (Kuwait)
KUWAIT
Ra's al Mish'āb
As Samāwah
An Nāṣirīyah
An Najaf
Ash Shaṭrah
Ad Dīwānīyah
Al 'Amārah
Al Ḩayy
Al Baṣrah
AL BAṢRAH
I R A Q
An Nu 'ayrīyah
Qurnah
Sūq ash Shuyūkh
Hafar al Bāṭin
Najd
Rafḩā'
'Ar'ar
Al Qaysūmah
Ḩafr al Bāṭin
RIYADH
AR RIYĀḌ (Riyadh)
Al Kharj
Al Ghāṭ
Al Majma'ah
Thādiq
Ruṃāḩ
Ḩawṭah
Al Quway'īyah
Marāt
Ad Dilam
Al Ḩilwah
Al Ḩarīq
As Sulayyīl
Layla
Al Bodi'
Al Hoddar
Al Hamar
Ghoţ
An Najaf
As Salmān
Ash Shabakah
Al 'Ukhayḍir
Ash Shabakah
Ash Shu'bah
An Nukhayb
Ad Dawādimī
Ḩuḷaylān
'Afīf
Al Qaṣīm
Buraydah
'Unayzah
Al Mithnab
Ar Rass
Fayd
Ḥā'il
An Nafūd
Jabal Shammar
Ṭābah
Sakākah
Al Jawf
Ṭurayf
Al Qurayyāt
'Ar'ar
Dūmat al Jandal
Jabal Ṭuwayq
Tabūk
Al Bad'
Ḍabā
Al Muwayliḥ
Al Wajh
Umm Lajj
Yanbu' al Baḥr
Al Madīnah (Medina)
Al Ḩamrā'
Khaybar
Harrat Khaybar
Ḩā'il
Qalat al Akhdar
Ḩarrat al Uwayriḍ
Madā'in Ṣāliḥ
Al 'Ulā
Ṭaymā'
Ḩarrat al Kishb
Mahd adh
Dhahab
Zalim
'Afīf
Ash Shu'bah
Al Ḩenākīyah
Wādi ar Rimah
Hanāk
Shaybārā
Ra's al Baridī
Al 'Aqīq
Masṭūrah
Rābigh
King Abdullah
Economic City
JIDDAH (Jedda)
Dhahabān
MAKKAH (Mecca)
2565
Al Hadā
At Ṭā'if
'Ushayrah
'Abūr
'Uṣfān
Ra'ja'
Qunfudhah
Ḥarrat Nawāṣif
Ūrūq Subay'
As Sirr
'Afīf
Al Musayjīd
Wādi Saḩbah
AD DAHNĀ'
'Irq as Subay'
AN NAFŪD
AR RUB' AL KHĀLĪ
S A U D I   A R A B I A

R E D   S E A

Es Sinā'
PETRA
Esh
Sharqīya
Es Sahrā'
en Nūbīya
EGYPT
EL QAHIRA (Cairo)
Ḥelwān
Es Suweis (Suez)
Būr Sa'id
Būr Safāga
Khalīg el Sueis
Gebel Kâtrina
2637
Ḥurghada
Ra's Gharib
Ras Banâs
HALAIB TRIANGLE
Gebel 'Ōda
1977
Gebel Oweinat
1934
Muḩammad Qol
Halaib
Ra's Hadârba
Gebel Elba
Ras Abû Mâdd
Yab'ū al Qurḥān
Ra's al Kasr
El Shalâtîn
278
36

SUDAN

THEBES
El Minyā
Beni Suef
El Faiyûm
Sohâg
Qena
Qûs
Luxor
Edfu
Kom Ombo
Aswân
El Ḥammâm
Naj' Ḥammâdî
Girga
Asyûṭ
Manfalûṭ
Deirût
Mallawî
El Khârga
Bâris
Baḩariya
PYRAMIDS
Dumqal
Wâdi Ḥalfa
Baḩr el Naṣr (Lake Nasser)
(Aswan High Dam)
TROPIC OF CANCER
Tropic of Cancer
Dunqunâb
Sidi Barrani
Siwa
El Faraḥira
El Bawîṭî
El Qasr
Bāwîṭî
Sîwa Oasis
Gebel Kâtrina
Beni Mazâr
Sadd el 'Âli

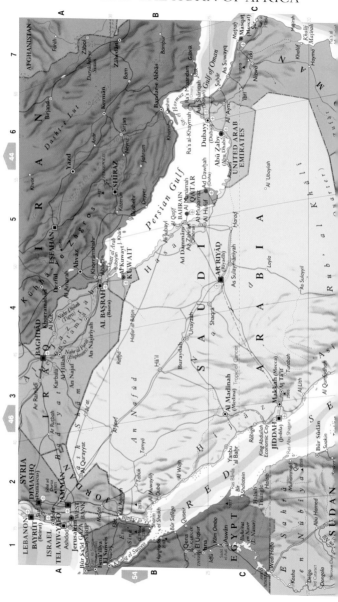

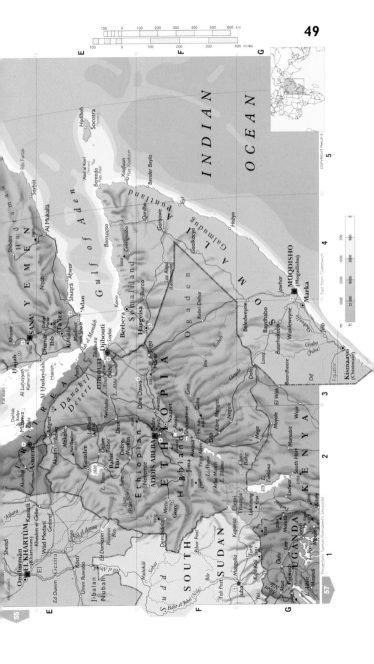

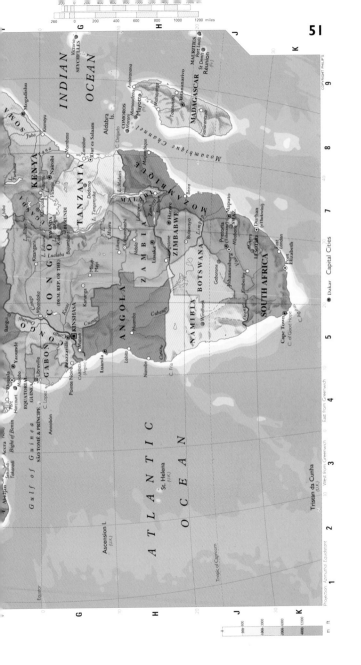

51

Projection: Azimuthal Equidistant

● Dakar Capital Cities

COPYRIGHT PHILIP'S

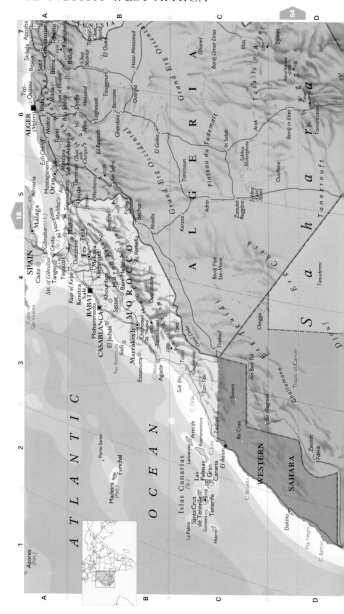

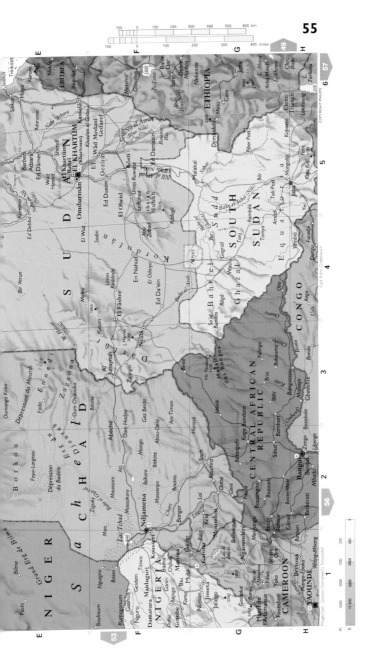

100 0 100 200 300 400 500 600 km
100   100   200   300   400 miles

COPYRIGHT PHILIP'S

E F G H

6 5 4 3 2 1

ERITREA

S   U   D   A   N

EL KHARTUM
(Khartoum)
El Khartum Bahri
Omdurman

Khasim el Girba
Kassala
Gedaref

Nhel Azraq
(Blue Nile)
Wad Medani
Ed Damazin

ETHIOPIA

Berber
Atbara
Ed Dâmer
Shendi

Wad Hamid

Ed Dueim
Kosti
El Gezira

El Obeid
Umm Ruwaba
En Nahud
El Odeiya

Malakal

SOUTH
SUDAN

Bahr el Jebel (Nile)

Bahr el Ghazal

Rumbek
Bor
Juba

Nyala
Ed Da'ein

CONGO

CENTRAL AFRICAN
REPUBLIC

Bangui

CAMEROON

YAOUNDÉ

NIGER

S   a   h   e   l

Ndjamena

NIGERIA

Maiduguri

Tchad

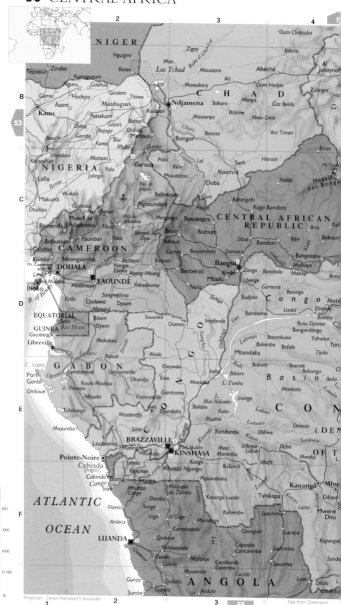

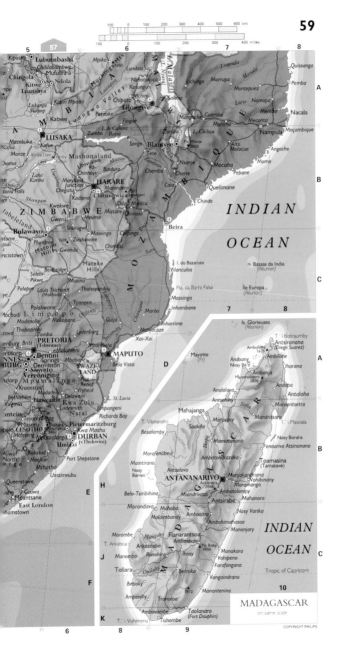

100 0 100 200 300 400 500 600 km
100 0 100 200 300 400 miles

A

Kipushi
Lubumbashi
Chililabombwe
Mufulira
Chingola
Kitwe Ndola
Luanshya

Mpika
Luangwa Valley
Lundazi
Lichinga
Marrupa
Mesalo
Lugenda
Quissanga
Pemba

Lukanga Swamp
Kopiri Mpashi
Petauke
Kabwe
Nkhotakota
Kasungu
Salima
Montepuez
Lirio
Namapa
Memba
Nacala

Mazabuka
LUSAKA
Kafue
Monze
Kariba Dam
Zumbo
L. de Cahora Bassa
Songo
Tete
Zomba
L. Chilwa
Alto Molocue
Angoche
Moma

Chinhoyi
Bindura
Kadoma
Chitungwiza
Marondera
Nsanje
Chemba
Mocuba
Pebane

HARARE

ZIMBABWE
Gweru
Kwekwe
Mvuma
Odzi Manica
Caia
Chinde
Quelimane

Bulawayo
Shurugwi
Masvingo
Chipinge
Chiredzi
Beira

B

INDIAN
OCEAN

I. do Bazaruto
Vilanculos
Bassas da India (Réunion)

Pta. da Barra Falsa
Île Europa (Réunion)

C

Massinga
Inhambane

Xai-Xai

Is. Glorieuses (Réunion)

MAPUTO

Mayotte (Fr)

Nosy Be
Andoany
Ambolobe
Antsiranana (Diego Suarez)
T. i Bobraumby

MADAGASCAR
on same scale

INDIAN
OCEAN

Tropic of Capricorn

COPYRIGHT PHILIPS

3   4   5   6

A

B

C

D

E

F

G

H

Sulawesi
(Celebes)
Mamuju Palopo
Kendari
Parepare
Watantone   Butung
MAKASSAR   I N D O N E S I A
Buru   Ambon
Banda Sea   Weber   Kep. Aru
5300   7260   Kep. Kai
3350
Kep.
Tanimbar   Pulau Dolak

Flores Sea   Wetar   Leti   Babar
Sumbawa   Alor   Dili   Arafura Sea
Raba   Flores   Timor   EAST   3310
Ende   TIMOR
Sumba   Savu Sea   Timor Sea   C. Croker
Kupang   Melville I.   C. Ar
6204   Darwin   Groo
Eyla

North   C. Londonderry   Joseph
Bonaparte   Katherine   Ce
Australia   Gulf
Basin   Wyndham   Larrimah
Daly Waters
Kimberley   NORTHERN   Barkly Tai
970   Halls Creek
Derby   Tanami   Tennant Creek
Broome   Desert
Great Sandy Desert   TERRITORY
Port   L. Mackay   MacDonnell Ranges   Alice Springs
Hedland   1531
N.W.   Dampier   Karratha   Mt. Zeil   Sim
Cape   Pannawonica   Lake   Gibson Desert   267   D
Mt. Meharry   Disappointment   Uluru   Mt.
1251   Newman   (Ayers Rock)   Woodroffe
Paraburdoo   Hamersley   1435
Range   A U S T R   A   SOU
Carnarvon   WESTERN   Musgrave Ranges
Shark Bay   Meekatharra   L. Carnegie   A U S T R
Geraldton   A U S T R A L I A   Great Victoria Desert   Coob
Murchison   Mount   Leonora   Tarcoola
Magnet   Lake   Penong   Lak
Barlee   Kalgoorlie-   Gaird
Boulder   Nullarbor   Plain
Norseman   Great Australian Bight   Port Lin
INDIAN   Northam   Esperance
OCEAN   PERTH   5632
Bunbury   Darling Range   South Australian Basin
Naturaliste   C. Leeuwin   Albany
Plateau   Augusta   S O U T H   E R N   O C

0
200   600
2000   6000
4000   12 000
6000   18 000
m   ft

Projection: Lambert's Equivalent Azimuthal   East from Greenwich
120   115   120   125   130
1   2   3   4   5

50 0 50 100 150 200 250 300 km
50 0 50 100 150 200 miles

QUEENSLAND

GREAT Dividing Range

CHESTERTON RANGE

Mt. Hutton 964

THRUSHTON

Darling

SOUTHWOOD Downs

Mt. Domville 645

Bundaberg
Waddy Pt.
Fraser I.
Hervey Bay
Maryborough
Tin Can Bay
GREAT SANDY
Gympie
Tewantin
Sunshine Coast
Nambour
Maroochydore
Caloundra
Bribie I.
Deception Bay
Caboolture
Redcliffe
Crows Nest
Ipswich
Toowoomba
BRISBANE
Beenleigh
Gold Coast
Southport
Warwick
Surfers Paradise
Tweed Hds.
Byron Bay
Ballina
Lismore
Casino
Grafton
Coffs Harbour
Nambucca Heads

GULGOA FLOOD PLAINS

Bourke
Darling
Cobar
Hermidale
Nyngan

NEW SOUTH WALES

Dubbo
Parkes
Orange
Bathurst
Lithgow
Katoomba
Penrith
Blacktown
SYDNEY
Campbelltown
Wollongong
Shellharbour
Kiama
Nowra

GOULBURN
Mudgee
Cessnock
Maitland
Kurri Kurri
Singleton
Muswellbrook
Raymond Terrace
Newcastle
Gosford

Armidale
Tamworth
Gunnedah
Narrabri
Moree

Port Macquarie
Taree
Tuncurry
Forster

Wagga Wagga
Canberra
Queanbeyan
Goulburn

Mt. Kosciuszko

Albury
Wodonga
Cooma
Bega
Eden

Shepparton
Benalla
Wangaratta
Bright

Gippsland
Bairnsdale
Sale
Morwell
Traralgon

Dandenong
Cranbourne

WILSONS PROMONTORY
Curtis Group
Kent Group
Deal I.

Flinders Island
Furneaux Group
Cape Barren I.
Clarke I.
Banks Strait

T A S M A N

S E A

COPYRIGHT PHILIP'S

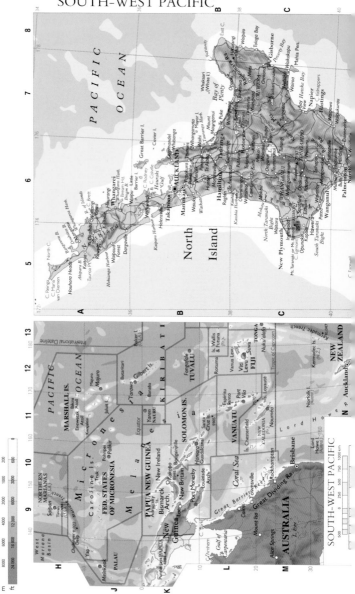

PACIFIC OCEAN

North Island

AUCKLAND

Whangarei

Hamilton

Tauranga

Rotorua

Gisborne

New Plymouth

Napier

Hastings

Wanganui

Palmerston North

Bay of Plenty

SOUTH-WEST PACIFIC

PACIFIC OCEAN

International Dateline

NORTHERN MARIANAS

Saipan

PALAU

Melekeok

FED. STATES OF MICRONESIA

Palikir

MARSHALL IS.

Majuro

KIRIBATI

Tarawa

NAURU

Yaren

Baker I.

Gilbert Is.

TUVALU

Fongafale

SOLOMON IS.

Honiara

PAPUA NEW GUINEA

Port Moresby

New Britain

New Ireland

Bismarck Arch.

Bougainville

Santa Cruz Is.

VANUATU

Port Vila

Espíritu Santo

FIJI

Suva

Viti Levu

Vanua Levu

TONGA

Nuku'alofa

Is. Wallis & Futuna (Fr.)

Rotuma

NEW CALEDONIA

Nouméa

Îs. Loyauté

Chesterfield

Norfolk I.

Lord Howe I.

Kermadec Is. (N.Z.)

NEW ZEALAND

Auckland Is.

AUSTRALIA

Brisbane

Cairns

Townsville

Rockhampton

Alice Springs

Mount Isa

L. Eyre

Great Dividing Ra.

Great Barrier Reef

Gulf of Carpentaria

Coral Sea

Lord Howe Rise

Kermadec Trench

Tropic of Capricorn

Equator

Caroline Islands

Truk

Yap

Pohnpei

Enewetak Atoll

Kwajalein

Jaluit

West Mariana Basin

Mi cr on es ia

Me la ne si a

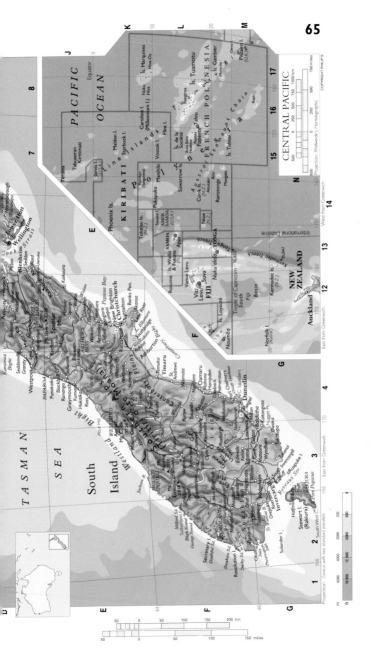

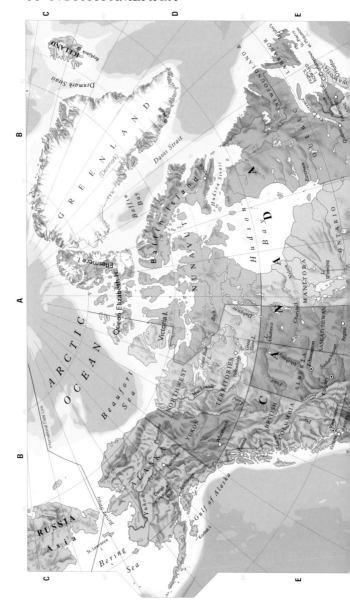

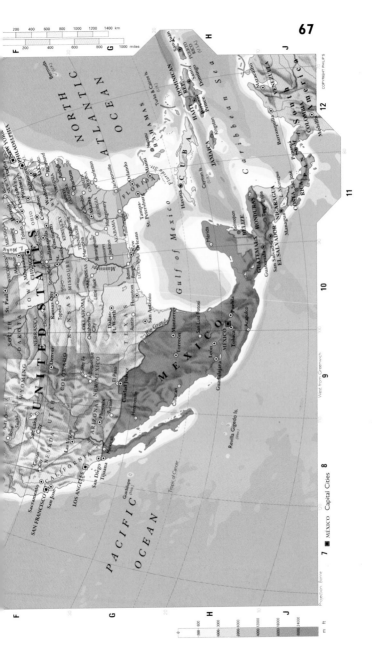

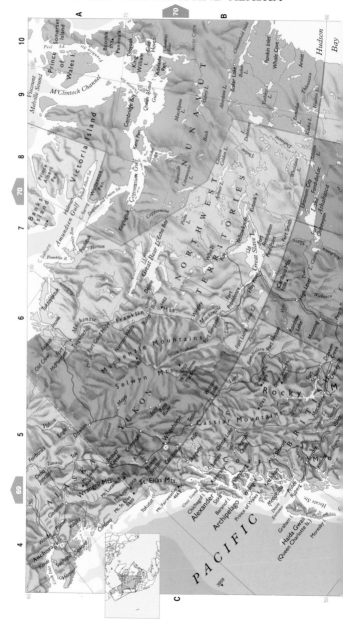

69

ALASKA

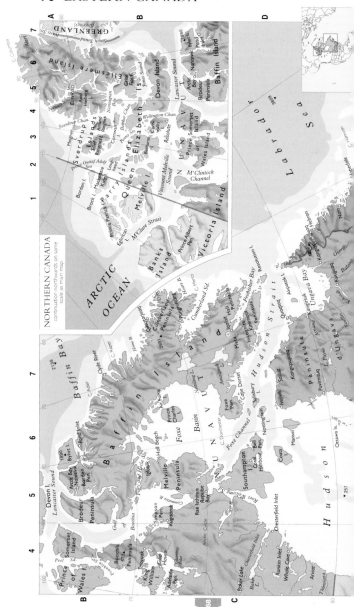

NORTHERN CANADA
continuation northwards on same
scale as main map

GREENLAND (Denmark)

C. Columbia
Alert
Smith Sound
Ellesmere Island
Hazen L.
Eureka
Eiland
Axel
Heiberg
I.
Norwegian
Bay
Grise
Fiord
Jones Sound
Pond
Inlet
Nanisivik
Arctic
Bay
Brodeur
Peninsula
Baffin Island
Devon Island
Sverdrup
Islands
Meighen I.
Ellef
Ringnes I.
Amund
Ringnes I.
Cornwallis
I.
Wellington Chan.
Cornwall
I.
Bathurst
I.
Devon Island
Lancaster Sound
Somerset
Island
Prince of
Wales Island
Resolute
Cornwallis
I.
Prince
Leopold I.
Prince Gustaf Adolf
Sea
Lougheed
I.
Kanheim
I.
Borden I.
Brock I.
Queen
Elizabeth
Islands
Parry Islands
Melville Island
NUNAVUT
M'Clintock
Channel
Viscount Melville
Sound
Victoria Island
Prince Patrick I.
Eglinton I.
M'Clure Strait
Prince Albert
Pen.
Banks
Island
ARCTIC
OCEAN

Labrador
Sea

Prince of
Wales
Island
Somerset
Island
Peel Sd.
Boothia
Peninsula
Gulf of
Boothia
Boothia
574
Pen.
Franklin Str.
Taloyoak
King
William I.
Gjoa
Haven
Spence
Bay
Pelly
Bay
Simpson
Pen.
Kugaaruk
Committee B.
Rae Isthmus
Repulse
Bay
Melville
Peninsula
Fury and Hecla Str.
Igloolik
Hall Beach
C. Dorchester
Foxe
Basin
Foxe Channel
Nottingham I.
Salisbury I.
Mansel
I.
Coats
I.
Southampton
Island
Roes
Welcome
Sd.
Bell
Pen.
Godthåb
Harbour
Coral Harbour
Baker Lake
Baker
Lake
Chesterfield Inlet
Chesterfield Inlet
Rankin Inlet
Whale Cove
Arviat
Arctic Circle
Baffin
Bay
Lancaster Sound
Devon I.
Bylot I.
Nanisivik
Pond Inlet
Borden
Pen.
Brodeur
Peninsula
Clyde River
Home B.
C. Raper
Baffin Island
Cumberland
Peninsula
Cumberland Sd.
Pangnirtung
Iqaluit
Hall
Peninsula
Frobisher Bay
Meta
Incognita
Peninsula
Kimmirut
Resolution I.
Hudson Strait
Akpatok I.
Ungava Bay
Kangiqsualujjuaq
Quaqtaq
Kangirsuk
Aupaluk
Tasiujaq
Kuujjuaq
Péninsule
d'Ungava
Salluit
Ivujivik
Kangiqsujuaq
Akulivik
Puvirnituq
Kangirsuk
NUNAVUT
Prince
Charles I.
Foxe
Pen.
Cape Dorset
C. Duchesne
Hudson
Bay
Ottawa Is.
257
Hebron
Nain
Labrador
George
Balatin

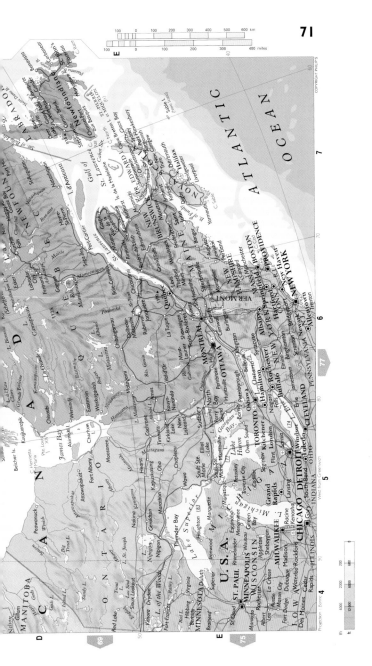

71

ATLANTIC OCEAN

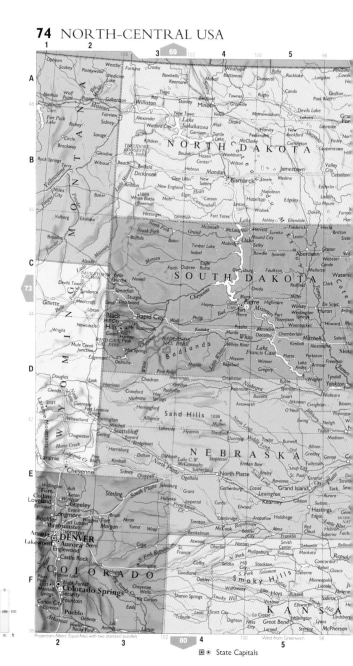

State Capitals

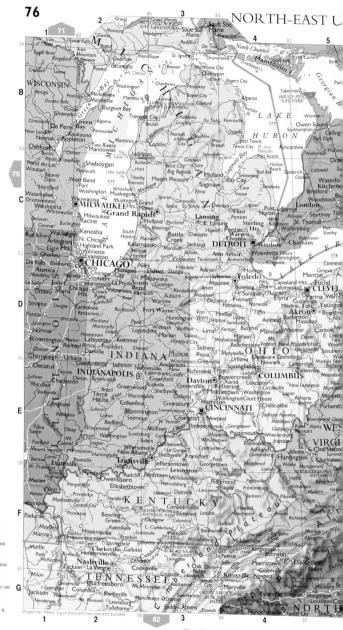

⊠ ⊛ State Capitals

PACIFIC OCEAN

N E V A D A

LOS ANGELES

SAN DIEGO

LAS VEGAS

Mojave Desert

Death Valley

Sonoran Desert

B A J A C A L I F O R N I A

Golfo de California (Mar de Cortés)

HAWAI'I

PACIFIC OCEAN

Hawaiian Islands

Honolulu

Kaua'i

O'ahu

Moloka'i

Maui

Hawai'i

Projection: Albers Equal Area with two standard parallels

⊠ ⊛ State Capitals

50 0 50 100 150 200 km
50 0 50 100 150 miles

6 73 112 7 110 8 108 9 106 10

COLORADO

Fillmore Richfield Ferron Green River Grand Junction Clifton Aspen Leadville Elbert Mt. 4389 Fairplay
Salina Green River Thompson Springs Orchard City Delta Hotchkiss Gunnison Buena Vista Pt. Antero
Marysvale Fremont Hanksville Mt. Peale Montrose Blue Mesa Res. Saguache SANGRE DE CRISTO RANGE
Beaver 3877 CANYONLANDS NATIONAL PARK Uncompahgre Pk. 4359 Gunnison Creede Rio Grande Blanca Pk. 4378
Parowan CAPITOL REEF NAT. PARK Moab Ouray Telluride Del Norte Monte Vista SANDDUNES NAT. MON.
Cedar City Torrey Monticello Dove Creek Silverton San Juan Mts. Alamosa La Garita
Tropic BRYCE CANYON NAT. PARK NATURAL BRIDGES NAT. MON. Cortez Durango 4045 Summit Peak Manassa
GRAND STAIRCASE ESCALANTE NAT. MON. Blanding HOVENWEEP NAT. MON. MESA VERDE NAT. PARK Pagosa Springs Monte Vista

U T A H

T

A

B

C

D

E

F

State Capitals

☒ ⊛ State Capitals

50 0 50 100 150 200 km
50 0 50 100 150 miles

6 77 82 **7** 80 **8** 9 76 **10**

NORTH CAROLINA

A

Middletown
Kingsport Bristol Abingdon Marion Martinsville Eden Danville Keff Emporia Murfreesboro Ahoskie
Johnson City Mountain City Air Golax Roxboro Oxford Henderson Enfield Rocky Mount Tarboro Williamston Plymouth CAPE HATTERAS
Morristown Elizabethton Elkin Reidsville Greensboro Burlington Wake Forest Raleigh Wilson Bethel Greenville Goldsboro NAT. SEASHORE
Knoxville Boone Winston-Salem High Point Durham Chapel Hill Smithfield Kinston New Bern Havelock C. Hatteras
Maryville Asheville Lenoir Hickory Statesville Lexington Siler City Sanford Clinton Jacksonville Wallace Morehead City
Mt. Mitchell Morganton Salisbury Kannapolis Albemarle Southern Pines Fayetteville Onslow Bay C. Lookout
Brevard Spartanburg Lincolnton Concord Monroe Rockingham Hamlet Laurinburg Beaufort

B

Greenville Gastonia Charlotte Rock Hill Cheraw Bennettsville Dillon Lumberton Wilmington
Easley Clemson Union Chester Lancaster Mullins C. Fear
Anderson Laurens Whiteville Conway
Greenwood Newberry Florence Marion North Myrtle Beach
Athens Abbeville Columbia Sumter Manning Myrtle Beach Long Bay
Aiken Orangeburg Andrews Georgetown

SOUTH CAROLINA

C

GEORGIA
Macon Warner Robins Dublin Statesboro Savannah Hilton Head Island
Cochran Swainsboro Garden City Hinesville
Eastman Vidalia Ridgeland Beaufort Parris I.
Hazlehurst Baxley Jesup Ossabaw I.
St. Catherines I.

D

ATLANTIC OCEAN

Jacksonville Jacksonville Beach
St. Augustine
Palm Coast

E

FLORIDA

OCEAN

Ocala Daytona Beach
Port Orange
New Smyrna Beach

Orlando Cocoa
Merritt Island
Melbourne

St. Petersburg TAMPA
Vero Beach
Fort Pierce Port St. Lucie
Stuart Hobe Sound

Sarasota

F

Great Sale Cay Little Abaco I.
Grand Cay Hope Town
Abaco I.

West Palm Beach
Boynton Beach
Delray Beach
Boca Raton Freeport Grand Bahama
Fort Lauderdale
Hollywood
Miami Beach
MIAMI

BAHAMAS

G

COPYRIGHT PHILIP'S

6 82 **7** 86 **8** 78 **9**

1 2 3 4

A

SAN DIEGO
TIJUANA Mexicali
Ensenada San Felipe
PHOENIX
Tucson
Casa Grande
Yuma
Sonoyta
Nogales
Douglas Agua Prieta
Deming
Las Cruces
CIUDAD JUÁREZ El Paso
Roswell
Lubbock
Wichita Fall

UNIT

Carlsbad
Fort W

B

Baja California
I. Ángel de la Guarda
I. Tiburón
Caborca
Magdalena de Kino
Cananea
Nacozari
Nuevo Casas Grandes
Villa Ahumada
Ojinaga
Pecos
Odessa
San Angelo
Abilene

Aus

SAN ANTONIO

G

Bahía Sebastián Vizcaíno
Santa Rosalía
Hermosillo
Guaymas
Empalme
Ciudad Obregón Navojoa
Huatabampo
Chihuahua
Cuauhtémoc
Madera
Delicias
Ciudad Camargo
Hidalgo del Parral
Jiménez
Eagle Pass
Del Rio
Ciudad Acuña
Piedras Negras
Nuevo Laredo
Laredo
Falcon Res.

C. San Lázaro
El Fuerte
Los Mochis Guasave
Guamúchil
Fuerte
Culiacán
Gómez Palacio
TORREÓN Saltillo
Monterrey
MONTERREY
Reynosa
McAlle
Br

C

C. San Lucas Cabo San Lucas
La Paz
B. de La Paz
Loreto
Topolobampo
Mazatlán
Rosario
El Salto
Durango
Concepción del Oro
Sombrerete
Fresnillo
Zacatecas
Matehuala
San Luis Potosí
Charcas
Montemorelos
Linares
Ciudad Victoria
Ciudad Mante
Ciudad Valles
Ciudad

Escuinapa
Acaponeta
Tuxpan
Tepic
Jerez

Islas Marías

D

Is. de Revillagigedo (Mex.)
Puerto Vallarta
C. Corrientes
Ameca
GUADALAJARA
L. de Chapala
Zamora
Ciudad Guzmán
Nevado de Colima
Manzanillo Colima
Tecomán
LEÓN
Guanajuato
Irapuato Celaya
Aguascalientes
Querétaro
Morelia
Uruapan
TOLUCA MÉXICO
Cuernavaca
Iguala
Popocatépetl
PUEBLA
Pachuca
Tulancingo

Lázaro Cárdenas
Balsas
Chilpancingo Chilapa
Tlapa
Oaxa

Acapulco
Omelepec

E

PACIFIC

F

I. Clipperton (Fr.)

OCEAN

Projection: Bonne

3 4 5

m ft
0
200 600
2000 6000
4000 12 000
6000 18 000

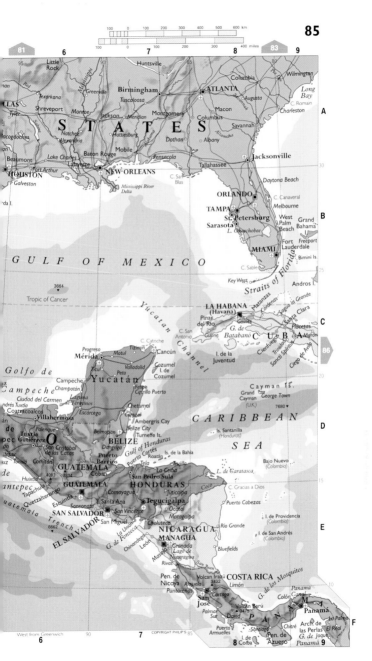

6 7 8 9

100 0 100 200 300 400 500 600 km
100 0 100 200 300 400 miles

Little Rock
Huntsville
Columbia
Wilmington
Texarkana
Greenville
Birmingham
ATLANTA
Augusta
Long Bay
LLAS
Tyler
Shreveport
Monroe
Jackson
Meridian
Montgomery
Columbus
Macon
Savannah
C. Romain
Charleston

A

acogdoches
Beaumont
Lake Charles
Natchez
Hattiesburg
Dothan
Albany

HOUSTON
Port Arthur
Galveston
Baton Rouge
Mobile
Pensacola
Tallahassee
Jacksonville

da I.
NEW ORLEANS
Mississippi River Delta
C. San Blas
Daytona Beach

B

ORLANDO
C. Canaveral
Melbourne
TAMPA
St. Petersburg
Sarasota
L. Okeechobee
West Palm Beach
Grand Bahama
Freeport
MIAMI
Fort Lauderdale
Bimini Is.

G U L F   O F   M E X I C O
C. Sable
Key West
Straits of Florida
Andros I.

3664
Tropic of Cancer

C

LA HABANA (Havana)
Matanzas
Cárdenas
Sagua la Grande
Yucatán
Pinar del Río
Güines
Santa Clara
Bahía Honda
Placetas
C. San Antonio
Güane
G. de Batabanó
C U B A
Morón
Cienfuegos
Trinidad
Sancti Spíritus
Ciego de Ávila

C. Catoche
Tizimín
Progreso
Motul
Cancún
Mérida
Valladolid
Peto
Cozumel
I. de Cozumel

Golfo de
Campeche
Champotón
Felipe Carrillo Puerto
I. de la Juventud

Campeche
Ciudad del Carmen
Laguna de Términos
Yucatán
Cayman Is.
Grand Cayman
(U.K.)
George Town
7680

ndrés Tuxtla
Coatzacoalcos
Escárcega
Chetumal
Corozal

de
Villahermosa
Ambergris Cay
Belize City
Turneffe Is.
C A R I B B E A N

D

Juxtla
Gutiérrez
Palenque
Belmopan
BELIZE
Dangriga
Is. Santanilla (Honduras)
S E A

San Cristóbal de las Casas
Puerto Barrios
Is. de la Bahía
Roatán
Trujillo
Bajo Nuevo (Colombia)

uz
Tonalá
Comitán
GUATEMALA
Cobán
Puerto Cortés
Tela
La Ceiba
L. de Caratasca

4083
3324
San Pedro Sula

antepec
Huixtla
GUATEMALA
HONDURAS
Coco
C. Gracias a Dios

atemala Trench
Tapachula
Quetzaltenango
Comayagua
Juticalpa
Puerto Cabezas

Escuintla
Santa Ana
Tegucigalpa

SAN SALVADOR
San Vincente
Ocotal
Matagalpa
I. de Providencia (Colombia)

E

6662
San Miguel
EL SALVADOR
La Unión
G. de Fonseca
Chinandega
León
Choluteca
NICARAGUA
MANAGUA
Río Grande
I. de San Andrés (Colombia)

Granada
Masaya
Lago de Nicaragua
Bluefields
Rivas

Pen. de Nicoya
Volcán Irazú
3432
COSTA RICA
Limón
G. de los Mosquitos
Panamá Canal

Alajuela
Puntarenas
Cartago
Colón
P A N A M A
Panamá
Arch. de las Perlas
La Palma

San José
Volcán Barú
3475
David
Chitré
El Real

Palmar Sur

F

Puerto Armuelles
Santiago
Pen. de Azuero
G. de San Miguel

I. de Coiba
Panamá

Mississippi River Delta

ORLANDO
TAMPA
St. Petersburg
Sarasota
L. Okeechobee

Daytona Beach
C. Canaveral
Melbourne
West Palm Beach
Grand Bahama
Freeport
Abaco I.

GULF OF
MEXICO

U.S.A.
MIAMI
Fort Lauderdale
Bimini Is.
New Providence I.
Eleuthera I.

C. Sable
Key West
Nassau
Cat I.

Straits of Florida
Andros I.
BAHAMAS

Tropic of Cancer

Great Exuma I.
Long

Yucatan Channel
LA HABANA (Havana)
Matanzas
Sagua la Grande
Santa Clara

Pinar del Río
Güines
G. de Batabanó
Cienfuegos
Sancti Spíritus
Trinidad
Placetas
Morón
Moa

C. San Antonio

Progreso
Motul
Tizimín
I. de la Juventud

CUBA
Greater

Camagüey
Nuevitas
Holguín
Gre

Mérida
Valladolid
Peto
Cozumel
I. de Cozumel

Las Tunas
Banes

Yucatán
Campeche
Champotón
Felipe Carrillo Puerto

Manzanillo
1972
Bay
Santiago de Cuba
Guantánamo

Jére

Cayman Is.
Grand Cayman
George Town (U.K.)
7680

MEXICO
Chetumal
Corozal
Ambergris Cay
Belize City
Turneffe Is.

Mandeville
Spanish Town
Kingston
Les C
I

Escárcega
Belmopan
Dangriga
BELIZE

JAMAICA
Pedro Cays (Jamaica)

Cobán
Puerto Barrios
Gulf of Honduras
Puerto Cortés
Is. de la Bahía
Roatán
Trujillo
Tela
La Ceiba
San Pedro Sula

Is. Santanilla (Honduras)

Bajo Nuevo (Colombia)

GUATEMALA
GUATEMALA
HONDURAS
Coco
L. de Caratasca

CARI

Santa Ana
SAN SALVADOR
Sonsonate
San Vicente
San Miguel
EL SALVADOR
La Unión
G. de Fonseca

Comayagua
Juticalpa
Tegucigalpa
Ocotal
Matagalpa
C. Gracias a Dios
Puerto Cabezas

I. de Providencia (Colombia)

Choluteca
NICARAGUA
MANAGUA
Granada
Lago de Nicaragua
Rivas
Río Grande
I. de San Andrés (Colombia)

Chinandega
León
Masaya
San Juan
Bluefields

Santa M

BARRANQUILLA
Cartagena
Sol

Pen. de Nicoya
Volcán Irazú 2432
Limón
G. de los Mosquitos
Panama Canal
Colón
G. del Darién
Sincelejo
Montería
Ma

Alajuela
Puntarenas
San José
Cartago
COSTA RICA
PANAMÁ
Panamá
La Palma
El Real
Riosucio

Palmar Sur
Volcán Barú 3475
David
Chitré
Arch. de las Perlas
Joaquí
Barraca
2960

Puerto Armuelles
Sonsonate
I. de Coiba
Pen. de Azuero
G. de Panamá
G. de Cupicas
C. Corrientes
Quindío
Bello
Manizales
Pereira

PACIFIC

I. del Coco (C. Rica)

Antioquia

Armenia

OCEAN
I. de Malpelo (Colombia)
Buenaventura
CALI
Huila
Neiva
Popayán
Palmira
Volcán Purace 4646

Projection : Bonne
West from Greenwich

m ft
0
200 600
2000 6000
4000 12 000
6000 18 000

100 0 100 200 300 400 500 600 km
100 0 100 200 300 400 miles

6   65   7   60   8   55

A

SARGASSO
SEA

ATLANTIC OCEAN

B

Tropic of Cancer

Turks & Caicos Is.
Cockburn (U.K.)
Town
Cap-Haïtien
Cap-à-Foux
Monte Cristi
Santiago de
los Caballeros
San Francisco
de Macorís
8605 Puerto Rico Trench
Arecibo
SAN JUAN
Charlotte
Amalie Virgin Is.
Anguilla (U.K.)
St-Martin (Fr./Neth.)
St-Barthélemy (Fr.)
ST. KITTS & NEVIS
ANTIGUA &
BARBUDA

C

Gonaïves
DOMINICAN
REP. La Romana
PRINCE
Barahona
Bani
San Pedro de Macorís
SANTO DOMINGO
Hispaniola
Mona
Mayagüez
Ponce
PUERTO RICO
(U.S.A.)
St. Croix
(U.S.A.)
Aguas (U.S.A./U.K.)
St-Eustatius
(Neth.)
Basseterre
St. John's
Montserrat (U.K.)
GUADELOUPE (Fr.)
Pointe-à-Pitre
Basse-Terre
DOMINICA
Roseau
MARTINIQUE (Fr.)
Fort-de-France
Castries
ST. LUCIA

t i l l e s

Leeward
Islands

Lesser

D

EAN SEA
Antilles
ST. VINCENT &
THE GRENADINES
Windward
Islands
Kingstown
Bridgetown
BARBADOS
GRENADA
St. George's

Pta. Gallinas
de la
Aajira
Jevada
a Marta
edupar
Aruba
Orangestad
Curaçao
Willemstad
Punto
Fijo
Bonaire
ABC Islands
(Neth.)
Coro
San
Felipe
Puerto Cabello
Maiquetía
MARACAY
La Blanquilla
(Ven.)
I. de Margarita
Porlamar
Carúpano
Tobago
Port of Spain
TRINIDAD & TOBAGO
San Fernando

E

MARACAIBO
Cabimas
Barquisimeto
VALENCIA
CARACAS
Barcelona
Cumaná
Puerto La
Cruz
Maturín
G. de Venezuela
La Tortuga
Guiria
G. de
Paria
L. de
Maracaibo
Valera
Mérida
Barinas
Acarigua
San Fernando
de Apure
El Tigre
Orinoco
Tucupita
Ciudad
Guayana
Ciudad Bolívar
Embalse de Guri
Tumeremo
Georgetown
New Amsterdam
Linden
Wismar
Apure

San Cristóbal
Pamplona
icaramanga
Barinas
Caicara
V E N E Z U E L A
G U Y A N A
SURINAME

Sogamoso
nja
TÁ
vicencio
O M B I A
Meta
Puerto Carreño
Arauca
Puerto Ayacucho
Vichada
Caura
Caroní
Mt. Roraima
2810
Sierra Pacaraima

Guanare
Puerto Inírida
Orinoco
Sierra
Parima

F

BRAZIL

Boa Vista

Equator

92

COPYRIGHT PHILIP'S

5   70   90   6   65   7   60   8

100 0 200 400 600 800 1000 1200 1400 km
100 0 200 400 600 800 1000 miles

COPYRIGHT PHILIP'S

PACIFIC

OCEAN

ATLANTIC

OCEAN

MINAS GERAIS
ESPÍRITO
SANTO
Belo
Horizonte
Juiz
de Fora
Campos
Vitória
Campinas
Niterói
RIO DE
JANEIRO
SÃO PAULO
Santos
MATO GROSSO
DO SUL
PARANÁ
Paranaguá
Santa Cruz
Pedro
SÃO PAULO
Curitiba
SANTA CATARINA
Uruguai
RIO GRANDE
DO SUL
Pôrto Alegre
Pelotas

PARAGUAY
Asunción
Pilcomayo
Paraná
Sucre
Salado
Pôrto
Resistencia
Corrientes
Paraná
URUGUAY
Montevideo
Rio de la Plata

San Miguel
de Tucumán
Santa Fe
Córdoba
Rosario
BUENOS AIRES
La Plata
San Juan
Mendoza
Mar del Plata
Salado

Iquique
Antofagasta

San Félix
(Chile)
San Ambrosio
(Chile)

Arch. de Juan Fernández
(Chile)

Viña del Mar
Valparaíso
SANTIAGO
Concepción
Valdivia
Puerto Montt
Colorado
Negro
Bahía
Blanca
Neuquén

A
R
G
E
N
T
I
N
A

C
H
I
L
E

Trelew
Chubut
Comodoro Rivadavia
Gulf of San Jorge

Gulf of Penas
Punta Arenas
Magellan's Str.
C. Horn
Tierra del Fuego

West Falkland
FALKLAND IS.
(U.K.)
Stanley
East Falkland

South Georgia
(U.K.)

Tropic of Capricorn

W West from Greenwich

■ LIMA Capital Cities

Projection: Lambert's Azimuthal Equal Area

m ft
600
3000
6000
12000
18000
24000

F G H
1 2 3 4 5 6 7

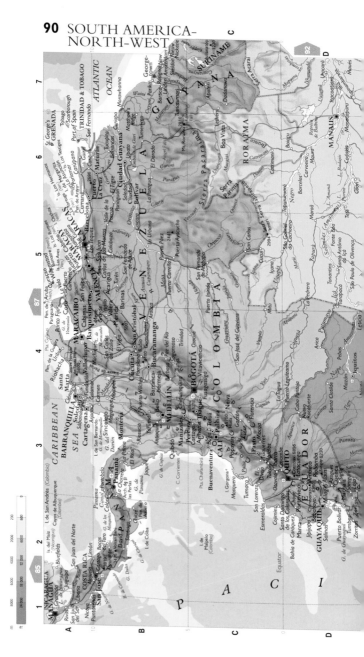

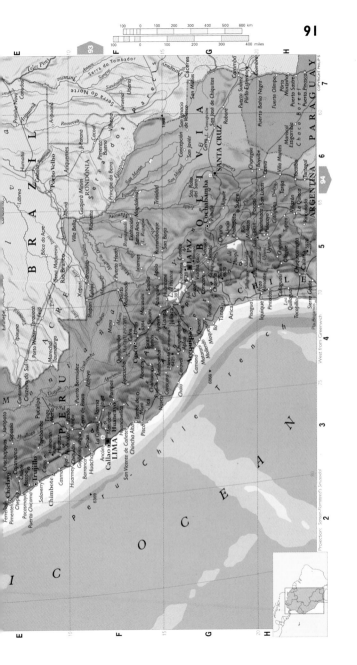

100 0 100 200 300 400 500 600 km
100 0 100 200 300 400 miles

93

94

Projection: Sanson-Flamsteed's Sinusoidal

West from Greenwich

COPYRIGHT PHILIP'S

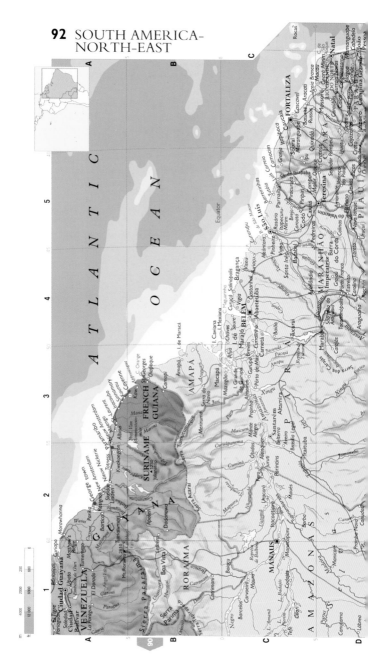

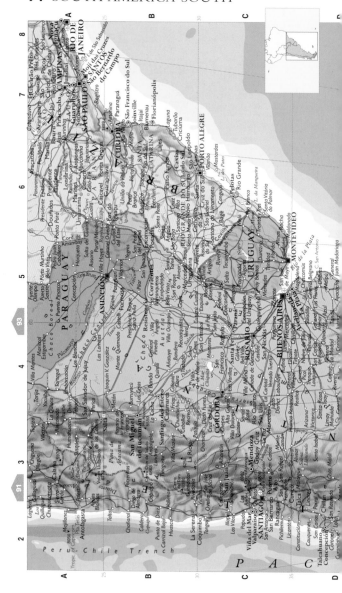

95

100 0 100 200 300 400 500 600 km
100 0 100 200 300 400 miles

E

A T L A N T I C

O C E A N

▲5930

F A L K L A N D   I S L A N D S
(ISLAS MALVINAS) (U.K.)
C. Dolphin
King George B. ▲700 ●Stanley
West Falkland 705▲ Port Darwin
Weddell I. C. Meredith East Falkland
Falkland Sd.

South Georgia
(U.K.)
▲2934 Grytviken

60° West from Greenwich 55°

Carmen de Patagones
San Antonio Oeste
Nécheta
Viedma
Golfo San Matías
Pen. Valdés
Pto. Lobos
G. Nuevo
Rawson
Puerto Madryn
Trelew
Telsen
Dos Bahías
Camarones
Gulf San Jorge
Pico Truncado
Comodoro Rivadavia
C. Tres Puntas
Puerto Deseado
Pto. Medanosa
Fitz Roy
Pico Molina
Laguna del Carbón
Puerto San Julián
Bahía Grande
Puerto Santa Cruz
Puerto Coig
C. Vírgenes
Río Gallegos
El Calafate
Estrecho de Magallanes
San Sebastián
Punta Arenas
Porvenir
Río Grande
Tierra del Fuego
▲2469
I. de los Estados (Staten I.)
C. San Diego
Le Maire (Str.)
Navarino
I. Wollaston
Hornos (C. Horn)

Puerto Montt
Osorno
Ancud
I. de Chiloé
Castro
Quellón
Chonchi
Is. Guaitecas
Arch. de los Chonos
I. Magdalena
Pen. de Taitao
G. de Penas
Pen. Tres Montes
I. Campana
I. Wellington
I. Madre de Dios
I. Santa Inés
Arch. Reina Adelaida
Estrecho de Magallanes
B. Otway
C. Froward

Projection: Sanson-Flamsteed's Sinusoidal

COPYRIGHT PHILIP'S

m ft
8000 24,000
6000 18,000
4000 12,000
2000 6000
200 680
0 0

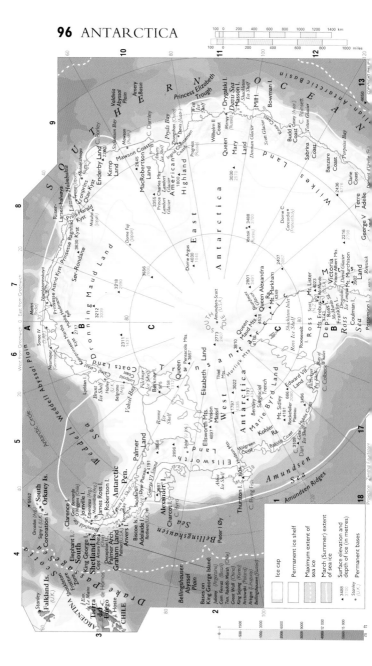

100 0 200 400 600 800 1000 1200 1400 km
100 0 200 400 600 800 1000 miles

SOUTHERN OCEAN

Valdivia Abyssal Plain
E. Basin
Princess Elizabeth Trough
Drygalski I.
Davis Sea
Masson I.
Bowman I.
West Ice Shelf
Mill I.
Shackleton Ice Shelf
Knox Coast
Budd Coast
Sabrina Coast
Banzare Coast
Clarie Coast
Terre Adélie
George V Land

Princess Elizabeth Land
Amery Ice Shelf
MacRobertson Land
American Highland
Queen Mary Land
Wilkes Land

Enderby Land
Kemp Land

East Antarctica

Dronning Maud Land
Coats Land
Queen Elizabeth Land
West Antarctica
Marie Byrd Land
Ellsworth Land
Palmer Land
Graham Land

Antarctic Pen.
Weddell Sea
Ronne Ice Shelf
Filchner Ice Shelf
Ross Ice Shelf
Ross Sea
Amundsen Sea
Bellingshausen Sea

Queen Maud Mts.
Horlick Mts.
Transantarctic Mts.
Pensacola Mts.
Ellsworth Mts.
Victoria Land
Mt. Erebus
Mt. Terror
Ross I.
Coulman I.
Possession I.

South Orkney Is.
South Shetland Is.
Elephant I.
Clarence I.
Coronation I.
Signy I.
King George I.
Joinville I.
James Ross I.
Robertson I.
Anvers I.
Adelaide I.
Alexander I.
Charcot I.
Thurston I.
Peter I Øy
Roosevelt I.
Siple I.

Scotia Sea
Drake Passage
Falkland Is.
Tierra del Fuego
ARGENTINA
CHILE
Stanley

Amundsen-Scott (U.S.A.)
SOUTH POLE

Bases on King George Island:
Jubany (Argentina)
Com. Ferraz (Brazil)
Ten. Rodolfo Marsh (Chile)
Great Wall (China)
King Sejong (Korea)
Artigas (Uruguay)
Bellingshausen (Russia)

Legend
- Ice cap
- Permanent ice shelf
- Maximum extent of sea ice
- March (Summer) extent of sea ice
- Surface elevation and depth of ice (in metres)
  - ▲ 3488
  - 3700
- ● Permanent bases

ft
15,000
12,000
9000
6000
3000
1500
-500

INDEX TO MAP PAGES

The index contains the names of all the principal places and features shown on the world maps. Physical features composed of a proper name (Erie) and a description (Lake) are positioned alphabetically by the proper name. The description is positioned after the proper name and is usually abbreviated:

Erie, L. **76 C5**

Where a description forms part of a settlement or administrative name, however, it is always written in full and put in its true alphabetical position:

Lake Charles **81 D7**

Names beginning St. are alphabetized under Saint, but Sankt, Sant, Santa and San are all spelt in full and are alphabetized accordingly.

The number in bold type which follows each name in the index refers to the number of the map page where that feature or place will be found. This is usually the largest scale at which the place or feature appears.

The letter and figure which are in bold type immediately after the page number give the grid square on the map page, within which the feature is situated.

Rivers are indexed to their mouths or confluences, and carry the symbol → after their names. The following symbols are also used in the index: ■ country, ☑ overseas territory or dependency, □ first order administrative area, △ national park.

A

A Coruña 18 A1
Aachen 14 C4
Aalborg 9 D7
Aarhus 9 D8
Aba 53 G7
Abaco I. 86 A4
Ābādān 47 E7
Abaetetuba 92 C4
Abakan 30 D7
Abancay 91 F4
Abaya, L. 57 C7
Abbeville 12 A4
Abbot Ice Shelf 96 B2
ABC Islands ☑ 87 D6
Abéché 55 F3
Abeokuta 53 G6
Aberdeen U.K. 10 C5
Aberdeen S. Dak., U.S.A. 74 C5
Aberdeen Wash., U.S.A. 72 C2
Aberystwyth 11 E4
Abidjan 53 G5
Abilene 80 C4
Abitibi, L. 71 E6
Abkhazia □ 25 E5
Åbo = Turku 9 C10
Abomey 53 G6
Absaroka Range 73 D9
Abu Dhabi = Abū Ẓaby 44 E3
Abu Hamed 55 E5
Abū Ẓaby 44 E3
Abuja 53 G7
Abunã 91 E5
Abunã → 91 E5
Acaponeta 84 C3
Acapulco 84 D5
Acarigua 90 B5
Accra 53 G5
Aceh □ 38 D1
Acharnes 23 E4

Acheloos → 23 E3
Achill I. 11 E1
Acklins I. 86 B5
Aconcagua, Cerro 94 C3
Acre = 'Akko 46 D3
Acre □ 91 E4
Acre → 91 E5
Ad Dammām 47 F7
Ad Dawḥah 44 E2
Ad Dīwānīyah 47 E6
Adair, C. 70 B6
Adamaoua, Massif de l' 55 G1
Adam's Bridge 43 Q11
'Adan 49 E4
Adana 46 C3
Adapazarı = Sakarya 25 E3
Adare, C. 96 B15
Addis Ababa = Addis Abeba 49 F2
Addis Abeba 49 F2
Adelaide 62 B2
Adelaide I. 96 A3
Adelaide Pen. 68 B3
Adélie, Terre 96 A14
Aden = 'Adan 49 E4
Aden, G. of 49 E4
Adige → 20 B4
Adirondack Mts. 77 C8
Adis Abeba = Addis Abeba 49 F2
Admiralty Is. 64 K9
Adour → 12 E3
Adrar 52 D6
Adrar des Iforas 52 E6
Adriatic Sea 20 C5
Adzhar Republic = Ajaria □ 25 E5
Ægean Sea 23 E5
Aerhtai Shan 34 B4
Afghanistan ■ 45 C6
Afyon 46 C2
Afyonkarahisar = Afyon 46 C2

Agadez 53 E7
Agadir 52 B4
Agartala 41 F8
Agen 12 D4
Agra 42 F10
Ağri 26 F5
Agrigento 21 F4
Agua Prieta 84 A3
Aguascalientes 84 C4
Agulhas, C. 58 E4
Ahaggar 52 D7
Ahmadabad 43 H8
Ahmadnagar 43 K9
Ahmadpur 42 E7
Ahmedabad = Ahmadabad 43 H8
Ahmednagar = Ahmadnagar 43 K9
Ahvāz 47 E7
Ahvenanmaa = Åland 9 C10
Ahwar 49 E4
Ahui = Heihe 35 A7
Air 53 E7
Air Force I. 70 C6
Aisne → 13 B5
Aix-en-Provence 13 E6
Aix-la-Chapelle = Aachen 14 C4
Aix-les-Bains 13 D6
Aizawl 41 F9
Aizuwakamatsu 33 E6
Ajaccio 13 F8
Ajanta Ra. 43 J9
Ajaria □ 25 E5
Ajdābiyā 54 B3
'Ajmān 44 E3
Ajmer 42 F9
Aketi 56 D4
Akhisar 23 E6
Akimiski I. 71 D5
Akita 32 D7
'Akko 46 D3
Aklavik 68 B6

Akola 43 J10
Akpatok I. 70 C7
Akranes 8 C1
Akron 76 D5
Aksai Chin 42 B11
Aksaray 46 C3
Aksu 34 B3
Aktyubinsk = Aqtöbe 29 D6
Akure 53 G7
Akureyri 8 C4
Akyab = Sittwe 41 G9
Al Aḥsā = Hasa 47 F7
Al 'Amārah 47 E6
Al 'Aqabah 47 E3
Al 'Aramah 47 F6
Al Baḥral Mayyit = Dead Sea 47 E3
Al Baṣrah 47 E6
Al Bayḍā 54 B3
Al Fallūjah 46 D5
Al Fāw 47 E7
Al Ḥillah Iraq 47 D6
Al Ḥillah Si. Arabia 47 G6
Al Hoceima 52 A5
Al Ḥudaydah 49 E3
Al Ḥufūf 47 F7
Al Jahrah 47 E6
Al Jawf Libya 54 D3
Al Jawf Si. Arabia 47 E4
Al Jazair = Algeria ■ 52 C6
Al Jazirah 46 D5
Al Jubayl 47 F7
Al Junaynah 55 F3
Al Khalīl 47 E3
Al Kufrah 54 D3
Al Kūt 47 D6
Al Kuwayt 47 E7
Al Lādhiqīyah 46 D3
Al Madīnah 47 F4
Al Maghreb = Morocco ■ 52 B4
Al Manāmah 44 E2
Al Mawşil 46 C5

Al Mubarraz 47 F7
Al Mukallā 49 E4
Al Musayyib 47 D6
Al Qāmishlī 46 C5
Al Qaṭīf 47 F7
Al Quds = Jerusalem 47 E3
Al Yaman = Yemen ■ 49 D4
Alabama □ 82 C4
Alabama → 82 D4
Alacant = Alicante 19 C5
Alagoas □ 93 D6
Alagoinhas 93 E6
Alamosa 79 B10
Åland 9 C10
Alanya 46 C2
Alappuzha 43 Q10
Alaşehir 23 E7
Alaska □ 69 B4
Alaska, G. of 69 C5
Alaska Peninsula 69 C4
Alaska Range 69 B4
Albacete 19 C5
Albania ■ 23 D3
Albany Australia 60 H2
Albany Ga., U.S.A. 83 D5
Albany N.Y., U.S.A. 77 C9
Albany Oreg., U.S.A. 72 D2
Albany → 71 D5
Albert, L. 57 D6
Albert Nile → 57 D6
Albertville 13 D7
Albi 12 E5
Ålborg = Aalborg 9 D7
Alborz, Reshteh-ye Kūhhā-ye 44 B3
Albuquerque 79 C9
Albury 63 C4
Alcalá de Henares 18 B4
Alchevsk 25 D4
Alcoy 19 C5
Aldabra Is. 51 G8

Aldan → 31 C10
Alderney 11 G5
Alegrete 94 B5
Alençon 12 B4
Aleppo = Ḥalab 46 C4
Alert 70 A7
Alès 13 D6
Alessándria 13 D8
Ålesund 8 D7
Aleutian Is. 69 C2
Alexander Arch. 69 C6
Alexander I. 96 A3
Alexandria = El
    Iskandarîya 54 B4
Alexandria *La., U.S.A.*
    81 D7
Alexandria *Va., U.S.A.*
    77 F7
Algarve 18 D1
Algeciras 18 D3
Alger 52 A6
Algeria ■ 52 C6
Algiers = Alger 52 A6
Alhucemas = Al Hoceïma
    52 A5
Alicante 19 C5
Alice Springs 60 E5
Aligarh 42 F11
Alipur Duar 41 D7
Aliwal North 59 E5
Alkmaar 14 B3
Allahabad 40 E3
Alleghey → 77 D5
Allegheny Mts. 77 F5
Allentown 77 D8
Alleppey = Alappuzha
    43 Q10
Allier → 13 C5
Alma Ata = Almaty 29 E8
Almada 18 C1
Almaty 29 E8
Almelo 14 B4
Almería 19 D4
Alnwick 10 D6
Alor 37 F2
Alor Setar 38 C2
Alps 14 E5
Alsace □ 13 B7
Altai = Aerhtai Shan
    34 B4
Altamira 92 C3
Altamura 21 D6
Altanbulag 35 A5
Altay 34 B3
Alton 75 F9
Altoona 77 D6
Altun Shan 34 C3
Alwar 42 F10
Alxa Zuoqi 35 C5
Amadjuak L. 70 C6
Amagasaki 33 F4
Amapá 92 B3
Amapá □ 92 B3
Amarillo 80 B3
Amazon → = Amazonas →
    92 C3
Amazonas □ 90 D6
Amazonas → 92 C3
Ambala 42 D10
Ambato 90 D3
Ambergris Cay 85 D7
Ambikapur 40 F4
Ambilobé 59 A9
Ambon 37 E3
Amchitka I. 69 C1
Amderma 28 C7
Ameca 84 C4
American Highland
    96 B10
American Samoa ☑
    65 L13
Ames 75 D8
Amherst 71 E7
Amiens 12 B5
Amirante Is. 26 K9
'Ammän 47 E3

Ammochostos =
    Famagusta 46 D3
Amos 71 E6
Amoy = Xiamen 35 D6
Amravati 43 J10
Amreli 43 J7
Amritsar 42 D9
Amroha 42 E11
Amsterdam 14 B3
Amudarya → 29 E6
Amund Ringnes I. 70 B4
Amundsen Gulf 68 A7
Amundsen Sea 96 B1
Amuntai 39 E5
Amur → 31 D12
An Nafūd 47 E5
An Najaf 47 D6
Anaconda 73 C7
Anadolu 25 F3
Anaheim 78 D4
Anambas, Kepulauan
    39 D3
Anamur 46 D3
Anápolis 93 F4
Anār 44 D3
Anatolia = Anadolu 25 F3
Añatuya 94 B4
Anchorage 69 B5
Ancohuma, Nevado
    91 G5
Ancona 20 C4
Ancud 95 E2
Ancud, G. de 95 E2
Andalgalá 94 B3
Andalucía □ 18 D3
Andalusia 82 D4
Andaman Is. 27 G11
Andaman Sea 38 B1
Anderson 76 D3
Anderson → 68 B7
Andes, Cord. de los
    91 G4
Andhra Pradesh □
    43 M11
Andijon 29 E8
Andorra ■ 19 A6
Andorra La Vella 12 E4
Andreanof Is. 69 C2
Ándria 20 D6
Andros 23 F5
Andros I. 86 B4
Ångara → 30 D7
Angarsk 30 D8
Ånge 8 C9
Angeles 36 A2
Ångermanälven → 8 C9
Angers 12 C3
Anglesey 11 E4
Angoche 59 B7
Angola ■ 58 A3
Angoulême 12 D4
Angoumois 12 D4
Anguilla ☑ 87 C7
Anhui □ 35 C6
Anjou 12 C3
Ankang 35 C5
Ankara 25 F3
Ann Arbor 76 D4
Annaba 52 A7
Annan 11 D5
Annapolis 77 E7
Annecy 13 D7
Anning 34 D5
Anniston 82 C5
Annobón 51 G4
Anqing 35 C6
Anshan 35 B7
Anshun 35 D5
Antakya = Hatay 46 C4
Antalaha 59 A10
Antalya 46 C2
Antalya Körfezi 46 C2
Antananarivo 59 B9
Antarctic Pen. 96 A4
Antarctica 96
Anti Atlas 52 C4
Antibes 13 E7

Anticosti, Î. d' 71 E7
Antigonish 71 E7
Antigua & Barbuda ■
    87 C7
Antioquia 90 B3
Antofagasta 94 A2
Antrim 11 D3
Antsirabe 59 B9
Antsiranana 59 A9
Antwerpen 14 C3
Anvers = Antwerpen
    14 C3
Anxi 34 B4
Anyang 35 C6
Ánzio 20 D4
Aomen = Macau 35 D6
Aomori 32 C7
Aoraki Mount Cook 65 F4
Aosta 13 D7
Aotearoa = New
    Zealand ■ 64 D7
Apaporis → 90 D5
Apeldoorn 14 B3
Apennines = Appennini
    20 B3
Apia 65 L13
Appalachian Mts. 77 F5
Appennini 20 B3
Appleton 76 B1
Apure → 90 B5
Apurímac → 91 F4
Aqaba = Al 'Aqabah
    47 E3
Aqaba, G. of 47 E3
Aqtöbe 29 D6
Aquitain, Bassin 12 D3
Ar Rachidiya = Er
    Rachidia 52 B5
Ar Ramādī 46 D5
Ar Riyāḍ 47 F6
Ara 40 E5
'Arab, Bahr el → 55 G4
Arab, Shatt al → 47 E7
Arabian Desert = Es
    Sahrâ' Esh Sharqîya
    54 C5
Arabian Gulf = Persian
    Gulf 44 E2
Arabian Sea 26 G8
Aracaju 93 E6
Aracati 92 C6
Araçatuba 93 G3
Araçuai 93 F5
Arad 16 E5
Arafura Sea 37 F4
Aragón □ 19 B5
Araguacema 92 D4
Araguaia → 92 D4
Araguari 93 F4
Arakan Coast 41 H9
Arakan Yoma 41 H10
Araks = Aras, Rüd-e →
    46 B7
Aral 29 E7
Aral Sea 29 E6
Aralsk = Aral 29 E7
Aralskoye More = Aral
    Sea 29 E6
Aran Is. 11 E2
Arapiraca 93 D6
Araraquara 93 G4
Ararat, Mt. = Ağrı Dağı
    25 F5
Araripe, Chapada do
    92 D6
Aras, Rüd-e → 46 B7
Arauca → 90 B5
Araxá 93 F4
Arbil 46 C6
Arbroath 10 C5
Arcachon 12 D3
Archangel = Arkhangelsk
    28 C5
Arctic Bay 70 B5
Arctic Ocean 4
Arctic Red River =
    Tsiigehtchic 68 B6
Ardabīl 46 C7

Ardenne 14 D3
Ardmore 80 B5
Arecibo 87 C6
Arendal 9 D7
Arequipa 91 G4
Arezzo 20 C3
Argentan 12 B3
Argentina ■ 94 D3
Argentino, L. 95 G2
Argostóli 23 E3
Århus = Aarhus 9 D8
Ária 91 G4
Arinos → 91 F7
Aripuanã → 90 E6
Arizona □ 79 C7
Arkansas □ 81 B7
Arkansas → 81 C8
Arkansas City 80 A5
Arkhangelsk 28 C5
Arklow 11 E3
Arles 13 E6
Arlington 77 E7
Arlon 14 D3
Armagh 11 D3
Armavir 25 D5
Armenia 90 C3
Armenia ■ 25 E5
Arnaud → 70 C6
Arnhem 14 C3
Arnhem, C. 60 C6
Arnhem Land 60 C5
Arno → 20 C3
Arrah = Ara 40 E5
Arran 10 D4
Arranmore 10 D2
Arras 13 A5
Arrecife 52 C3
Artigas 94 C5
Artois 12 A5
Artvin 25 E5
Aru, Kepulauan 37 F4
Arua 57 D6
Aruanã 93 E3
Aruba ☑ 87 D6
Arunachal Pradesh □
    41 C10
Arusha 57 E7
Aruwimi → 56 D4
Arviat 68 B10
Arxan 35 B6
Arzamas 24 B5
As Sohar = Şuḩār 44 E4
As Sulaymānīyah *Iraq*
    46 D6
As Sulaymānīyah *Si. Arabia* 47 F6
Aş Şuwayrah 47 D6
Asahikawa 32 B8
Asansol 40 F6
Ascension I. 51 G2
Áscoli Piceno 20 C4
Aseb 49 E3
Asenovgrad 22 C5
Ashgabat = Ashgabat
    29 F6
Ash Shāriqah 44 E3
Asheville 83 B6
Ashford 11 F7
Ashgabat 29 F6
Ashkhabad = Ashgabat
    29 F6
Ashqelon 47 E3
Ashtabula 76 D5
Ashuanipi, L. 71 D7
Asinara 20 D2
'Asīr 48 D3
Asir, Ras 49 E5
Asmera 57 A7
Assab = Aseb 49 E3
Assam □ 41 D9
Assen 14 B4
Assiniboia 69 D9
Assiniboine → 69 D10
Assisi 20 C4
Astana 29 D8
Asti 13 D8
Astipálaia 23 F6

Astoria 72 C2
Astrakhan 25 D6
Asturias □ 18 A3
Asunción 94 B5
Aswân 54 C5
Aswân Dam = Sadd el
    Aali 54 D5
Asyût 54 C5
At Tā'if 48 C3
Atacama, Desierto de
    94 A3
Atbara 55 E5
Atbara, Nahr → 55 E5
Athabasca 69 C8
Athabasca → 68 C8
Athabasca, L. 68 C8
Athens = Athina 23 F4
Athens 83 C6
Athina 23 F4
Athínai = Athina 23 F4
Athlone 11 E3
Athos 23 D5
Athy 11 E3
Atlanta 83 C5
Atlantic City 77 E8
Atlas Mts. = Haut Atlas
    52 B4
Attapuerca 18 A4
Attawapiskat 71 D5
Attawapiskat → 71 D5
Atyraū 29 E6
Aube □ 13 B5
Aubusson 12 D5
Auch 12 E4
Auckland 64 B6
Aude → 13 E5
Augsburg 14 D6
Augusta *Ga., U.S.A.*
    83 C7
Augusta *Maine, U.S.A.*
    77 B11
Aujuittuq = Grise Fiord
    70 B5
Aunis □ 12 C3
Aurangabad *Bihar, India*
    40 E5
Aurangabad *Maharashtra, India* 43 K9
Aurillac 12 D5
Aurora *Colo., U.S.A.*
    74 F2
Aurora *Ill., U.S.A.* 76 D1
Austin 80 D5
Austral Is. = Tubuaï, Îs.
    65 M16
Austral Seamount Chain
    65 M16
Australia ■ 60 E6
Australian Capital
    Territory □ 63 C4
Austria ■ 15 E8
Autun 13 C6
Auvergne □ 13 D5
Auvergne, Mts. d' 13 D5
Auxerre 13 C5
Avallon 13 C5
Avellaneda 94 C5
Avellino 21 D5
Aversa 21 D5
Aviemore 10 C5
Avignon 13 E6
Ávila 18 B3
Avilés 18 A3
Avranches 12 B3
Awash 49 F3
Awbārī, Idehan 54 C1
Axel Heiberg I. 70 B5
Axios → 23 D4
Ayacucho *Argentina*
    94 D5
Ayacucho *Peru* 91 F4
Aydın 23 F6
Ayers Rock = Uluru 60 F5
Ayeyarwady =
    Irrawaddy → 41 K10
Aylmer, L. 68 B8
Ayr 10 D4
Ayvalık 23 E6

Aẓ Ẕahrān 47 F7
Az Zarqā 46 D4
Azamgarh 40 D4
Azärbayjan =
  Azerbaijan ■ 25 E6
Azare 53 F8
Azbine = Aïr 53 E7
Azerbaijan ■ 25 E6
Azores 50 C1
Azov 25 D4
Azov, Sea of 25 D4
Azuero, Pen. de 86 E3
Azul 94 D5

B

Bab el Mandeb 49 E3
Bābā, Koh-i- 42 B5
Bābol 44 B3
Babruysk 17 B9
Babuyan Chan. 36 A2
Babylon 46 D5
Bacabal 92 C5
Bacău 17 E8
Back ➝ 68 B9
Bacolod 36 B2
Badagara 43 P9
Badajoz 18 C2
Badalona 19 B7
Baden-Baden 14 D5
Baden-Württemberg □
  14 D5
Bādghīs □ 42 B3
Badlands 74 D3
Baffin B. 70 B7
Baffin I. 70 C6
Bafoulabé 53 F3
Bagamoyo 57 F7
Bagé 94 C6
Baghdād 46 D6
Baghlān 42 A6
Bago = Pegu 41 J11
Baguio 36 A2
Bahamas ■ 86 A4
Baharampur 40 E7
Bahawalpur 42 E7
Bahía = Salvador 93 E6
Bahía □ 93 E5
Bahía Blanca 94 D4
Bahr el Ghazal 55 G4
Bahraich 40 D3
Bahrain ■ 44 E2
Baia Mare 17 E7
Baie-Comeau 71 E7
Baie Verte 71 E8
Ba'ijī 46 D5
Baikal, L. = Baykal, Oz.
  30 D8
Baile Atha Cliath = Dublin
  11 E3
Bairiki = Tarawa 64 J12
Baiyin 35 C5
Baja, Pta. 84 B1
Baja California 84 A1
Baker, L. 68 B10
Baker I. 64 J13
Baker Lake 68 B10
Bakers Dozen Is. 71 D6
Bakersfield 78 C3
Bākhtarān = Kermānshāh
  46 D6
Bakı 25 E6
Bakony 16 E3
Baku = Bakı 25 E6
Baky = Bakı 25 E6
Balabac Str. 38 C5
Balaghat Ra. 43 K10
Balaklava 25 E3
Balakovo 24 C6
Balashov 24 C5
Balasore = Baleshwar
  40 G6
Balaton 16 E3
Balbina, Reprêsa de
  90 D7
Baleares, Is. 19 C7

Balearic Is. = Baleares, Is.
  19 C7
Baleine = Whale ➝
  70 D7
Balaghat 43 G6
Bali 39 F5
Balikeşir 23 E6
Balikpapan 39 E5
Balkan Mts. = Stara
  Planina 22 C4
Balkanabat 29 F6
Balkhash, Ozero =
  Balqash Köli 29 E8
Ballarat 62 C3
Ballari 43 M10
Ballater 10 C5
Ballina 11 D2
Ballinasloe 11 E2
Ballymena 11 D3
Balochistan =
  Baluchistan □ 42 F4
Balqash Köli 29 E8
Balrampur 40 D4
Balsas ➝ 84 D4
Bālṭī 17 E8
Baltic Sea 9 D9
Baltimore 77 E7
Baluchistan □ 42 F4
Bam 44 D4
Bamako 53 F4
Bambari 55 G3
Bamberg 14 D6
Bamenda 53 G8
Bāmīān □ 42 B5
Banaba 64 K11
Bananal, I. do 93 E3
Banaras = Varanasi 40 E4
Banda, Kepulauan 37 E3
Banda Aceh 38 C1
Banda Sea 37 F3
Bandar = Machilipatnam
  40 J3
Bandar-e Abbās 44 E4
Bandar-e Anzalī 46 C7
Bandar-e Bushehr =
  Büshehr 44 D2
Bandar-e Torkeman
  44 B3
Bandar Lampung 39 F3
Bandar Maharani = Muar
  39 D2
Bandar Penggaram =
  Batu Pahat 39 D2
Bandar Seri Begawan
  38 D5
Bandırma 23 D7
Bandjarmasin =
  Banjarmasin 39 E4
Bandon 11 F2
Bandundu 56 E3
Bandung 39 F3
Banff Canada 69 C8
Banff U.K. 10 C5
Bangalore = Bengaluru
  43 N10
Bangassou 56 D4
Banggai, Kepulauan
  37 E2
Banghāzī 54 B3
Bangka 39 E3
Bangkok 38 B2
Bangladesh ■ 41 E7
Bangor Down, U.K. 11 D4
Bangor Gwynedd, U.K.
  11 E4
Bangor U.S.A. 77 B11
Bangui 56 D3
Bangweulu, L. 57 G6
Bani 87 C5
Banja Luka 20 B6
Banjarmasin 39 E4
Banjul 53 F2
Banks I. 68 A7
Bannu 42 C7
Bantry 11 F2
Banyak, Kepulauan
  39 D1

Baoding 35 C6
Baoji 35 C5
Baoshan 34 D4
Baotou 35 B6
Ba'qūbah 46 D6
Bar-le-Duc 13 B6
Baracoa 86 B5
Barail Range 41 E9
Barakaldo 19 A4
Baranavichy 17 B8
Baranof I. 69 C6
Barbacena 93 G5
Barbados ■ 87 D8
Barcelona Spain 19 B7
Barcelona Venezuela
  90 A6
Barddhaman 40 F6
Bardīyah 54 B4
Bareilly 42 E11
Barhi 40 E5
Bari 20 D6
Bari Doab 42 D8
Barinas 90 B4
Baring, C. 68 B8
Barisal 41 F8
Barkly Tableland 60 D6
Barlee, L. 60 F2
Barletta 20 D6
Barmer 42 G7
Barnsley 11 E6
Barnstaple 11 F4
Baroda = Vadodara
  43 H8
Barotseland 58 B4
Barquisimeto 90 A5
Barra Brazil 93 E5
Barra U.K. 10 C3
Barra do Corda 92 D4
Barraigh = Barra 10 C3
Barrancabermeja 90 B4
Barranquilla 90 A4
Barreiras 93 E5
Barreiro 18 C1
Barretos 93 G4
Barrie 71 E6
Barrow 69 A4
Barrow-in-Furness 11 D5
Barry 11 F5
Barstow 78 C4
Bartle Frere 61 G8
Bartlesville 81 A6
Barysaw 17 A9
Basarabia = Bessarabia
  17 E9
Basel 14 E4
Bashkortostan □ 29 D6
Basilan 36 C2
Basildon 11 F7
Basingstoke 11 F6
Basle = Basel 14 E4
Basque Provinces = País
  Vasco □ 19 A4
Basra = Al Baṣrah 47 E6
Bass Str. 61 H8
Bassas da India 59 C7
Basse-Terre 87 C7
Bassein 41 J10
Basseterre 87 C7
Basti 40 D4
Bastia 13 E8
Bata 56 D1
Batabanó, G. de 86 B3
Batangas 36 B2
Batdambang 38 B2
Bath 11 F5
Bathurst Australia 63 B4
Bathurst Canada 71 E7
Bathurst, C. 68 A7
Bathurst Inlet 68 B9
Batman 46 C5
Batna 52 A7
Baton Rouge 81 D8
Battambang =
  Batdambang 38 B2
Battle Creek 76 C3

Batu, Kepulauan 39 E1
Batu Pahat 39 D2
Batumi 25 E5
Bauld, C. 71 D8
Bauru 93 G4
Bavaria = Bayern □
  15 D6
Bay City 76 C4
Bayamo 86 B4
Bayan Har Shan 34 C4
Bayan Hot = Alxa Zuoqi
  35 C5
Bayanhongor 35 B5
Baydhabo 49 G3
Bayeux 12 B3
Baykal, Oz. 30 D8
Bayonne 12 E3
Bayrūt 46 D3
Beagle, Canal 95 G3
Beardmore Glacier
  96 C14
Béarn 12 E3
Beauce, Plaine de la
  12 B4
Beaufort Sea 66 B6
Beaufort West 58 E4
Beaumont 81 D6
Beaune 13 C6
Beauvais 12 B5
Beaver ➝ 69 C9
Beawar 42 F9
Béchar 52 B5
Bedford 11 E6
Be'er Sheva 47 E3
Beersheba = Be'er Sheva
  47 E3
Bei Jiang ➝ 35 D6
Bei'an 35 B7
Beihai 35 D5
Beijing 35 C6
Beinn na Faoghla =
  Benbecula 10 C3
Beira 59 B6
Beirut = Bayrūt 46 D3
Beitbridge 59 C6
Béja 54 A1
Bejaïa 52 A7
Békéscsaba 16 E5
Bela 42 F5
Belarus ■ 24 C2
Belau = Palau ■ 36 C4
Belaya Tserkov = Bila
  Tserkva 17 D10
Belcher Chan. 70 B7
Belcher Is. 71 D6
Beledweyne 49 G4
Belém 92 C4
Belfast 11 D4
Belfort 13 C7
Belgaum 43 M9
Belgium ■ 14 C3
Belgorod 24 C4
Belgrade = Beograd
  22 B3
Belitung 39 E3
Belize ■ 85 D7
Belize City 85 D7
Bell Peninsula 70 C5
Bell Ville 94 C4
Belle-Île 12 C2
Belle Isle 71 D8
Belle Isle, Str. of 71 D8
Belleville Canada 71 E6
Belleville U.S.A. 75 F10
Bellin = Kangirsuk 70 D7
Bellingham 72 B2
Bellingshausen Sea
  96 A2
Bellinzona 13 C8
Belmonte 93 F6
Belmopan 85 D7
Belo Horizonte 93 F5
Beloit 75 D10
Belomorsk 28 C4
Belorussia = Belarus ■
  24 C2

Beloye, Ozero 24 A4
Beloye More 8 B13
Beltsy = Bălţi 17 E8
Bemidji 75 B7
Ben Nevis 10 C4
Benares = Varanasi 40 E4
Benbecula 10 C3
Bend 72 D3
Bendery = Tighina 17 E9
Bendigo 63 C3
Benevento 20 D5
Bengal, Bay of 41 J7
Bengaluru 43 N10
Bengbu 35 C6
Benghazi = Banghāzī
  54 B3
Bengkulu 39 E2
Benguela 58 A2
Beni ➝ 91 F5
Beni Mellal 52 B4
Beni Suef 54 C5
Benidorm 19 C5
Benin ■ 53 G6
Benin, Bight of 53 H6
Benin City 53 G7
Benjamin Constant 90 D4
Benoni 59 D5
Bentley Subglacial Trench
  96 C18
Benton Harbor 76 C2
Benue ➝ 53 G7
Benxi 35 B7
Beograd 22 B3
Beppu 33 G2
Berber 55 E5
Berbera 49 E4
Berbérati 56 D3
Berbice ➝ 90 B7
Berdichev = Berdychiv
  17 D9
Berdyansk 25 D4
Berdychiv 17 D9
Berezina = Byarezina ➝
  17 B10
Berezniki 28 D6
Bérgamo 13 D8
Bergen 8 C7
Bergerac 12 D4
Berhampore =
  Baharampur 40 E7
Berhampur = Brahmapur
  40 H5
Bering Sea 69 C1
Bering Strait 69 B3
Berkeley 72 H2
Berkner I. 96 B4
Berlin 15 B7
Bermejo ➝ 94 B5
Bermejo, Paso =
  Uspallata, P. de 94 C3
Bermuda ☑ 67 F13
Bern 14 E4
Berne = Bern 14 E4
Berry 12 C5
Berwick-upon-Tweed
  10 D6
Besançon 13 C7
Bessarabia 17 E9
Bethel 69 B3
Bethlehem S. Africa
  59 D5
Bethlehem U.S.A. 77 D8
Béthune 13 A5
Bettiah 40 D5
Betul 43 J10
Beverley 11 E6
Beyneu 29 E6
Beypazarı 25 E3
Beyşehir Gölü 46 C2
Béziers 13 E5
Bezwada = Vijayawada
  40 J3
Bhagalpur 40 E6
Bhanrer Ra. 43 H11
Bharat = India ■ 43 J10
Bharatpur 42 F10
Bhatpara 41 F7

Bhavnagar 43 J8
Bhilai = Bhilainagar-Durg
  40 G3
Bhilainagar-Durg 40 G3
Bhilwara 43 G9
Bhima → 43 L10
Bhiwandi 43 K8
Bhiwani 42 E10
Bhopal 43 H10
Bhubaneshwar 40 G5
Bhuj 43 H6
Bhusawal 43 J9
Bhutan ■ 41 D8
Biafra, B. of = Bonny,
  Bight of 56 D1
Biała Podlaska 17 B6
Białystok 17 B6
Biarritz 12 E3
Bida 53 G7
Biddeford 77 C10
Bié, Planalto de 58 A3
Bielefeld 14 B5
Biella 13 D8
Bielsko-Biała 16 D4
Bien Hoa 38 B3
Bienville, L. 71 D6
Big Horn Mts. = Bighorn
  Mts. 73 D10
Big Spring 80 C3
Big Trout L. 71 D5
Biggar 69 C9
Bighorn → 73 C10
Bighorn Mts. 73 D10
Bihar 40 E5
Bihar □ 40 E5
Bijagós, Arquipélago dos
  53 F2
Bijapur 43 L9
Bikaner 42 E8
Bikini Atoll 64 H11
Bila Tserkva 17 D10
Bilaspur 40 F4
Bilbao 19 A4
Bilbo = Bilbao 19 A4
Bilecik 25 E3
Bilhorod-Dnistrovskyy
  25 D3
Billings 73 D9
Billiton Is. = Belitung
  39 E3
Bilma 55 E1
Biloxi 81 D9
Binghamton 77 C8
Binzert = Bizerte 54 A1
Bioko 53 H7
Birmingham U.K. 11 E6
Birmingham U.S.A. 82 C4
Birnin Kebbi 53 F6
Birr 11 E3
Biscay, B. of 12 D2
Bishkek 29 E8
Biskra 52 B7
Bismarck 74 B4
Bismarck Arch. 64 K9
Bissagos = Bijagós,
  Arquipélago dos 53 F2
Bissau 53 F2
Bitola 22 D3
Bitolj = Bitola 22 D3
Bitterfontein 58 E3
Bitterroot Range 73 D6
Biu 55 F1
Biwa-Ko 33 F5
Bizerte 54 A1
Björneborg = Pori 8 C10
Black Forest =
  Schwarzwald 14 D5
Black Hills 74 D3
Black Sea 25 E3
Blackburn 11 E5
Blackpool 11 E5
Blackwater → 11 E2
Blagoevgrad 22 C4
Blagoveshchensk 31 D10
Blanc, Mont 13 D7
Blanca, B. 95 D4
Blanca Peak 79 B10

Blantyre 59 B6
Blenheim 65 D5
Blida 52 A6
Bloemfontein 59 D5
Blois 12 C4
Bloomington Ill., U.S.A.
  75 E10
Bloomington Ind., U.S.A.
  76 E2
Blue Mts. 72 D4
Blue Nile = Nîl el Azraq →
  55 E5
Blue Ridge 83 A7
Bluefields 86 D3
Blumenau 94 B7
Bo 53 G3
Bo Hai 35 C6
Boa Vista 90 C6
Bobo-Dioulasso 53 F5
Bóbr → 16 B2
Bochum 14 C4
Boden 8 B10
Bodensee 13 C8
Bodø 8 B8
Bodrog → 16 D5
Bodrum 23 F6
Bogalusa 81 D9
Bogor 39 F3
Bogotá 90 C4
Bogra 41 E7
Bohemian Forest =
  Böhmerwald 15 D7
Böhmerwald 15 D7
Bohol Sea 36 C2
Boise 72 E5
Bole 34 B3
Bolivia ■ 91 G6
Bologna 20 B3
Bologoye 24 B3
Bolsena, L. di 20 C3
Bolshoy Kavkas =
  Caucasus Mountains
  25 E5
Bolton 11 E5
Bolu 25 E3
Bolvadin 46 C2
Bolzano 20 A3
Bom Jesus da Lapa
  93 E5
Boma 56 F2
Bombala 63 C4
Bombay = Mumbai 43 K8
Bomu → 56 D4
Bon, C. 21 F3
Bonaire 87 D6
Bonavista 71 E8
Bongor 55 F2
Bonifacio 13 F8
Bonin Is. 27 F16
Bonn 14 C4
Bonny, Bight of 56 D1
Boosaaso 49 E4
Boothia, Gulf of 70 B5
Boothia Pen. 68 A10
Borås 9 D8
Bordeaux 12 D3
Borden I. 70 B2
Borden Pen. 70 B5
Borger 80 B3
Borhoyn Tal 35 B6
Borisoglebsk 24 C5
Borkou 55 E2
Borneo 39 D4
Bornholm 9 D9
Borovichi 24 B3
Borūjerd 46 D7
Bosnia-Herzegovina ■
  20 B6
Bosporus = İstanbul
  Boğazı 22 D7
Bossangoa 55 G2
Bosten Hu 34 B3
Boston U.K. 11 E6
Boston U.S.A. 77 D10
Bothnia, G. of 8 C10
Botletle → 58 C4
Botoșani 17 E8

Botswana ■ 58 C4
Botucatu 93 G4
Bouaké 53 G4
Bouar 56 C3
Bouârfa 52 B5
Bougainville I. 64 K10
Boulder 74 E2
Boulder Dam = Hoover
  Dam 78 B5
Boulogne-sur-Mer 12 A4
Bourbonnais 13 C5
Bourg-en-Bresse 13 C6
Bourgas = Burgas 22 C6
Bourges 12 C5
Bourgogne □ 13 C6
Bourke 63 B4
Bournemouth 11 F6
Boyne → 11 E3
Boyoma, Chutes 57 D5
Bozeman 73 D8
Bozen = Bolzano 20 A3
Bozoum 55 G2
Brač 20 C7
Bräcke 8 C9
Bradenton 83 F6
Bradford 11 E6
Braga 18 B1
Bragança 92 C4
Brahestad = Raahe 8 C10
Brahmanbaria 41 F8
Brahmani → 40 G6
Brahmapur 40 H5
Brahmaputra → 41 F7
Brăila 17 F8
Branco → 90 D6
Brandenburg 15 B7
Brandenburg □ 15 B7
Brandon 69 D10
Brantford 76 C5
Bras d'Or L. 71 E7
Brasil = Brazil ■ 93 E4
Brasília 93 F4
Brașov 17 F7
Bratislava 16 D3
Bratsk 30 D8
Braunschweig 14 B6
Bravo del Norte, Rio =
  Grande, Rio → 84 B5
Bray 11 E3
Brazil ■ 93 E4
Brazos → 81 E6
Brazzaville 56 E3
Brecon 11 F5
Breda 14 C3
Bregenz 14 E5
Breiðafjörður 8 B1
Bremen 14 B5
Bremerhaven 14 B5
Bremerton 72 C2
Brennerpass 15 E6
Bréscia 13 D9
Breslau = Wrocław 16 C3
Brest Belarus 17 B7
Brest France 12 B1
Brest-Litovsk = Brest
  17 B6
Bretagne □ 12 B2
Briançon 13 D7
Bridgeport 77 D9
Bridgetown 87 D8
Bridgewater 71 E7
Bridlington 11 D6
Brigham City 73 F7
Brighton 11 F6
Bríndisi 21 D6
Brisbane 63 A5
Bristol 11 F5
Bristol B. 69 C3
Bristol Channel 11 F4
British Indian Ocean
  Terr. = Chagos Arch. □
  26 J9
British Isles 11 D4
Brittany = Bretagne □
  12 B2
Brive-la-Gaillarde 12 D4
Brno 16 D3
Brock I. 70 B2

Brocken 14 C6
Brodeur Pen. 70 B5
Broken Hill 62 B3
Brooks Range 69 B5
Broome 60 D3
Broughton Island =
  Qikiqtarjuaq 70 C7
Brownsville 81 G5
Brownwood 80 D4
Bruay-la-Buissière 13 A5
Bruges = Brugge 14 C2
Brugge 14 C2
Brumado 93 E5
Brunei = Bandar Seri
  Begawan 38 D5
Brunei ■ 38 D4
Brunswick =
  Braunschweig 14 B6
Brunswick 83 D7
Brussel 14 C3
Brussels = Brussel 14 C3
Bruxelles = Brussel 14 C3
Bryan 81 D5
Bryansk 24 C3
Bucaramanga 90 B4
Buchanan 53 G3
Bucharest = București
  22 B6
Buckie 10 C5
București 22 B6
Budapest 16 E4
Bude 11 F4
Buenaventura 90 C3
Buenos Aires 94 C4
Buenos Aires, L. 95 F2
Buffalo 77 C6
Bug → Buh → 25 D3
Bug → 16 B5
Bugursulan 29 D6
Buh → 25 D3
Buir Nur 35 B6
Bujumbura 57 E5
Bukavu 57 E5
Bukhara = Buxoro 29 F7
Bukittinggi 39 E2
Bulawayo 59 C5
Bulgan 35 B5
Bulgaria ■ 22 C5
Bunbury 60 G2
Buncrana 11 D3
Bundaberg 63 A5
Bundi 43 G9
Bundoran 11 D2
Buon Ma Thuot 38 B3
Bur Acaba 49 G3
Bûr Safâga 54 C5
Bûr Sa'îd 54 B5
Bûr Sûdân 55 E6
Buraydah 47 F5
Burco 49 F4
Burdur 46 C2
Burdwan = Barddhaman
  40 F6
Burgas 22 C6
Burgos 18 A4
Burgundy = Bourgogne □
  13 C6
Burhanpur 43 J10
Burkina Faso ■ 53 F5
Burlington Iowa, U.S.A.
  75 E9
Burlington Vt., U.S.A.
  77 B9
Burma ■ 41 G11
Burnie 62 D4
Burnley 11 E5
Burnside → 68 B9
Burqin 34 B3
Bursa 23 D7
Buru 37 E3
Burundi ■ 57 E6
Bury St. Edmunds 11 E7
Busan 35 C7
Büshehr 44 D2
Busto Arsízio 13 D8
Buta 57 D4
Butare 57 E5

Butaritari 64 J12
Butembo 57 D5
Butha Qi 35 B7
Butte 37 E2
Butte 73 C7
Butterworth 38 C2
Butuan 36 C3
Butung = Buton 37 E2
Buurhakaba 49 G3
Buxoro 29 F7
Buyant-Uhaa 35 B6
Buzău 17 F8
Buzuluk 29 D6
Byarezina → 17 B10
Bydgoszcz 16 B3
Byelorussia = Belarus ■
  24 C2
Bylot I. 70 B6
Byrranga, Gory 30 B8
Bytom 16 C4

C

Ca Mau 38 C3
Cabanatuan 36 A2
Cabedelo 92 D7
Cabimas 90 A4
Cabinda 56 F2
Cabinda □ 56 F2
Cabo Frio 93 G5
Cabo Verde ■ 50 E1
Cabonga, Réservoir
  71 E6
Cabora Bassa Dam =
  Cahora Bassa, Reprêsa
  de 59 B6
Cabot Str. 71 E8
Čačak 22 C3
Cáceres Brazil 91 G7
Cáceres Spain 18 C2
Cachimbo, Serra do
  93 D2
Cachoeira 93 E6
Cachoeira do Sul 94 C6
Cachoeiro de Itapemirim
  93 G5
Cádiz 18 D2
Cádiz, G. de 18 D2
Caen 12 B3
Caetité 93 E5
Cagayan de Oro 36 C2
Cágliari 21 E2
Caguas 87 C6
Cahora Bassa, Reprêsa
  de 59 B6
Cahors 12 D4
Cairns 61 D8
Cairo = El Qâhira 54 B5
Cairo 81 A9
Cajamarca 91 E3
Calabar 53 H7
Calábria □ 21 E6
Calais 12 A4
Calama 94 A3
Calamian Group 36 B1
Calapan 36 B2
Calbayog 36 B2
Calcutta = Kolkata 41 F7
Caldera 94 B2
Caldwell 72 E5
Calgary 69 C8
Cali 90 C3
Calicut = Kozhikode
  43 P9
California □ 78 B3
California, G. de 84 B2
Callao 91 F3
Caltanissetta 21 F5
Calvi 13 E8
Calvinia 58 E3
Camagüey 86 B4
Camargue 13 E6
Cambay = Khambhat
  43 H8
Cambodia ■ 38 B3
Cambrai 13 A5

Cambrian Mts. 11 E5
Cambridge *U.K.* 11 E7
Cambridge *U.S.A.* 77 C10
Cambridge Bay = Ikaluktutiak 68 B9
Camden *Ark., U.S.A.* 81 C7
Camden *N.J., U.S.A.* 77 E8
Cameroon ■ 56 C2
Cameroun, Mt. 53 H7
Cametá 92 C4
Camocim 92 C5
Campana, I. 95 F1
Campánia □ 21 D5
Campbellton 71 E7
Campbelltown 10 D4
Campeche 85 D6
Campeche, Golfo de 85 D6
Campina Grande 92 D6
Campinas 94 A7
Campo Grande 93 G3
Campobasso 20 D5
Campos 93 G5
Campos Belos 93 E4
Camrose 69 C8
Can Tho 38 B3
Canada ■ 68 C8
Çanakkale 23 D6
Çanakkale Boğazı 23 D6
Cananea 84 A2
Canarias, Is. 52 C2
Canary Is. = Canarias, Is. 52 C2
Canavieiras 93 F6
Canberra 63 C4
Candia = Iraklio 23 G5
Canea = Chania 23 G5
Caniapiscau → 70 D7
Caniapiscau, L. 71 D7
Çankırı 25 E3
Cannanore 43 P9
Cannes 13 E7
Canoas 94 B6
Canora 69 C9
Cantabria □ 18 A4
Cantabrian Mts. = Cantábrica, Cordillera 18 A3
Cantábrica, Cordillera 18 A3
Canterbury 11 F7
Canterbury Bight 65 F4
Canterbury Plains 65 E4
Canton = Guangzhou 35 D6
Canton 76 D5
Cap-Haitien 87 C5
Cape Breton I. 71 E7
Cape Coast 53 G5
Cape Dorset 70 C6
Cape Girardeau 81 A9
Cape Town 58 E3
Cape Verde Is. = Cabo Verde ■ 52 E7
Cape York Peninsula 61 C7
Capela 93 E6
Capri 21 D5
Caprivi Strip 58 B4
Caquetá → 90 D5
Caracas 90 A5
Caracol 93 D5
Caratasca, L. 86 C3
Caratinga 93 F5
Caravelas 93 F6
Carbón, L. del 95 F3
Carbondale 81 A9
Carbonear 71 E8
Carcassonne 12 E5
Carcross 68 B6
Cardamon Hills 43 Q10
Cárdenas 86 B3
Cardiff 11 F5
Cardigan B. 11 E4

Cardston 69 D8
Cariacica 93 G5
Caribbean Sea 86 D5
Cariboo Mts. 69 C7
Carinhanha 93 E5
Carinthia = Kärnten □ 15 E7
Carlisle 11 D5
Carlow 11 E3
Carlsbad 80 C1
Carmacks 68 B6
Carmarthen 11 F4
Carmaux 12 D5
Carnarvon *Australia* 60 E1
Carnarvon *S. Africa* 58 E4
Carnegie, L. 60 F3
Caroline I. 65 K15
Caroline Is. 64 J10
Caroní → 90 B6
Caronie = Nébrodi, Monti 21 F5
Carpathians 16 D5
Carpaţii Meridionali 17 F7
Carpentaria, G. of 60 C6
Carpentras 13 D6
Carpi 20 B3
Carrara 13 D9
Carrauntoohill 11 E2
Carrick-on-Suir 11 E3
Carson City 72 G4
Cartagena *Colombia* 90 A3
Cartagena *Spain* 19 D5
Cartago 90 C3
Cartwright 70 D8
Caruaru 92 D6
Carúpano 90 A6
Casablanca 52 B4
Cascade Ra. 72 C3
Cascavel 94 A6
Caserta 20 D5
Caseyr, Raas = Asir, Ras 49 E5
Casiquiare → 90 C5
Casper 73 E10
Caspian Sea 29 E6
Castellammare di Stábia 21 D5
Castelló de la Plana 19 C5
Castelsarrasin 12 D4
Castilla-La Mancha □ 18 C4
Castilla y Leon □ 18 A3
Castlebar 11 E2
Castleblaney 11 D3
Castres 12 E5
Castries 87 D7
Castro 95 E2
Castro Alves 93 E6
Cat I. 86 B4
Catalão 93 F4
Catalonia = Cataluña □ 19 B6
Cataluña □ 19 B6
Catamarca 94 B3
Catanduanes □ 36 B2
Catanduva 93 G4
Catánia 21 F5
Catanzaro 21 E6
Catoche, C. 85 C7
Catskill Mts. 77 C8
Cauca → 90 B4
Caucaia 92 C6
Caucasus Mountains 25 E5
Caura → 90 B6
Cauvery → 43 P11
Cavan 11 D3
Caviana, I. 92 B3
Cawnpore = Kanpur 40 D3
Caxias 92 C5
Caxias do Sul 94 B6
Cayenne 92 A3
Cayman Is. ☑ 86 C3

Ceará = Fortaleza 92 C6
Ceará □ 92 D6
Cebu 36 B2
Cedar L. 69 C10
Cedar Rapids 75 E9
Cefalù 21 E5
Ceglèd 16 E4
Celaya 84 C4
Celebes = Sulawesi 37 E2
Celebes Sea 37 D2
Celtic Sea 11 F2
Central, Cordillera 90 C3
Central African Rep. ■ 56 C4
Central Makran Range 42 F4
Cephalonia = Kefalonia 23 E3
Ceram = Seram 37 E3
Ceram Sea = Seram Sea 37 E3
Cerignola 20 D5
Cerigo = Kythira 23 F4
Cesena 20 B4
Çeské Budějovice 16 D2
Českomoravská Vrchovina 16 D2
Çeşme 23 E6
Ceuta 18 E3
Cévennes 13 D5
Chachapoyas 91 E3
Chad ■ 55 E2
Chad, L. = Tchad, L. 55 F1
Chagai Hills = Chāh Gay Hills 42 E3
Chagos Arch. ☑ 26 J9
Chāh Gay Hills 42 E3
Chakradharpur 40 F5
Chalisgaon 43 J9
Chalon-sur-Saône 13 C6
Châlons-en-Champagne 13 B6
Chambal → 42 F11
Chambéry 13 D6
Chamonix-Mont Blanc 13 D7
Champagne 13 B6
Champaign 76 D1
Champlain, L. 77 B9
Chañaral 94 B2
Chandigarh 42 D10
Chandpur 41 F8
Chandrapur 43 K11
Chang Jiang → 35 C7
Changchun 35 B7
Changde 35 D6
Changhua 35 D7
Changsha 35 D6
Changzhi 35 C6
Changzhou 35 C6
Chania 23 G5
Channel Is. 11 G5
Channel-Port aux Basques 71 E8
Chantrey Inlet 68 B10
Chaozhou 35 D6
Chapala, L. de 84 C4
Chapayevsk 24 C6
Chapleau 71 E5
Chapra = Chhapra 40 E5
Charaña 91 G5
Chardzhou = Türkmenabat 29 F7
Chari → 55 F1
Chärikär 42 B6
Chärjew = Türkmenabat 29 F7
Charleroi 14 C3
Charles, C. 77 G8
Charleston *S.C., U.S.A.* 83 C8

Charleston *W. Va., U.S.A.* 76 E5
Charleville 63 A4
Charleville-Mézières 13 B6
Charlotte 83 B7
Charlotte Amalie 87 C6
Charlottesville 77 E6
Charlottetown 71 E7
Charlton I. 71 D6
Charolles 13 C6
Charters Towers 61 E8
Chartres 12 B4
Chascomús 94 D5
Châteaubriant 12 C3
Châteaulin 12 B1
Châteauroux 12 C4
Châtellerault 12 C4
Chatham = Miramichi 71 E7
Chatham *Canada* 76 C4
Chatham *U.K.* 11 F7
Chattagåm = Chittagong 41 F8
Chattanooga 82 B5
Chaumont 13 B6
Cheb 16 C1
Cheboksary 24 B6
Chech, Erg 52 D5
Chechenia □ = Chechnya □ 25 E6
Chechnya = Chechenia □ 25 E6
Cheduba I. 41 H9
Chegutu 59 B6
Cheju-do = Jeju-do 35 C7
Chekiang = Zhejiang □ 35 D7
Cheleken = Hazar 29 F6
Chełm 17 C6
Chelmsford 11 F7
Cheltenham 11 F5
Chelyabinsk 29 D7
Chelyuskin, Mys 30 B8
Chemnitz 15 C7
Chenab → 42 D7
Chengchou = Zhengzhou 35 C6
Chengde 35 B6
Chengdu 35 C5
Chengjiang 34 D5
Ch'engtu = Chengdu 35 C5
Chennai 43 N12
Cher → 12 C4
Cherbourg 12 B3
Cherepovets 24 B4
Chergui, Chott ech 52 B6
Cherkasy 24 D3
Chernigov = Chernihiv 24 C3
Chernihiv 24 C3
Chernivtsi 17 D7
Chernobyl = Chornobyl 17 C10
Chernovtsy = Chernivtsi 17 D7
Cherrapunji 41 E8
Chervonohrad 17 C7
Chesapeake B. 77 E7
Cheshskaya Guba 28 C5
Chester *U.K.* 11 E5
Chester *U.S.A.* 77 E8
Chesterfield, Îs. 64 L10
Chesterfield Inlet 68 B10
Chetumal 85 D7
Cheviot Hills 10 D5
Chew Bahir 55 H6
Cheyenne 74 E2
Cheyenne → 74 C4
Chhapra 40 E5
Chi → 38 A2
Chiai 35 D7
Chiávari 13 D8
Chiba 33 F7
Chibougamau 71 E6

Chicacole = Srikakulam 40 H4
Chicago 76 D2
Chichagof I. 69 C6
Chichester 11 F6
Chickasha 80 B5
Chiclayo 91 E3
Chico 72 G3
Chico → *Chubut, Argentina* 95 E3
Chico = *Santa Cruz, Argentina* 95 F3
Chicoutimi 71 E6
Chidley, C. 70 C7
Chieti 20 C5
Chihli, G. of = Bo Hai 35 C6
Chihuahua 84 B3
Chilapa 84 D5
Chilaw 43 R11
Chile ■ 94 D2
Chililabombwe 59 A5
Chilin = Jilin 35 B7
Chilka L. 40 H5
Chillán 94 D2
Chiloé, I. de 95 E2
Chilpancingo 84 D5
Chilung 35 D7
Chilwa, L. 59 B7
Chimborazo 90 D3
Chimbote 91 E3
Chimkent = Shymkent 29 E7
Chin □ 41 F9
China ■ 35 C5
Chinandega 85 E7
Chincha Alta 91 F3
Chindwin → 41 G10
Chingola 59 A5
Chinhoyi 59 B6
Chiniot 42 D8
Chinnampo = Namp'o 35 C7
Chinon 12 C4
Chióggia 20 B4
Chios 23 E6
Chipata 59 A6
Chiquinquira 90 B4
Chirchiq 29 E7
Chiredzi 59 C6
Chisasibi 71 D6
Chisimaio = Kismaayo 49 H3
Chişinău 17 E9
Chistopol 24 B7
Chita 30 D9
Chitral 42 B7
Chittagong 41 F8
Chittagong □ 41 E8
Chitungwiza 59 B6
Chkalov = Orenburg 29 D6
Cholet 12 C3
Choluteca 85 E7
Chomolungma = Everest, Mt. 40 C6
Chon Buri 38 B2
Ch'ŏngjin 35 B7
Chongqing 35 D5
Chonos, Arch. de los 95 F2
Chornobyl 17 C10
Chorzów 16 C4
Choybalsan 35 B6
Christchurch 65 E5
Christmas I. = Kiritimati 65 J15
Chubut □ 95 E3
Chudskoye, Ozero 24 B2
Chuncheon 35 C7
Chungking = Chongqing 35 D5
Chuquicamata 94 A3
Chur 13 C8
Churchill 68 C10

Churchill → *Man., Canada* 68 C10
Churchill → *Nfld. & L., Canada* 71 D7
Churchill, C. 68 C10
Churchill Falls 71 D7
Churu 42 E9
Chusovoy 28 D6
Chuuk = Truk 64 J10
Chuvashia □ 24 B6
Cicero 76 D2
Ciechanów 16 B5
Ciego de Ávila 86 B4
Cienfuegos 86 B3
Cill Chainnigh = Kilkenny 11 E3
Cincinnati 76 E3
Cinto, Mte. 13 E8
Circle 69 B5
Cirebon 39 F3
Citlaltépetl = Orizaba, Pico de 84 D5
Città del Vaticano = Vatican City ■ 20 D4
Ciudad Bolívar 90 B6
Ciudad de México 84 D5
Ciudad del Carmen 85 D6
Ciudad Delicias = Delicias 84 B3
Ciudad Guayana 90 B6
Ciudad Juárez 84 A3
Ciudad Madero 84 C5
Ciudad Mante 84 C5
Ciudad Obregón 84 B3
Ciudad Real 18 C4
Ciudad Victoria 84 C5
Civitavécchia 20 C3
Cizre 46 C5
Clarksdale 81 B8
Clarksville 82 A4
Clear, C. 11 F2
Clearwater 83 F6
Clearwater Mts. 73 C6
Clermont-Ferrand 13 D5
Cleveland 76 D5
Clinton 75 E9
Clinton Colden L. 68 B9
Clones 11 D3
Clonmel 11 E3
Clovis 80 B2
Cluj-Napoca 17 E6
Clyde → 10 D4
Clyde, Firth of 10 D4
Clyde River 70 B7
Coast Mts. 68 C7
Coast Ranges 72 F2
Coats I. 70 C5
Coats Land 96 B5
Coatzacoalcos 85 D6
Cobar 63 B4
Cobh 11 F2
Cobija 91 F5
Cocanada = Kakinada 40 J4
Cochabamba 91 G5
Cochin = Kochi 43 Q10
Cochin China = Nam-Phan 38 B3
Cochrane 71 E5
Cockburn, Canal 95 G2
Coco → 86 D3
Cod, C. 77 C10
Codó 92 C5
Coeur d'Alene 72 C5
Cognac 12 D3
Coimbatore 43 P10
Coimbra 18 B1
Colatina 93 F5
Colchester 11 F7
Coleraine 11 D3
Colima 84 D4
Coll 10 C3
Colmar 13 B7
Cologne = Köln 14 C4

Colomb-Béchar = Béchar 52 B5
Colombia ■ 90 C4
Colombo 43 R11
Colonsay 10 C3
Colorado □ 79 A10
Colorado → *Argentina* 95 D4
Colorado → *N. Amer.* 78 E5
Colorado Plateau 79 B7
Colorado Springs 74 F2
Columbia Mo., U.S.A. 75 F8
Columbia S.C., U.S.A. 83 B7
Columbia Tenn., U.S.A. 82 B4
Columbia → 72 C1
Columbia, District of □ 77 E7
Columbus Ga., U.S.A. 82 C5
Columbus Miss., U.S.A. 82 C3
Columbus Ohio, U.S.A. 76 E4
Colville → 69 A4
Colwyn Bay 11 E5
Comilla 41 F8
Committee B. 70 C5
Communism Pk. = imeni Ismail Samani, Pik 29 F8
Como 13 D8
Como, Lago di 13 D8
Comodoro Rivadavia 95 F3
Comorin, C. = Kanyakumari 43 Q10
Comoros ■ 51 H8
Compiègne 13 B5
Conakry 53 G3
Conceição da Barra 93 F6
Concepción Chile 94 D2
Concepción Paraguay 94 A5
Concepción del Oro 84 C4
Concepción del Uruguay 94 C5
Conchos → 84 B3
Concord 77 C10
Concórdia 94 C5
Condeúba 93 E5
Congo (Brazzaville) = Congo ■ 56 E3
Congo (Kinshasa) = Congo, Dem. Rep. of the ■ 56 E4
Congo ■ 56 E3
Congo → 56 F2
Congo, Dem. Rep. of the ■ 56 E4
Conjeeveram = Kanchipuram 43 N11
Conn, L. 11 D2
Connaught □ 11 E2
Connecticut □ 77 D9
Connecticut → 77 D9
Connemara 11 E2
Conselheiro Lafaiete 93 G5
Constance = Konstanz 14 E5
Constance, L. = Bodensee 13 C8
Constanța 22 B7
Constantine 52 A7
Constitución 94 D2
Contas → 93 E6
Coober Pedy 62 A1
Cooch Behar = Koch Bihar 41 D7
Cook, Mt. = Aoraki Mount Cook 65 E4

Cook Inlet 69 C4
Cook Is. ☑ 65 L14
Cook Strait 65 D6
Cooktown 61 B4
Coondapoor 43 N9
Copenhagen = København 9 D8
Copiapó 94 B2
Coppermine = Kugluktuk 68 B8
Coppermine → 68 B8
Coquimbo 94 C2
Coracora 91 G4
Coral Harbour 70 C5
Coral Sea 64 L10
Corby 11 E6
Corcaigh = Cork 11 F2
Córdoba Argentina 94 C4
Córdoba Spain 18 D3
Córdoba, Sierra de 94 C4
Cordova 69 B5
Corfu = Kerkyra 23 E2
Corinth = Korinthos 23 F4
Corinth, G. of = Korinthiakos Kolpos 23 E4
Corinto 93 F5
Cork 11 F2
Corner Brook 71 E8
Cornwall 71 B8
Cornwall I. 70 B4
Cornwallis I. 70 B4
Coro 90 A5
Corocoro 91 G5
Coronation Gulf 68 B8
Coronel 94 D2
Coronel Suárez 94 D4
Corpus Christi 80 F5
Corrib, L. 11 E2
Corrientes 94 B5
Corrientes, C. Colombia 90 B3
Corrientes, C. Mexico 84 C3
Corse □ 13 E8
Corse, C. 13 E8
Corsica = Corse □ 13 E8
Corsicana 81 C5
Corte 13 E8
Cortés, Mar de = California, G. de 84 B2
Çorum 25 B5
Corumbá 91 G7
Corunna = A Coruña 18 A1
Corvallis 72 D2
Cosenza 21 E6
Costa Blanca 19 C5
Costa Brava 19 B7
Costa del Sol 18 D3
Costa Dorada 19 B6
Costa Rica ■ 86 E3
Cotabato 36 C2
Côte d'Azur 13 E7
Côte-d'Ivoire = Ivory Coast ■ 53 G4
Cotentin 12 B3
Cotonou 53 G6
Cotopaxi 90 D3
Cotswold Hills 11 F5
Cottbus 14 C7
Council Bluffs 75 E7
Courantyne → 90 B7
Courtrai = Kortrijk 14 C2
Coventry 11 E6
Covington 76 E3
Cox's Bazar 41 G8
Cozumel, Isla 85 C7
Cradock 59 E5
Craigavon 11 D3
Craiova 22 B4
Cranbrook 69 D8
Crateús 92 D5
Crato 92 D6
Crawley 11 F6
Cremona 13 D9

Cres 20 B5
Crete = Kriti 23 G5
Créteil 12 B5
Creuse → 12 C4
Crewe 11 E5
Crimean Pen. = Krymskyy Pivostriv 25 D3
Crișul Negru → 16 E5
Crișul Repede → 16 E5
Crna Gora = Montenegro ■ 22 C2
Croatia ■ 20 B6
Croker, C. 60 C5
Cromer 11 E7
Cross Sound 69 C6
Crotone 21 E6
Crowsnest Pass 69 D8
Cruzeiro do Sul 91 E4
Cuando → 58 B4
Cuango = Kwango → 56 E3
Cuanza → 56 F2
Cuba ■ 86 B4
Cubango → 58 B4
Cúcuta 90 B4
Cuddalore 43 P11
Cuenca Ecuador 90 D3
Cuenca Spain 19 B4
Cuernavaca 84 D5
Cuiabá 93 F2
Cuito → 58 B4
Culiacán 84 C3
Cumaná 90 A6
Cumberland 77 E6
Cumberland Pen. 70 C7
Cumberland Plateau 76 F3
Cumberland Sd. 70 C7
Cunene → 58 B2
Cúneo 13 D7
Cunnamulla 63 A4
Curaçao 87 D6
Curicó 94 C2
Curitiba 94 B7
Cusco 91 F4
Cuttack 40 G5
Cuxhaven 14 B5
Cuzco = Cusco 91 F4
Cwmbran 11 F5
Cyclades 23 F5
Cyprus ■ 46 D3
Cyrenaica 54 C3
Czech Rep. ■ 16 D2
Częstochowa 16 C4

D

Da Hinggan Ling 35 B7
Da Lat 38 B3
Da Nang 38 A3
Da Qaidam 34 C4
Daba Shan 35 C5
Dacca = Dhaka 41 F8
Dadra & Nagar Haveli □ 43 J8
Dadu 42 F5
Daegu 35 C7
Daejeon 35 C7
Dagestan □ 25 E6
Dagö = Hiiumaa 24 B1
Dagupan 36 A2
Dahod 43 H9
Dakar 53 F2
Dakhla 52 D2
Dakhla, El Wâhât el- 54 C4
Dalandzadgad 35 B5
Dalap-Uliga-Darrit = Majuro 64 J12
Dali 34 D5
Dalian 35 C7
Daliang Shan 34 D5
Dallas 81 C5
Dalmacija 20 C6
Dalmatia = Dalmacija 20 C6
Daloa 53 G4

Daly Waters 60 D5
Daman 43 J8
Damanhûr 54 B5
Damaraland 58 C3
Damascus = Dimashq 46 D4
Damâvand, Qolleh-ye 44 C3
Dâmbovița → 22 B6
Damietta = Dumyât 54 B5
Dammam = Ad Dammâm 47 F7
Dampier 60 D2
Danbury 77 D9
Dandong 35 B7
Danger Is. = Pukapuka 65 L14
Dangla Shan = Tanggula Shan 34 C4
Danmark = Denmark ■ 9 D7
Danube = Dunărea → 17 F9
Danville 83 A10
Danzig = Gdańsk 16 A4
Dar el Beida = Casablanca 52 B4
Dar es Salaam 57 F7
Darbhanga 40 D5
Dardanelles = Çanakkale Boğazı 23 D6
Dârfûr 55 F3
Darién, G. del 90 B3
Darjeeling = Darjiling 40 D7
Darjiling 40 D7
Darling → 62 B3
Darling Ra. 60 G2
Darlington 11 D6
Darmstadt 14 D5
Darnah 54 B3
Darnley, C. 96 A10
Darnley B. 68 B7
Dartmoor 11 F5
Dartmouth 71 E7
Darwin 60 C5
Daryoi Amu = Amudarya → 29 E6
Dashen, Ras 57 B7
Dasht → 42 G2
Daşoguz 29 E6
Datong 35 B6
Daugava → 24 B1
Daugavpils 24 B1
Dauphin 69 C9
Dauphiné 13 D6
Davangere 43 M9
Davao 36 C3
Davenport 75 E9
David 86 E3
Davis Str. 6 C14
Dawna Ra. 41 J12
Dawson 68 B6
Dax 12 E3
Daxian 35 C5
Daxue Shan 34 C5
Dayr az Zawr 46 D5
Dayton 76 E3
Daytona Beach 83 E7
De Aar 58 E4
Dead Sea 47 E3
Death Valley 78 B4
Debre Markos 55 F6
Debrecen 16 E5
Decatur Ala., U.S.A. 82 B4
Decatur Ill., U.S.A. 75 F10
Deccan 43 L11
Dee → 10 C5
Deer Lake 71 E8
Dehra Dun 42 D11
Delaware □ 77 E8
Delaware → 77 E8
Delgado, C. 57 G8
Delhi 42 E10
Delicias 84 B3
Déline 68 B7

Demanda, Sierra de la 18 A4
Demavend = Damāvand, Qolleh-ye 44 C3
Den Bosch = 's-Hertogenbosch 14 C3
Den Haag = 's-Gravenhage 14 B3
Den Helder 14 B3
Denali 69 B4
Denia 19 C6
Denizli 46 C2
Denmark ■ 9 D7
Denmark Str. 66 C17
Denpasar 39 F5
Denton 80 C5
D'Entrecasteaux Is. 61 B9
Denver 74 F2
Deoghar 40 E6
Deolali 43 K8
Deosai Mts. 42 B9
Dera Ghazi Khan 42 D7
Dera Ismail Khan 42 D7
Derbent 25 E6
Derby Australia 60 D3
Derby U.K. 11 E6
Derg, L. 11 E2
Derry = Londonderry 11 D3
Des Moines 75 E8
Des Moines → 75 E9
Dese 49 E2
Desolation, I. 95 G2
Dessau 15 C7
Dessye = Dese 49 E2
Detroit 76 D4
Deutsche Bucht 14 A5
Deutschland = Germany ■ 14 C6
Deventer 14 B4
Devon I. 70 B5
Dezfūl 47 D7
Dezhneva, Mys 31 C16
Dhahran = Aẓ Ẓahrān 47 F7
Dhaka 41 F8
Dhaka □ 41 E8
Dhamtari 40 G3
Dhanbad 40 F6
Dhaulagiri 40 C4
Dhenkanal 40 G5
Dhubri 41 D7
Dhule 43 J9
Diamantina 93 F5
Diamantina → 62 A2
Diamantino 93 E2
Dibrugarh 41 D10
Diefenbaker, L. 69 C9
Diego Suarez = Antsiranana 59 A9
Dieppe 12 B4
Digby 71 D7
Digne-les-Bains 13 D7
Dihang = Brahmaputra → 41 F7
Dijlah, Nahr → 47 E6
Dijon 13 C6
Dikson 28 B9
Dili 37 F3
Dilli = Delhi 42 E10
Dillingham 69 C4
Dimashq 46 D4
Dimbovița = Dâmbovița → 22 B6
Dimitrovgrad Bulgaria 22 C5
Dimitrovgrad Russia 24 C6
Dimitrovo = Pernik 22 C4
Dinajpur 41 E7
Dinan 12 B2
Dinant 14 C3
Dinara Planina 20 B6
Dinaric Alps = Dinara Planina 20 B6

Dingle 11 E1
Dingwall 10 C4
Dipolog 36 C2
Dire Dawa 49 F3
Dirranbandi 63 A4
Disappointment, L. 60 D3
District of Columbia □ 77 E7
Distrito Federal □ 93 F4
Diu 43 J7
Divinópolis 93 G5
Diyarbakır 46 C5
Djakarta = Jakarta 39 F3
Djawa = Jawa 39 F3
Djerba, Î. de 54 B1
Djerid, Chott 52 B7
Djibouti 49 E3
Djibouti ■ 49 E3
Djourab, Erg du 55 E2
Dnepr = Dnipro → 25 D3
Dneprodzerzhinsk = Dniprodzerzhynsk 25 D3
Dnepropetrovsk = Dnipropetrovsk 25 D4
Dnestr = Dnister → 17 E10
Dnieper = Dnipro → 25 D3
Dniester = Dnister → 17 E10
Dnipro → 25 D3
Dniprodzerzhynsk 25 D3
Dnipropetrovsk 25 D4
Dnister → 17 E10
Dnyapro = Dnipro → 25 D3
Doba 55 G2
Doberai, Jazirah 37 E4
Dobrich 22 C6
Dobruja 22 B7
Dodecanese 23 F6
Dodekanisa = Dodecanese 23 F6
Dodge City 80 A3
Dodoma 57 F7
Doha = Ad Dawḥah 44 E2
Dokdo = Liancourt Rocks 33 E2
Dolbeau-Mistassini 71 E6
Dole 13 C6
Dolomites = Dolomiti 20 A3
Dolomiti 20 A3
Dolores 94 D5
Dolphin and Union Str. 68 B8
Dominica ■ 87 C7
Dominican Rep. ■ 87 C5
Don → Russia 25 D4
Don → U.K. 10 C5
Donau = Dunărea → 17 F9
Doncaster 11 E6
Donegal 11 D2
Donets → 25 D5
Donetsk 25 D4
Dongola 55 E5
Dongting Hu 35 D6
Donostia-San Sebastián 19 A5
Dorchester, C. 70 C6
Dordogne → 12 D3
Dordrecht 14 C3
Dörö̈ Nuur 34 B4
Dortmund 14 C4
Dos Bahías, C. 95 E3
Dos Hermanas 18 D3
Dothan 82 D5
Douai 13 A5
Douala 53 H7
Doubs → 13 C6
Douglas I. of Man 11 D4
Douglas U.S.A. 79 E8
Dourados 94 A6

Douro → 18 B1
Dover 11 F7
Dover, Str. of 11 F7
Dovrefjell 8 C7
Draguignan 13 E7
Drakensberg 59 E5
Drammen 9 D8
Drau = Drava → 20 B7
Drava → 20 B7
Dresden 15 C7
Dreux 12 B4
Drina → 20 B7
Drobeta-Turnu Severin 22 B4
Drogheda 11 E3
Drogobych = Drohobych 17 D6
Drohobych 17 D6
Droichead Atha = Drogheda 11 E3
Dronning Maud Land 96 B7
Druk Yul = Bhutan ■ 41 D8
Drumheller 69 C8
Drygalski I. 96 A11
Dubā 44 F7
Dubai = Dubayy 44 E3
Dubawnt → 68 B9
Dubawnt, L. 68 B9
Dubayy 44 E3
Dubbo 63 B4
Dublin Ireland 11 E3
Dublin U.S.A. 82 D6
Dubrovnik 20 C7
Dudinka 30 C6
Duero = Douro → 18 B1
Dugi Otok 20 B5
Duisburg 14 C4
Dulce → 94 C4
Duluth 75 B8
Dumaguete 36 C2
Dumfries 11 D5
Dumyât 54 B5
Dún Dealgan = Dundalk 11 D3
Dún Laoghaire 11 E3
Duna = Dunărea → 17 F9
Dunaj = Dunărea → 17 F9
Dunărea → 17 F9
Dunav = Dunărea → 17 F9
Dunbar 10 D5
Duncan 80 B5
Dundalk 11 D3
Dundee U.K. 10 C5
Dunedin 65 F4
Dunfermline 10 C5
Dungarvan 11 E3
Dunhuang 34 B4
Dunkerque 12 A5
Dunkirk = Dunkerque 12 A5
Dúnlaoghaire = Dún Laoghaire 11 E3
Durance → 13 E6
Durango 84 C4
Durazno 94 C5
Durazzo = Durrës 22 D2
Durban 59 D6
Düren 14 C4
Durg = Bhilainagar-Durg 40 G3
Durgapur 40 F6
Durham U.K. 11 C6
Durham U.S.A. 83 B8
Durrës 22 D2
Dushanbe 29 F7
Düsseldorf 14 C4
Dutch Harbor 69 C3
Duyun 35 D5
Dvina, Severnaya → 28 C5
Dvinsk = Daugavpils 24 B2
Dwarka 43 H6
Dyer, C. 70 C7

Dyersburg 81 A9
Dzerzhinsk 24 B5
Dzhambul = Taraz 29 E8
Dzhankoy 25 D3
Dzhezkazgan = Zhezqazghan 29 E7
Dzhizak = Jizzax 29 E7
Dzungaria = Junggar Pendi 34 B3
Dzüünmod 35 B5

E

East Bengal 41 E7
East Beskids = Vychodné Beskydy 17 D5
East C. = Dezhneva, Mys 31 C16
East China Sea 35 C7
East Falkland 95 G5
East Kilbride 10 D4
East London 59 E5
East Main = Eastmain 71 D6
East St. Louis 75 F9
East Sea = Japan, Sea of 32 D4
East Timor ■ 37 F3
Eastbourne 11 F7
Eastern Ghats 43 N11
Eastmain 71 D6
Eastmain → 71 D6
Eau Claire 75 C9
Eau Claire, L. à l' 71 D6
Eberswalde-Finow 15 B7
Ebetsu 32 B7
Ebolowa 56 D2
Ebro → 19 B6
Ech Chéliff 52 A6
Echo Bay 68 B8
Eclipse Sd. 70 B6
Ecuador ■ 90 D3
Ed Dar el Beida = Casablanca 52 B4
Edinburgh 10 D5
Edirne 22 D6
Edmonton 69 C8
Edmundston 71 E7
Edremit 23 E6
Edson 69 C8
Edward, L. 57 E5
Edward VII Land 96 C17
Edwards Plateau 80 D4
Eesti = Estonia ■ 24 B2
Égadi, Ísole 21 F4
Eger = Cheb 16 C1
Eger 16 E5
Eglinton I. 70 B2
Egmont, Mt. = Taranaki, Mt. 64 C6
Eğridir 46 C2
Eğridir Gölü 46 C2
Egypt ■ 54 C5
El Aaiún 52 C3
El Asnam = Ech Chéliff 52 A6
El Centro 78 D5
El Djouf 53 D4
El Dorado 81 C7
El Faiyûm 54 C5
El Fâsher 55 F4
El Ferrol = Ferrol 18 A1
El Fuerte 84 B3
El Geneina = Al Junaynah 55 F3
El Gîza 54 C5
El Iskandarîya 54 B4
El Jadida 52 B4
El Khârga 54 C5

El Khartûm 55 E5
El Mahalla el Kubra 54 B5
El Mansûra 54 B5
El Minyâ 54 C5
El Obeid 55 F5
El Oued 52 B7
El Paso 79 E9
El Puerto de Santa Maria 18 D2
El Qâhira 54 B5
El Reno 80 B5
El Salvador ■ 85 E7
El Suweis 54 C5
El Tigre 90 B6
El Uqsur 54 C5
Elat 47 E3
Elâzığ 46 C4
Elba 20 C3
Elbe → 14 B5
Elbert, Mt. 79 A9
Elbeuf 12 B4
Elbing = Elbląg 16 A4
Elbląg 16 A4
Elbrus 25 E5
Elburz Mts. = Alborz, Reshteh-ye Kūhhā-ye 44 B3
Elche 19 C5
Elda 19 C5
Eldoret 57 D7
Elefantes → 59 C6
Elektrostal 24 B4
Elephant I. 96 A4
Eleuthera 86 A4
Elgin U.K. 10 C5
Elgin U.S.A. 76 C1
Elgon, Mt. 57 D6
Elista 25 D5
Elizabeth 77 D8
Elizabeth City 83 A9
Elkhart 76 D3
Elko 72 F6
Ellas = Greece ■ 23 E4
Ellef Ringnes I. 70 B3
Ellesmere I. 70 B6
Ellice Is. = Tuvalu ■ 64 K12
Elliot Lake 71 E5
Ellore = Eluru 40 J3
Ellsworth Land 96 B2
Eluru 40 J3
Elx = Elche 19 C5
Ely 11 E7
eMalahleni 59 D5
Emâmrūd 44 B3
Embarcación 94 A4
Emden 14 B4
Emmen 14 B4
Empalme 84 B2
Empangeni 59 D6
Empedrado 94 B5
Empty Quarter = Rub' al Khâlî 48 D4
Ems → 14 B4
En Nahud 55 F4
Enare = Inarijärvi 8 B11
Encarnación 94 B5
Encounter B. 62 C2
Ende 37 F2
Enderby Land 96 A9
Enewetak Atoll 64 H11
Enez 23 D6
Engels 24 C6
Enggano 39 F2
England □ 11 E6
English Bazar = Ingraj Bazar 40 E7
English Channel 11 F5
Enid 80 B5
Ennedi 55 E3
Ennis 11 E2
Enniskillen 11 D3
Enns → 15 D8
Enschede 14 B4
Ensenada 84 A1
Entebbe 57 D6
Entre Ríos □ 94 C5

Enugu 53 G7
Eólie, Is. 21 E5
Épernay 13 B5
Épinal 13 B7
Equatoria 55 G4
Equatorial Guinea ■ 56 D1
Er Rachidia 52 B5
Erāwadī Myit = Irrawaddy → 41 K10
Erbil = Arbil 46 C6
Erciyaş Dağı 46 C6
Erebus, Mt. 96 B15
Ereğli Konya, Turkey 46 C3
Ereğli Zonguldak, Turkey 25 E3
Erfurt 15 C6
Erie 77 C5
Erie, L. 76 C5
Eritrea ■ 49 E2
Erlangen 15 D6
Erne, Lower L. 11 D3
Erode 43 P10
Erramala Hills 43 M11
Ertis = Irtysh → 28 C7
Ergzebirge 15 C7
Erzincan 25 F4
Erzurum 25 F5
Es Sahrā' Esh Sharqīya 54 C5
Es Sînā' 54 C5
Esbjerg 9 D7
Esbo = Espoo 9 C10
Esch-sur-Alzette 13 B6
Escuinapa de Hidalgo 84 C3
Esfahān 44 C2
Esh Sham = Dimashq 46 D4
Esil = Ishim → 29 D8
Esker 71 D7
Eskilstuna 9 D9
Eskimo Point = Arviat 68 B10
Eskişehir 25 F3
Eslämäbäd-e Gharb 46 D6
España = Spain ■ 18 C4
Esperance 60 G3
Espinazo, Sierra del = Espinhaço, Serra do 93 F5
Espinhaço, Serra do 93 F5
Espírito Santo □ 93 G5
Espíritu Santo 64 L11
Espoo 9 C10
Essaouira 52 B4
Essen 14 C4
Essequibo → 90 B7
Esslingen 14 D5
Estados, I. de Los 95 G4
Estância 93 E6
Estevan 69 D9
Estonia ■ 24 B2
Estrela, Serra da 18 B2
Estrondo, Serra do 92 D4
Etawah 42 F11
eThekwini = Durban 59 D6
Ethiopia ■ 49 F2
Ethiopian Highlands 49 F2
Etna 21 F5
Etosha Pan 58 B3
Euboea = Evia 23 E5
Eugene 72 E2
Euphrates = Furāt, Nahr al → 47 E6
Eureka Canada 70 B5
Eureka U.S.A. 72 F1
Europa, Île 59 C8
Europa, Picos de 18 A3
Evanston 76 C2
Evansville 76 F2
Everest, Mt. 40 C6
Everett 72 C2

Everglades △ 83 G7
Evia 23 E5
Évora 18 C2
Évreux 12 B4
Evros → 22 D6
Évvoia = Evia 23 E5
Exeter 11 F5
Exmoor 11 F5
Exmouth 11 F5
Extremadura □ 18 C2
Eyasi, L. 57 E6
Eyre, L. = Kati Thanda-Lake Eyre 60 F6
Eyre Pen. 62 B2

F

F.Y.R.O.M. = Macedonia ■ 22 D3
Faenza 20 B3
Færoe Is. = Føroyar ☑ 6 C4
Fair Isle 10 B6
Fairbanks 69 B5
Fairweather, Mt. 69 C6
Faisalabad 42 D8
Faizabad 40 D4
Falkland Is. ☑ 95 G5
Fall River 77 D10
Falmouth 11 F4
Falun 9 C9
Famagusta 46 D3
Fano 20 B4
Fao = Al Fāw 47 E7
Farāh 42 C3
Farasān, Jazā'ir 49 D3
Farasan Is. = Farasān, Jazā'ir 49 D3
Fareham 11 F6
Fargo 74 B6
Faro 18 D2
Fārs □ 44 D3
Fāryāb □ 45 B6
Fatehgarh 42 F11
Fatehpur Raj., India 42 F9
Fatehpur Ut. P., India 40 E3
Fazilka 42 D9
Fécamp 12 B4
Fehmarn 15 A6
Feira de Santana 93 E6
Felipe Carrillo Puerto 85 D7
Felixstowe 11 F9
Fenyang 35 C6
Feodosiya 25 D4
Fermont 71 D7
Fernando Póo = Bioko 53 H7
Ferozepore = Firozpur 42 D9
Ferrara 20 B3
Ferret, C. 12 D3
Ferrol 18 A1
Fès 52 B5
Fetlar 10 A6
Feuilles → 70 D6
Fez = Fès 52 B5
Fezzan 54 C2
Fianarantsoa 59 C9
Figeac 12 D5
Figueres 19 A7
Fiji ■ 64 L12
Finike 46 C2
Finisterre, C. = Fisterra, C. 18 A1
Finland ■ 8 C11
Finland, G. of 9 D11
Finlay → 68 C7
Firat = Furāt, Nahr al → 47 E6
Firenze 20 C3

Firozabad 42 F11
Firozpur 42 D9
Fish → 58 D3
Fishguard 11 E4
Fisterra, C. 18 A1
Fiume = Rijeka 20 B5
Flagstaff 79 C7
Flanders = Flandre 14 C2
Flandre 14 C2
Flathead L. 73 C7
Flattery, C. 72 B1
Flensburg 14 A5
Flers 12 B3
Flin Flon 69 C9
Flinders → 61 D7
Flinders I. 62 C4
Flinders Ranges 62 B2
Flint 76 D4
Flint I. 65 L15
Florence = Firenze 20 C3
Florence 83 B8
Flores 37 F2
Florianópolis 94 B7
Florida □ 83 F6
Florida, Straits of 86 B3
Floro 8 C7
Flushing = Vlissingen 14 C2
Fly → 61 B7
Foçani 17 F8
Fóggia 20 D5
Foix 12 E4
Foligno 20 C4
Folkestone 11 F7
Fond du Lac 76 D10
Fongafale 64 K12
Fontainebleau 13 B5
Fontenay-le-Comte 12 C3
Foochow = Fuzhou 35 D6
Forfar 10 C5
Forlì 20 B4
Formentera 19 C6
Formosa = Taiwan ■ 35 D7
Formosa 94 B5
Forøyar ☑ 6 C4
Forsayth 61 B7
Fort Albany 71 D5
Fort Collins 74 E2
Fort Dauphin = Taolanaro 59 D9
Fort-de-France 87 D7
Fort Dodge 75 D7
Fort Franklin = Déline 68 B7
Fort George = Chisasibi 71 D6
Fort Good Hope 68 B7
Fort Lauderdale 83 F7
Fort Liard 68 B7
Fort Macleod 69 D8
Fort McPherson 68 B6
Fort Myers 83 F7
Fort Norman = Tulita 68 B7
Fort Peck L. 73 C10
Fort Providence 68 B8
Fort Resolution 68 B8
Fort Rupert = Waskaganish 71 D6
Fort Scott 81 A6
Fort Shevchenko 29 E6
Fort Simpson 68 B7
Fort Smith Canada 68 B8
Fort Smith U.S.A. 81 B6
Fort Wayne 76 D3
Fort William 10 C4
Fort Worth 80 C5
Fort Yukon 69 B5
Fortaleza 92 C6
Foshan 35 D6
Fougères 12 B3
Foula 10 A5
Fouta Djalon 53 F3
Foxe Basin 70 C6

Foxe Chan. 70 C5
Foxe Pen. 70 C6
Foz do Iguaçu 94 B6
Franca 93 G4
France ■ 13 C5
Franceville 56 E2
Franche-Comté □ 13 C6
Francistown 59 C5
Frankfurt Brandenburg, Germany 15 B8
Frankfurt Hessen, Germany 14 C5
Fränkische Alb 15 D6
Franklin B. 68 B7
Franklin Mts. 68 B7
Franklin Str. 68 A10
Frantsa Iosifa, Zemlya 28 A6
Fraser → 69 D7
Fraserburgh 10 C5
Fredericksburg 77 E7
Fredericton 71 E7
Frederikshavn 9 D8
Fredrikstad 9 D8
Free State □ 59 D5
Freeport Bahamas 86 A4
Freeport U.S.A. 75 D10
Freetown 53 G3
Freiburg 14 E4
Fréjus 13 E7
French Guiana ☑ 92 B3
French Polynesia ☑ 65 M16
Fresnillo 84 C4
Fresno 78 B3
Fria, C. 58 B2
Friedrichshafen 14 E5
Frobisher B. 70 C7
Frobisher Bay = Iqaluit 70 C7
Frunze = Bishkek 29 E8
Frutal 93 F4
Frýdek-Místek 16 D8
Fuchou = Fuzhou 35 D6
Fuchū 33 F3
Fuengirola 18 D3
Fuerte → 84 B3
Fuerteventura 52 C3
Fuhai 34 B3
Fuji 33 F6
Fuji-San 33 F6
Fujian □ 35 D6
Fujiyama, Mt. = Fuji-San 33 F6
Fukien = Fujian □ 35 D6
Fukui 33 E5
Fukuoka 33 G2
Fukushima 33 E7
Fukuyama 33 F3
Fulda 14 C5
Fulda → 14 C5
Funabashi 33 F7
Funafuti = Fongafale 64 K12
Funchal 52 B2
Fundy, B. of 71 E7
Furāt, Nahr al → 47 E6
Furneaux Group 62 D4
Fürth 14 D6
Fury and Hecla Str. 70 C5
Fushun 35 B7
Fuxin 35 B7
Fuzhou 35 D6
Fyn 9 D8

G

Gaalkacyo 49 F4
Gabès 54 B1
Gabès, G. de 54 B1
Gabon ■ 56 E2
Gaborone 59 C5
Gabrovo 22 C5
Gachsärän 44 D2
Gadarwara 43 H11
Gadsden 82 B4
Gafsa 52 B7

Gagnoa 53 G4
Gagnon 71 D7
Gaillimh = Galway 11 E2
Gainesville Fla., U.S.A. 83 E6
Gainesville Ga., U.S.A. 83 B6
Gairdner, L. 62 B2
Galashiels 10 D5
Galați 17 F9
Galdhøpiggen 8 C7
Galesburg 75 E9
Galicia □ 18 A2
Galilee, Sea of = Yam Kinneret 46 D3
Gallinas, Pta. 90 A4
Gallipoli = Gelibolu 23 D6
Gällivare 8 B10
Galloway, Mull of 11 D4
Galmudug 49 G4
Galveston 81 E6
Galway 11 E2
Galway B. 11 E2
Gambia ■ 53 F2
Gambia → 53 F2
Gan Jiang → 35 D6
Gâncâ 25 E6
Gand = Gent 14 C2
Gandak → 40 E5
Gander 71 E8
Gandhi Sagar 43 G9
Gandía 19 C5
Ganga → 41 F8
Ganganagar 42 E8
Gangdisê Shan 40 B3
Ganges = Ganga → 41 F8
Gangneung 35 C7
Gangtok 41 D7
Gansu □ 34 C5
Ganzhou 35 D6
Gaoxiong = Kaohsiung 35 D7
Gap 13 D7
Gar 34 C2
Garabogazköl Aylagy 29 E6
Garagum 29 F6
Garanhuns 92 D6
Garda, L. di 20 B3
Garden City 80 A3
Gardêz 42 C6
Garmisch-Partenkirchen 14 E6
Garonne → 12 D3
Garoowe 49 F4
Garoua 55 G1
Garrison Res. = Sakakawea, L. 74 B4
Garry, L. 68 B9
Garwa = Garoua 55 G1
Gary 76 D2
Garzê 34 C5
Gascogne 12 E4
Gascogne, G. de 12 D2
Gascony = Gascogne 12 E4
Gaspé 71 E7
Gaspé, C. 71 E7
Gaspésie, Pén. de la 71 E7
Gasteiz = Vitoria-Gasteiz 19 A4
Gata, Sierra de 18 B2
Gateshead 11 D6
Gauhati = Guwahati 41 D8
Gävle 9 C9
Gawilgarh Hills 43 J10
Gaxun Nur 34 B5
Gaya 40 E5
Gaza 47 E3
Gaza Strip → 47 E3
Gaziantep 46 C4
Gazimağosa = Famagusta 46 D3
Gdańsk 16 A4
Gdynia 16 A4

Gebze 22 D7
Gedaref 55 F6
Gedser 9 E8
Geelong 63 C3
Gejiu 34 D5
Gela 21 F5
Gelibolu 23 D6
Gelsenkirchen 14 C4
General Acha 94 D4
General Alvear 94 D3
General Pico 94 D4
General Santos 36 C3
Geneva = Genève 14 E4
Geneva, L. = Léman, L.
  13 C7
Genève 14 E4
Gennargentu, Mti. del
  21 D7
Genoa = Génova 13 D8
Génova, G. di 20 C2
Gent 14 C2
George 58 E4
George → 70 D7
George River =
  Kangiqsualujjuaq
  70 D7
George Town Cayman Is.
  86 C3
George Town Malaysia
  38 C2
George V Land 96 A14
Georgetown 90 B7
Georgia □ 83 C6
Georgia ■ 25 E5
Georgian B. 71 E5
Georgiyevsk 25 E5
Gera 15 C7
Geraldton 60 F1
Germany ■ 14 C6
Germiston 59 D5
Gerona = Girona 19 B7
Getafe 18 B4
Gettysburg 77 E7
Ghaghara → 40 E5
Ghana ■ 53 G5
Ghardaïa 52 B6
Gharyān 54 B1
Ghats, Eastern 43 N11
Ghats, Western 43 N9
Ghawdex = Gozo 21 F5
Ghazâl, Bahr el → Chad
  55 F2
Ghazâl, Bahr el →
  South Sudan 55 G5
Ghaziabad 42 E10
Ghazipur 40 E4
Ghazni 42 C6
Ghent = Gent 14 C2
Ghowr □ 42 C4
Gibraltar □ 18 D3
Gibraltar, Str. of 18 E3
Gibson Desert 60 E4
Giebnegáisi = Kebnekaise
  8 B9
Gifu 33 F5
Gijón 18 A3
Gila → 78 D5
Gīlān □ 46 C7
Gilbert Is. 64 J12
Gilgit 42 B9
Giresun 25 E4
Girga 54 C5
Girne = Kyrenia 46 D3
Giron = Kiruna 8 B10
Girona 19 B7
Gironde → 12 D3
Girvan 10 D4
Gisborne 64 C7
Gitega 57 E5
Giuba → 49 G3
Giza = El Gîza 54 C5
Gjøa Haven 68 B10
Glace Bay 71 E8
Gladstone 61 E9
Glåma = Glomma →
  9 C8
Glasgow 10 D4

Glazov 28 D6
Gleiwitz = Gliwice 16 C4
Glendale 78 C3
Glenrothes 10 C5
Glens Falls 77 C9
Gliwice 16 C4
Głogów 16 C3
Glomma → 9 C8
Gloucester 11 F5
Gniezno 16 B3
Goa 43 M8
Goa □ 43 M8
Gobi 35 B6
Godavari → 40 J4
Godhra 43 H8
Gods → 69 C10
Gods L. 69 C10
Godthåb = Nuuk 66 C14
Goeie Hoop, Kaap die =
  Good Hope, C. of
  58 E3
Gogra = Ghaghara →
  40 E5
Goiânia 93 F4
Goiás 93 F3
Goiás □ 93 E4
Goio-Erê 94 A6
Gold Coast 63 A5
Golden Gate 72 H2
Goldsboro 83 B9
Golspie 10 C5
Goma 57 E5
Gomel = Homyel 17 B10
Gomera 52 C2
Gómez Palacio 84 B4
Gonaïves 87 C5
Gonbad-e Kāvūs 44 B3
Gonda 40 D3
Gonder 55 F6
Gonghe 34 C5
Good Hope, C. of 58 E3
Gorakhpur 40 D4
Gore 55 G6
Gorgān 44 B3
Gorkiy = Nizhniy
  Novgorod 24 B5
Görlitz 15 C8
Gorlovka = Horlivka
  25 D4
Gorna Dzhumaya =
  Blagoevgrad 22 C4
Gorno-Altay □ 29 D9
Gorontalo 37 D2
Górzów Wielkopolski
  16 B2
Göta kanal 9 D9
Göteborg 9 D8
Gotha 14 C6
Gothenburg = Göteborg
  9 D8
Gotland 9 D9
Gotō-Rettō 33 G1
Göttingen 14 C5
Gottwaldov = Zlín 16 D3
Gouda 14 B3
Gouin, Rés. 71 E6
Goulburn 63 B4
Governador Valadares
  93 F5
Goya 94 B5
Gozo 21 F5
Graaff-Reinet 58 E4
Gracias a Dios, C. 86 D3
Grafton 63 A5
Graham Land 96 A3
Grahamstown 59 E5
Grampian Mts. 10 C4
Gran Canaria 52 C2
Gran Chaco 94 B4
Gran Sasso d'Itália 20 C4
Granada Nic. 85 E7
Granada Spain 18 D4
Granby 71 E6
Grand Bahama I. 86 A4
Grand Canyon 79 B6
Grand Cayman 86 C3
Grand Coulee Dam 72 C4

Grand Falls 71 E7
Grand Falls-Windsor
  71 E8
Grand Forks 74 B6
Grand Island 74 E5
Grand Rapids Canada
  69 C10
Grand Rapids U.S.A.
  76 C3
Grand St-Bernard, Col du
  13 D7
Grand Teton 73 E8
Grande → Bolivia 91 G6
Grande → Brazil 93 E5
Grande, B. 95 G3
Grande, Río → 84 B5
Grande Baleine, R. de
  la → 71 D6
Grantham 11 E6
Grasse 13 E7
Graulhet 12 E4
's-Gravenhage 14 B3
Graz 15 E8
Great Abaco I. = Abaco I.
  86 A4
Great Australian Bight
  60 G4
Great Barrier Reef 61 D8
Great Basin 72 G5
Great Bear → 68 B7
Great Bear L. 68 B7
Great Belt = Store Bælt
  9 D8
Great Divide, The = Great
  Dividing Ra. 61 E8
Great Dividing Ra. 61 E8
Great Falls 73 C8
Great Inagua I. 86 B5
Great Indian Desert =
  Thar Desert 42 F7
Great Karoo 58 E4
Great Khingan Mts. = Da
  Hinggan Ling 35 B7
Great Ouse → 11 E7
Great Saint Bernard
  Pass = Grand St-
  Bernard, Col du 13 D7
Great Salt Desert = Kavīr,
  Dasht-e 44 C3
Great Salt L. 73 F7
Great Salt Lake Desert
  73 F7
Great Sandy Desert
  60 E3
Great Sangi = Sangihe,
  Pulau 37 D3
Great Slave L. 68 B8
Great Smoky Mts. △
  83 B6
Great Victoria Desert
  60 F4
Great Wall 35 C5
Great Yarmouth 11 E7
Great Zab = Zāb al
  Kabīr → 46 C5
Greater Antilles 86 C5
Greater Sunda Is. 39 F4
Greece ■ 23 E4
Greeley 74 E2
Green → 79 A8
Green Bay 76 B2
Greenland ☒ 66 C9
Greenock 10 D4
Greensboro 83 A8
Greenville Ala., U.S.A.
  82 D4
Greenville Miss., U.S.A.
  81 C8
Greenville S.C., U.S.A.
  83 B6
Greenwood 81 C8
Gremikha 28 C4
Grenada ■ 87 D7
Grenoble 13 D6
Grey Ra. 63 A3
Greymouth 65 E4
Griffith 63 B4

Grimsby 11 E6
Gris-Nez, C. 12 A4
Grise Fiord 70 B5
Grodno = Hrodna 17 B6
Groningen 14 B4
Grosseto 20 C3
Grossglockner 15 E7
Groznyy 25 E6
Grudziądz 16 B4
Guadalajara Mexico
  84 C4
Guadalajara Spain 18 B4
Guadalcanal 64 K11
Guadalete → 18 D2
Guadalquivir → 18 D2
Guadalupe =
  Guadeloupe ☒ 87 C7
Guadalupe, Sierra de
  18 C3
Guadarrama, Sierra de
  18 B4
Guadeloupe ☒ 87 C7
Guadiana → 18 D2
Guadix 18 D4
Guafo, Boca del 95 E2
Guajará-Mirim 91 F5
Guajira, Pen. de la 90 A4
Gualeguaychú 94 C5
Guam ☒ 64 H9
Guamúchil 84 B3
Guanahaní = San
  Salvador I. 86 B5
Guanajuato 84 C4
Guangdong □ 35 D6
Guangxi Zhuangzu
  Zizhiqu □ 35 D5
Guangzhou 35 D6
Guantánamo 86 B4
Guantánamo B. 86 B5
Guaporé → 91 F5
Guaqui 91 G5
Guarapuava 94 B6
Guardafui, C. = Asir, Ras
  49 E5
Guatemala 85 E6
Guatemala ■ 86 D2
Guaviare → 90 C5
Guaxupé 93 G4
Guayaquil 90 D3
Guayaquil, G. de 90 D2
Guaymas 84 B2
Guelph 76 D5
Guéret 12 C4
Guernsey 11 G5
Guidónia-Montecélio
  20 C4
Guildford 11 F6
Guilin 35 D6
Guinea ■ 53 F3
Guinea, Gulf of 51 F3
Guinea-Bissau ■ 53 F3
Guingamp 12 B2
Guiyang 35 D5
Guizhou □ 35 D5
Gujarat □ 43 H7
Gujranwala 42 C9
Gujrat 42 C9
Gulf, The = Persian Gulf
  44 E2
Gulu 57 D6
Guna 43 G10
Gunsan 35 C7
Guntur 40 J3
Gurkha 40 C5
Gurupi → 92 C4
Guryev = Atyraū 29 E6
Gusau 53 F7
Guwahati 41 D8
Guyana ■ 90 B7
Guyane française =
  French Guiana ☒ 92 B3
Guyenne 12 D4
Güzelyurt = Morphou
  46 D3
Gwädar 42 G3
Gwalior 42 F11
Gwanda 59 C5

Gwangju 35 C7
Gwanju = Gwangju 35 C7
Gweru 59 B5
Gyandzha = Gäncä 25 E6
Gyaring Hu 34 C4
Gympie 63 A5
Győr 16 E3
Gyumri 25 E5
Gyzylarbat = Serdar
  29 F6

H

Haarlem 14 B3
Hachinohe 32 C7
Ḥadd, Ra's al 45 F4
Hadejia 53 F7
Haḍramawt 49 D4
Haeju 35 C7
Haerhpin = Harbin 35 B7
Hafizabad 42 C8
Hagen 14 C4
Hagerstown 77 E7
Hague, C. de la 12 B3
Hague, The =
  's-Gravenhage 14 B3
Haguenau 13 B7
Haida Gwaii 68 C6
Haidarābād = Hyderabad
  43 L11
Haifa = Ḥefa 46 D3
Haikou 35 D6
Ḥā'il 47 F5
Hailar 35 B6
Hainan □ 35 E5
Haiphong 35 D5
Haiti ■ 87 C5
Hajji Ibrahim 46 C6
Hakodate 32 C7
Halab 46 C4
Halberstadt 15 C6
Halden 9 D8
Haldwani 42 E11
Halifax Canada 71 E7
Halifax U.K. 11 E6
Hall Beach = Sanirajak
  70 C5
Hall Pen. 70 C7
Halle 15 C6
Halmahera 37 D3
Halmstad 9 D8
Hälsingborg =
  Helsingborg 9 D8
Hamadān 46 D7
Ḥamāh 46 C4
Hamamatsu 33 F5
Hamar 8 C10
Hamburg 14 B5
Hämeenlinna 8 C10
Hameln 14 B5
Hamersley Ra. 60 E2
Hamhŭng 35 C7
Hami 34 B4
Hamilton Canada 71 E6
Hamilton N.Z. 64 B6
Hamilton U.K. 10 D4
Hamlin = Hameln 14 B5
Hamm 14 C4
Hammerfest 8 A10
Hammond 76 D2
Hampton 77 F7
Handan 35 C6
Hangayn Nuruu 34 B4
Hangzhou = Hangzhou
  35 C7
Hangzhou 35 C7
Hangzhou Wan 35 C7
Hania = Chania 23 G5
Hankö 9 D10
Hanna 69 C8
Hannibal 75 F9
Hannover 14 B5
Hanoi 35 D5
Hanover = Hannover
  14 B5
Hanover, I. 95 G2
Hanzhong 35 C5

Haora 40 F7
Haparanda 8 B10
Happy Valley-Goose Bay 71 D7
Har Hu 34 C4
Har Us Nuur 34 B4
Haraḍ 47 F7
Harbin 35 B7
Hardangerfjorden 8 C7
Hardwar = Haridwar 42 E11
Harer 49 F3
Hargeisa 49 F3
Haridwar 42 E11
Haringhata → 41 G7
Harlingen 80 F5
Harlow 11 F7
Härnösand 8 C9
Harricana → 71 D6
Harris 10 C3
Harrisburg 77 D7
Harrison, C. 70 D8
Harrogate 11 D6
Hartford 77 D9
Hartlepool 11 D6
Harvey 76 D2
Harwich 11 F7
Haryana □ 42 E10
Harz 14 C6
Hasa 47 F7
Haskovo = Khaskovo 22 D5
Hastings N.Z. 64 C7
Hastings U.K. 11 F7
Hastings U.S.A. 74 E5
Hatay 46 C4
Hatgal 34 A4
Hathras 42 F11
Hatia 41 F8
Hatteras, C. 83 B10
Hattiesburg 81 D9
Haugesund 9 D7
Hauraki G. 64 B6
Haut Atlas 52 B4
Havana = La Habana 86 B3
Havant 11 F6
Havel → 15 B7
Havre 73 B9
Havre-St.-Pierre 71 D7
Hawai'i □ 78 H12
Hawaiian Is. 78 H12
Hawick 10 D5
Hawke B. 64 C7
Hay 63 B3
Hay River 68 B8
Hayastan = Armenia ■ 25 E5
Hayes → 69 C10
Hazar 29 F6
Hazaribag 40 F5
Hearst 71 E5
Hebei □ 35 C6
Hebron = Al Khalîl 47 E3
Hebron 70 D7
Hechi 35 D5
Hechuan 35 C5
Heerlen 13 A6
Hefei 35 C6
Hegang 35 B8
Heidelberg 14 D5
Heihe 35 A7
Heilbronn 14 D5
Heilongjiang □ 35 B7
Heimaey 8 C1
Hejaz = Ḥijāz 47 F4
Hekou 34 D5
Helena 73 C7
Helgoland 14 A4
Heligoland B. = Deutsche Bucht 14 A5
Hellas = Greece ■ 23 E4
Hellespont = Çanakkale Boğazı 23 D6

Helmand → 42 D2
Helmsdale 10 B5
Helsingborg 9 D8
Helsinki 9 C11
Helwân 54 C5
Hemel Hempstead 11 F6
Henan □ 35 C6
Hengyang 35 D6
Henrietta Maria, C. 71 D5
Hentiyn Nuruu 35 B5
Herāt 42 B3
Hereford 11 E5
Herford 14 B5
Hermosillo 84 B2
Hernád → 16 E5
Heroica Nogales = Nogales 84 A2
's-Hertogenbosch 14 C3
Hessen □ 14 C5
Hexham 11 D5
Hialeah 83 G7
Hibbing 75 B8
Hidalgo del Parral 84 B3
Higashiōsaka 33 F4
High River 69 C8
High Tatra = Tatry 16 D4
High Wycombe 11 F6
Hiiumaa 24 B1
Ḥijāz 47 F4
Hildesheim 14 B5
Hilo 78 J13
Hilversum 14 B3
Himachal Pradesh □ 42 D10
Himalaya 40 C5
Himeji 33 F4
Ḥimṣ 46 D4
Hindu Kush 42 B7
Hingoli 43 K10
Hirosaki 32 C7
Hiroshima 33 F3
Hisar 42 E9
Hispaniola 87 C5
Hitachi 33 E7
Hjälmaren 9 D9
Hkakabo Razi 41 C11
Ho Chi Minh City = Thanh Pho Ho Chi Minh 38 B3
Hoare B. 70 C7
Hobart 62 D4
Hódmezővásárhely 16 E5
Hodna, Chott el 52 A6
Hōfu 33 F2
Hoggar = Ahaggar 52 D7
Hoh Xil Shan 34 C3
Hoher Rhön = Rhön 14 C5
Hohhot 35 B6
Hokkaidō □ 32 B8
Holguín 86 B4
Hollywood 83 G7
Holman 68 A8
Holstebro 9 D7
Holyhead 11 E4
Home B. 70 C7
Homer 69 C4
Homs = Ḥimṣ 46 D4
Homyel 17 B10
Honan = Henan □ 35 C6
Honduras ■ 85 E7
Honduras, G. de 85 D7
Hønefoss 9 C8
Hong Kong □ 35 D5
Hongjiang 35 D5
Hongshui He → 35 D5
Hongze Hu 35 C6
Honiara 64 K10
Honolulu 78 H12
Honshū 33 F4
Hood, Mt. 72 D3
Hooghly = Hugli → 40 G7
Hoorn 14 B3
Hoover Dam 78 B5

Hopedale 70 D7
Hopei = Hebei □ 35 C6
Horlivka 25 D4
Hormozgān □ 44 E3
Hormuz, Str. of 44 E4
Horn, Cape = Hornos, C. de 95 H3
Hornavan 8 B9
Hornos, C. de 95 H3
Horqin Youyi Qianqi 35 B7
Horsham 62 C3
Horton → 68 B7
Hoste, I. 95 H3
Hot Springs 81 B7
Hotan 34 C2
Houlton 77 A12
Houma 81 E8
Houston 81 E6
Hövsgöl Nuur 34 A5
Howe, C. 63 C5
Howrah = Haora 40 F7
Hoy 10 B5
Høyanger 8 C7
Hradec Králové 16 C2
Hrodna 17 B6
Hrvatska = Croatia ■ 20 B5
Hsiamen = Xiamen 35 D6
Hsian = Xi'an 35 C5
Huacho 91 F3
Huai He → 35 C6
Huainan 35 C6
Huallaga → 90 E3
Huambo 58 A3
Huancavelica 91 F3
Huancayo 91 F3
Huang Hai = Yellow Sea 35 C7
Huang He → 35 C6
Huangshan 35 D6
Huangshi 35 C6
Huánuco 91 E3
Huaraz 91 E3
Huascarán, Nevado 91 E3
Huasco 94 B2
Huatabampo 84 B3
Hubballi 43 M9
Hubei □ 35 C6
Huddersfield 11 E6
Hudiksvall 8 C9
Hudson → 77 D8
Hudson Bay 70 C5
Hudson Str. 70 C7
Hue 38 A3
Huelva 18 D2
Huesca 19 A5
Hughenden 61 E7
Hugli → 40 G7
Huila, Nevado del 90 C3
Huize 34 D5
Hull = Kingston upon Hull 11 E6
Hull 71 E6
Hulun Nur 35 B6
Humaitá 91 E6
Humber → 11 E6
Humboldt 69 C9
Humboldt → 72 F4
Húnaflói 8 B1
Hunan □ 35 D6
Hungary ■ 16 E4
Hüngnam 35 C7
Hunsrück 14 D4
Huntington 76 E4
Huntington Beach 78 D3
Huntly 10 C5
Huntsville Canada 71 E6
Huntsville U.S.A. 82 B4
Hupeh = Hubei □ 35 C6
Huron, L. 76 B4
Húsavík 8 B2
Hutchinson 80 A5
Hvar 20 C6
Hwang Ho = Huang He → 35 C6

Hwange 59 B5
Hyargas Nuur 34 B4
Hyderabad India 43 L11
Hyderabad Pakistan 42 G6
Hyères 13 E7
Hyères, Îs. d' 13 E7

I

Ialomiţa → 22 B6
Iaşi 17 E8
Ibadan 53 G6
Ibagué 90 C3
Ibarra 90 C3
Ibiá 93 F4
Ibiapaba, Sa. da 92 C5
Ibiza = Eivissa 19 C6
Ibotirama 93 E5
Iça 91 F3
İçel = 90 D5
İçel 46 C3
Iceland ■ 8 B2
Ichihara 33 F7
Ichinomiya 33 F5
Idaho □ 73 D7
Idaho Falls 73 E7
Idar-Oberstein 14 D4
Idensalmi = Iisalmi 8 C11
Idfû 54 D5
Idlib 46 D4
Ife 53 G6
Iforas, Adrar des 52 E6
Igarapava 93 G4
Igarka 28 C9
Iglésias 21 E2
Igloolik 70 C5
Iglulligaarjuk = Chesterfield Inlet 68 B10
Igluuik = Igloolik 70 C5
Igoumenitsa 23 E3
Iguaçu → 94 B6
Iguaçu, Cat. del 94 B6
Iguala 84 D5
Iguassu = Iguaçu → 94 B6
Iguatu 92 D6
Iisalmi 8 C11
Ijebu-Ode 53 G6
IJsselmeer 14 B3
Ikaluktutiak 68 B9
Ikaria 23 F6
Ikeda 33 F3
Ikparjuk = Arctic Bay 70 B5
Ilagan 36 A2
Ilām 46 D6
Ile → 29 E8
Île-de-France □ 12 B5
Ilebo 56 E4
Ilesha 53 G6
Ilhéus 93 E6
Ili = Ile → 29 E8
Iligan 36 C2
Illampu = Ancohuma, Nevado 91 G5
Illapel 94 C2
Iller → 14 D5
Illimani, Nevado 91 G5
Ilmen, Ozero 24 B3
Iloilo 36 B2
Ilorin 53 G6
Imabari 33 F3
Imandra, Ozero 28 C4
Imatra 8 C11
imeni Ismail Samani, Pik 29 F8
Imola 20 B3
Imperatriz 92 D4
Impéria 13 E8
Imphal 41 E9
In Salah 52 C6
Inari 8 B11
Inarijärvi 8 B11
Ince Burun 25 E3
Incheon 35 C7

Incomáti → 59 D6
Indalsälven → 8 C9
Independence 75 F7
India ■ 43 J10
Indiana □ 76 D3
Indiana □ 76 E3
Indianapolis 76 E2
Indigirka → 31 B12
Indira Gandhi Canal 42 F8
Indonesia ■ 39 E4
Indore 43 H9
Indre → 12 C4
Indus → 43 G5
İnebolu 25 E3
Ingolstadt 15 D6
Ingraj Bazar 40 E7
Inland Sea 33 F3
Inn → 15 D7
Inner Hebrides 10 C3
Inner Mongolia = Nei Mongol Zizhiqu □ 35 B6
Innsbruck 15 E6
Inoucdjouac = Inukjuak 70 D6
Inowrocław 16 B4
Insein 41 J11
International Falls 75 A8
Inukjuak 70 D6
Inuvik 68 B6
Invercargill 65 G3
Invergordon 10 C4
Inverness 10 C4
Inverurie 10 C5
Ioannina 23 E3
Ionian Is. = Ionioi Nisoi 23 E3
Ionian Sea 21 F6
Ionioi Nisoi 23 E3
Ios 23 F5
Iowa □ 75 D8
Iowa City 75 E9
Ipameri 93 F4
Ipatinga 93 F5
Ipiales 90 C3
Ipin = Yibin 35 D5
Ipoh 38 D2
Ipswich Australia 63 A5
Ipswich U.K. 11 E7
Iqaluit 70 C7
Iquique 91 H4
Iquitos 90 D4
Iraklio 23 G5
Iráklion = Iraklio 23 G5
Iran ■ 44 C3
Irapuato 84 C4
Iraq ■ 46 D5
Ireland ■ 11 E3
Irian Jaya = Papua □ 37 E5
Iringa 57 F7
Irish Sea 11 E4
Irkutsk 30 D8
Iron Gate = Portile de Fier 22 B4
Ironwood 75 B9
Irrawaddy → 41 K10
Irtysh → 28 C7
Irún 19 A5
Irvine 10 D4
Ísafjörður 8 B1
Isar → 15 D7
İschia 21 D4
Isère → 13 D6
Isfahan = Eşfahān 44 C2
Ishim → 29 D8
Ishinomaki 32 D7
Isiro 57 D5
Iskenderun 46 C4
Islamabad 42 C8
Island = Iceland ■ 8 B2
Island L. 69 C10
Islay 10 D3
Isle of Wight □ 11 F6
Ismail = Izmayil 17 F9
Ismâ'îlîya 47 E3
Isparta 46 C2
Israel ■ 46 E3

Issoire 13 D5
Issyk-Kul, Ozero =
 Ysyk-Köl 29 E8
İstanbul 22 D7
İstanbul Boğazı 22 D7
Istra 20 B4
Istres 13 E6
Istria = Istra 20 B4
Itaberaba 93 E5
Itabira 93 F5
Itabuna 93 E6
Itajaí 94 B7
Italy ■ 20 C4
Itaperuna 93 G5
Itapicuru → 93 E6
Ivanava 17 B7
Ivano-Frankivsk 17 D7
Ivanovo = Ivanava 17 B7
Ivanovo 24 B5
Ivory Coast ■ 53 G4
Ivujivik 70 C6
Iwaki 33 E7
Iwakuni 33 F3
Iwo 53 G6
Izhevsk 28 D6
Izmayil 17 F9
İzmir 23 E6
İznik Gölü 23 D7
Izumi-Sano 33 F4

J

Jabalpur 43 H11
Jaboatão 92 D6
Jacareí 94 A7
Jackson Mich., U.S.A.
 76 C3
Jackson Miss., U.S.A.
 81 C8
Jackson Tenn., U.S.A.
 82 B3
Jacksonville Fla., U.S.A.
 83 D7
Jacksonville Ill., U.S.A.
 75 F9
Jacmel 87 C5
Jacobabad 42 E6
Jacobina 93 E5
Jaén 18 D4
Jaffa = Tel Aviv-Yafo
 46 D3
Jaffna 43 Q12
Jahrom 44 D3
Jaipur 42 F9
Jakarta 39 F3
Jalālābād 42 B7
Jalapa Enríquez = Xalapa
 84 D5
Jalgaon 43 J9
Jalna 43 K9
Jalpaiguri 41 D7
Jaluit I. 64 J11
Jamaica ■ 86 C4
Jamalpur Bangla. 41 E7
Jamalpur India 40 E6
Jambi 39 E2
James → 74 D6
James B. 71 D5
Jamestown N. Dak.,
 U.S.A. 74 B5
Jamestown N.Y., U.S.A.
 77 C6
Jammu 42 C9
Jammu & Kashmir □
 42 B10
Jamnagar 43 H7
Jamshedpur 40 F6
Janesville 75 D10
Januária 93 F5
Jaora 43 H9
Japan ■ 33 F5
Japan, Sea of 32 D4
Japen = Yapen 37 E5
Japurá → 90 D5
Jarvis I. 65 K15
Jäsk 44 E4

Jaú 93 G4
Jauja 91 F3
Jaunpur 40 E4
Java = Jawa 39 F3
Java Sea 39 E3
Jawa 39 F3
Jaya, Puncak 37 E5
Jebel, Bahr el → 55 G5
Jedburgh 10 D5
Jedda = Jiddah 47 G4
Jeju-do 35 C7
Jelenia Góra 16 C2
Jelgava 24 B1
Jena 15 C6
Jeonju 35 C7
Jequié 93 E5
Jequitinhonha 93 F5
Jequitinhonha → 93 F6
Jérémie 86 C5
Jerez de la Frontera
 18 D2
Jerid, Chott el = Djerid,
 Chott 52 B7
Jersey 11 G5
Jersey City 77 D8
Jerusalem 47 E3
Jessore 41 F7
Jhang Maghiana 42 D8
Jhansi 43 G11
Jhelum 42 C8
Jhelum → 42 D8
Jiamusi 35 B8
Ji'an 35 D6
Jiangmen 35 D6
Jiangsu □ 35 C6
Jiangxi □ 35 D6
Jiaxing 35 C7
Jiayi = Chiai 35 D7
Jiddah 47 G4
Jihlava → 16 D3
Jijiga 49 F3
Jilin 35 B7
Jilong = Chilung 35 D7
Jima 55 G6
Jiménez 84 B4
Jinan 35 C6
Jingdezhen 35 D6
Jinggu 34 D5
Jinhua 35 D6
Jining
 Nei Monggol Zizhiqu,
 China 35 B6
Jining Shandong, China
 35 C6
Jinja 57 D6
Jinzhou 35 B7
Jipijapa 90 D2
Jiujiang 35 D6
Jixi 35 B8
Jizzax 29 E7
João Pessoa 92 D7
Jodhpur 42 F8
Joensuu 8 C11
Jogjakarta = Yogyakarta
 39 F4
Johannesburg 59 D5
Johnson City 83 A6
Johnstown 77 D6
Johor Bahru 39 D2
Joinville 94 B7
Joliet 76 D1
Joliette 71 E6
Jolo 36 C2
Jones Sound 70 B5
Jonesboro 81 B8
Jönköping 9 D8
Jonquière 71 E6
Joplin 81 A6
Jos 53 G7
Jotunheimen 8 C7
Jowzjān □ 45 B6
Juan de Fuca, Str of
 72 B1
Juan Fernández, Arch. de
 89 G3
Juàzeiro 93 D5

Juàzeiro do Norte 92 D6
Juba = Giúba → 49 G3
Juba 55 H5
Jubbulpore = Jabalpur
 43 H11
Juchitán de Zaragoza
 85 D5
Juiz de Fora 93 G5
Juliaca 91 G4
Jullundur 42 D9
Jumna = Yamuna →
 40 E3
Junagadh 43 J7
Jundiaí 94 A7
Juneau 69 C6
Junggar Pendi 34 B3
Junín 94 C4
Jur, Nahr el → 55 G4
Jura = Jura, Mts. du
 13 C7
Jura → Schwäbische Alb
 14 D5
Jura 10 D4
Jura, Mts. du 13 C7
Juruá → 90 D5
Juruena → 91 E7
Jutland = Jylland 9 D7
Juventud, I. de la 86 B3
Jylland 9 D7
Jyväskylä 8 C11

K

K2 42 B10
Kaapstad = Cape Town
 58 E3
Kabardino-Balkaria □
 25 E5
Kābul 42 B6
Kabwe 59 A5
Kachchh, Gulf of 43 H6
Kachchh, Rann of 43 G6
Kachin □ 41 D11
Kaçkar 25 E5
Kadiyevka = Stakhanov
 25 D4
Kadoma 59 B5
Kaduna 53 F7
Kaesŏng 35 C7
Kafue → 59 B5
Kaga Bandoro 55 G2
Kagoshima 33 H2
Kaho'olawe 78 H12
Kahramanmaraş 46 C4
Kai, Kepulauan 37 F4
Kaieteur Falls 90 B7
Kaikoura 65 F4
Kainji Res. 53 F6
Kairouan 54 A1
Kaiserslautern 14 D4
Kaitaia 64 A5
Kajaani 8 C11
Kajabbi 61 D6
Kakamega 57 D6
Kakhovske Vdskh. 25 D3
Kakinada 40 J4
Kalaallit Nunaat =
 Greenland ☑ 66 C9
Kalaburagi 43 L10
Kalahari 58 C4
Kalakan 30 D8
Kalamata 23 F4
Kalamazoo 76 C3
Kalemie 57 F5
Kalgoorlie-Boulder 60 G3
Kalimantan 39 E4
Kálimnos 23 F6
Kaliningrad 24 C1
Kalispell 73 B6
Kalisz 16 C4
Kallsjön 8 C8
Kalmar 9 D9
Kalmykia □ 25 D6
Kaluga 24 C4
Kalutara 43 R11
Kama → 29 D6
Kamchatka, Poluostrov
 31 D13

Kamchatka Pen. =
 Kamchatka, Poluostrov
 31 D13
Kamina 57 F5
Kamloops 69 C7
Kampala 57 D6
Kampong Saom 38 B2
Kampuchea =
 Cambodia ■ 38 B3
Kamyanets-Podilskyy
 17 D8
Kamyshin 24 C6
Kanaaupscow 71 D6
Kananga 56 F4
Kanash 24 B6
Kanazawa 33 E5
Kanchenjunga 40 D7
Kanchipuram 43 N11
Kandahār 42 D4
Kandalaksha 8 B12
Kandi 53 F6
Kandy 43 R12
Kangaroo I. 62 C2
Kangiqliniq = Rankin Inlet
 68 B10
Kangiqsualujjuaq 70 D7
Kangiqsujuaq 70 C6
Kangiqtugaapik = Clyde
 River 70 B7
Kangirsuk 70 D7
Kaniapiskau =
 Caniapiscau → 70 D7
Kaniapiskau, L. =
 Caniapiscau, L. 71 D7
Kanin, Poluostrov 28 C5
Kanin Nos, Mys 28 C5
Kankakee 76 D2
Kankan 53 F4
Kankendy = Xankändi
 25 F6
Kano 53 F7
Kanpur 40 D3
Kansas □ 74 F5
Kansas City Kans., U.S.A.
 75 F7
Kansas City Mo., U.S.A.
 75 F7
Kansu = Gansu □ 34 C5
Kanyakumari 43 Q10
Kanye 59 C5
Kaohsiung 35 D7
Kaolack 53 F2
Kapiri Mposhi 59 A5
Kāpīsā □ 45 C7
Kaposvár 16 E3
Kaptai L. 41 F9
Kapuas → 39 E3
Kara Bogaz Gol, Zaliv =
 Garabogazköl Aylagy
 29 E6
Kara Kalpak Republic =
 Qoraqalpog'iston □
 29 E6
Kara Kum = Garagum
 29 F6
Kara Sea 28 B8
Karabük 46 B3
Karachi 43 G5
Karaganda = Qaraghandy
 29 E8
Karakalpakstan =
 Qoraqalpog'iston □
 29 E6
Karakoram Ra. 42 B10
Karaman 46 C3
Karamay 34 B3
Karbalā' 47 D6
Karelia □ 8 C12
Kariba, L. 59 B5
Kariba Dam 59 B5
Karimata, Selat 39 E3
Karkuk = Kirkūk 46 D6
Karlovac 20 B6
Karlskrona 9 D9
Karlsruhe 14 D5
Karlstad 9 D8
Karnal 42 E10

Karnaphuli Res. = Kaptai
 L. 41 F9
Karnataka □ 43 N10
Kärnten □ 15 E7
Karpathos 23 G6
Kars 25 E5
Karshi = Qarshi 29 F7
Karwar 43 M9
Kasai → 56 E3
Kasaragod 43 N9
Kasba L. 68 B9
Kāshān 44 C2
Kashgar = Kashi 34 C2
Kashi 34 C2
Kasongo 57 E5
Kassalâ 55 E6
Kassel 14 C5
Kastamonu 25 E3
Kasur 42 D9
Katanga □ 57 F4
Kathiawar 43 H7
Kathmandu = Katmandu
 40 F6
Kati Thanda-Lake Eyre
 60 F6
Katihar 40 E6
Katima Mulilo 58 B4
Katiola 53 G4
Katmandu 40 D5
Katowice 16 C4
Katsina 53 F7
Kattegat 9 D8
Kaua'i 78 G11
Kaunas 24 C1
Kavala 22 D5
Kavīr, Dasht-e 44 C3
Kawagoe 33 F6
Kawaguchi 33 F6
Kawardha 40 G3
Kawasaki 33 F6
Kawawachikamach
 71 D7
Kawthule = Kayin □
 41 H11
Kayah □ 41 H11
Kayes 53 F3
Kayin □ 41 H11
Kayseri 46 C3
Kazakhstan ■ 29 E7
Kazan 24 B6
Kazanlük 22 C5
Kea 23 F5
Kebnekaise 8 B9
Kebri Dehar 49 F3
Kecskemét 16 E4
Kediri 39 F4
Keelung = Chilung 35 D7
Keetmanshoop 58 D3
Kefalonia 23 E3
Keflavík 8 C1
Keighley 11 E6
Kelang = Klang 39 D2
Kells 11 E3
Kelowna 69 D8
Keluang = Kluang 39 D2
Kem 28 C4
Kemerovo 29 D9
Kemi 8 B10
Kemi älv = Kemijoki →
 8 B10
Kemijoki → 8 B10
Kemp Land 96 A9
Kempten 14 E6
Kendari 37 E2
Kenema 53 G3
Kenitra 52 B4
Kennewick 72 C4
Kenogami → 71 D5
Kenosha 76 C2
Kent Pen. 68 B9
Kentucky □ 76 F3
Kentville 71 E7
Kenya ■ 57 D7
Kenya, Mt. 57 E7
Kerala □ 43 P10
Kerch 25 D4
Kericho 57 E7
Kerinci 39 E2

Kerkyra 23 E2
Kermadec Is. 64 M13
Kermadec Trench 65 N13
Kermān 44 D4
Kermānshāh 46 D6
Kerrobert 69 C9
Kerulen → 36 B6
Ketchikan 69 C6
Key West 86 B3
Khabarovsk 31 E11
Khairpur 42 F6
Khakassia □ 30 D6
Khambhat 43 H8
Khambhat, G. of 43 J8
Khanewal 42 D7
Khaniá = Chania 23 G5
Khanka, L. 32 A3
Khankendy = Xankändi 25 F6
Kharagpur 40 F6
Kharg = Khārk, Jazīreh-ye 47 E7
Khārga, El Wāhât-el 54 C5
Khārk, Jazīreh-ye 47 E7
Kharkiv 24 D4
Kharkov = Kharkiv 24 D4
Khartoum = El Khartûm 55 E5
Khaskovo 22 D5
Khatanga 30 B8
Khenchela 52 A7
Kherson 25 E3
Khios = Hios 23 E6
Khiuma = Hiiumaa 24 B1
Khmelnytskyy 17 D8
Khodzent = Khüjand 29 E7
Khojak Pass 42 D5
Kholm 45 B6
Khon Kaen 38 A2
Khorat = Nakhon Ratchasima 38 B2
Khorramābād 46 D7
Khorrāmshahr 47 E7
Khouribga 52 B4
Khudzhand = Khüjand 29 E7
Khüjand 29 E7
Khulna 41 F7
Khulna □ 41 F7
Khushab 42 C8
Khuzdar 42 F5
Khvoy 46 C6
Khyber Pakhtunkhwa □ 42 B8
Khyber Pass 42 B7
Kiangsi = Jiangxi □ 35 D6
Kiangsu = Jiangsu □ 35 C6
Kıbrıs = Cyprus ■ 46 D3
Kicking Horse Pass 69 C8
Kiel 14 A6
Kiel Canal = Nord-Ostsee-Kanal 14 A5
Kielce 16 C5
Kieler Bucht 14 A6
Kiev = Kyyiv 17 C10
Kigali 57 E6
Kigoma-Ujiji 57 F5
Kikládhes = Cyclades 23 F5
Kikwit 56 F3
Kilimanjaro 57 E7
Kilkenny 11 E3
Killarney 11 E2
Killeen 80 D5
Kilmarnock 10 D4
Kilrush 11 E2
Kilwa Kivinje 57 F7
Kimberley Australia 60 D4
Kimberley S. Africa 58 D4
Kimmirut 70 C7
Kimry 24 B4
Kinabalu, Gunung 38 C5

Kindia 53 F3
Kindu 57 E5
Kineshma 24 B5
King Abdullah Economic City 46 G4
King George I. 96 A4
King George Is. 71 D5
King I. 62 C3
King William I. 68 B10
Kingait = Cape Dorset 70 C6
Kingaok = Bathurst Inlet 68 B9
Kings Canyon △ 78 B3
King's Lynn 11 E7
Kingston Canada 71 E6
Kingston Jamaica 86 C4
Kingston upon Hull 11 E6
Kingstown 87 D7
Kingsville 80 F5
Kinsale 11 F2
Kinshasa 56 E3
Kirghizia = Kyrgyzstan ■ 29 E8
Kiribati ■ 64 K12
Kırıkkale 25 F5
Kirin = Jilin 35 B7
Kirinyaga = Kenya, Mt. 57 E7
Kiritimati 65 J15
Kirkcaldy 10 C5
Kirkcudbright 11 D4
Kirkland Lake 71 E5
Kırklareli 22 D6
Kirkūk 46 D6
Kirkwall 10 B5
Kirov 28 D5
Kirovabad = Gäncä 25 E6
Kirovohrad 25 D3
Kırşehir 25 F5
Kirthar Range 42 F5
Kiruna 8 B10
Kiryū 33 F6
Kisangani 57 D5
Kishanganj 40 D7
Kishinev = Chişinău 17 E9
Kisii 57 E6
Kislovodsk 25 E5
Kismaayo 49 H3
Kisumu 57 E6
Kitakyūshū 33 G2
Kitale 57 D7
Kitami 32 B8
Kitchener 71 E5
Kitega = Gitega 57 E5
Kíthira = Kythira 23 F4
Kithnos 23 F5
Kitwe 59 A5
Kivu, L. 57 E5
Kıyev = Kyyiv 17 C10
Kızıl Irmak → 25 E4
Kizlyar 25 E6
Kizyl-Arvat = Serdar 29 F6
Kladno 16 C8
Klagenfurt 15 E8
Klaipėda 24 B1
Klamath Falls 72 E3
Klang 39 D2
Klarälven → 9 C8
Klerksdorp 59 D5
Kluane L. 68 B6
Kluang 39 D2
Knossos 23 G5
Knoxville 83 B6
Koartac = Quaqtaq 70 C7
Kōbe 33 F4
København 9 D8
Koblenz 14 C4
Kocaeli 25 E4
Koch Bihar 41 D7
Kōchi India 43 Q10
Kōchi Japan 33 G3
Kochiu = Gejiu 34 D5
Kodiak 69 C4
Kodiak I. 69 C4

Koforidua 53 G5
Kōfu 33 F6
Kohat 42 C7
Kohima 41 E10
Ko'qo'on 29 E8
Kokchetav = Kökshetaū 29 D7
Koko Kyunzu 41 K9
Kokomo 76 D2
Kokopo 64 K10
Kökshetaū 29 D7
Koksoak → 70 D7
Kola Pen. = Kolskiy Poluostrov 8 B13
Kolar Gold Fields 43 N11
Kolguyev, Ostrov 28 C5
Kolhapur 43 L9
Kolkata 41 F7
Kollam 43 Q10
Köln 14 C4
Kolomna 24 B4
Kolomyya 17 D7
Kolpino 24 B3
Kolskiy Poluostrov 8 B13
Kolwezi 57 G5
Kolyma → 31 C13
Komatsu 33 E5
Komi □ 28 C6
Kommunarsk = Alchevsk 25 D4
Kommunizma, Pik = imeni Ismail Samani, Pik 29 F8
Kompong Cham 38 B3
Kompong Som = Kampong Saom 38 B2
Komsomolsk-na-Amur 31 D11
Konar □ 42 B7
Kondoz 45 B7
Konin 16 B4
Konosha 28 C5
Konotop 24 C3
Konstanz 14 E5
Konya 46 C3
Kootenay L. 69 D8
Korçë 23 D3
Korčula 20 C6
Kordestan = Kurdistan 46 D5
Kordestān □ 46 D6
Kordofân 55 F4
Korea, North ■ 35 C7
Korea, South ■ 35 C7
Korea Bay 35 C7
Korea Strait 35 C7
Korhogo 53 G4
Korinthiakos Kolpos 23 E4
Korinthos 23 F4
Kōriyama 33 F7
Koror 36 C4
Körös → 16 E5
Korosten 17 C9
Kortrijk 14 C2
Kos 23 F6
Kosciuszko, Mt. 63 C4
Košice 16 D5
Kosovo ■ 22 C3
Kosovska Mitrovica = Mitrovica 22 C3
Kôstî 55 F5
Kostroma 24 B5
Koszalin 16 A3
Kota 43 G9
Kota Bharu 38 C2
Kota Kinabalu 38 C5
Kotabumi 39 E2
Kotelnich 24 B6
Kotka 9 C11
Kotor 22 C2
Kotri 42 G6
Kotuy → 30 B8
Kotzebue 69 B3
Koudougou 53 F5
Koumra 55 G2

Kovel 17 C7
Kovrov 24 B5
Koyampattur = Coimbatore 43 P10
Kozhikode 43 P9
Kra, Isthmus of = Kra, Kho Khot 38 B1
Kra, Kho Khot 38 B1
Kragujevac 22 B3
Krakatau = Rakata, Pulau 39 F3
Kraków 16 C4
Kraljevo 22 C3
Kramatorsk 25 D4
Krasnodar 25 D4
Krasnoturinsk 28 D7
Krasnoyarsk 30 D7
Krasnyy Luch 25 D4
Krefeld 14 C4
Kremenchuk 24 D3
Kribi 56 D1
Krishna → 40 K3
Kristiansand 9 D7
Kristiansund 8 C7
Kriti 23 G5
Krivoy Rog = Kryvyy Rih 25 D3
Krk 20 B5
Kronshtadt 24 B2
Kroonstad 59 D5
Kropotkin 25 D5
Krung Thep = Bangkok 38 B2
Kruševac 22 C3
Krymskyy Pivostriv 25 D3
Kryvyy Rih 25 D3
Ksar el Kebir 52 B4
Ksar es Souk = Er Rachidia 52 B5
Kuala Lumpur 39 D2
Kuala Terengganu 38 C2
Kuangchou = Guangzhou 35 D6
Kuantan 39 D2
Kuching 39 D4
Kucing = Kuching 39 D4
Kudymkar 28 D6
Kueiyang = Guiyang 35 D5
Kufra Oasis = Al Kufrah 54 D3
Kugaaruk = Pelly Bay 70 C5
Kugluktuk 68 B8
Kuito 58 A3
Külob 29 F7
Kulyab = Külob 29 F7
Kuma → 25 E6
Kumagaya 33 E6
Kumamoto 33 G2
Kumanovo 22 C3
Kumasi 53 G5
Kumba 53 H7
Kumbakonam 43 P11
Kungrad = Qŭnghirot 29 E6
Kungur 29 D6
Kunlun Shan 34 C3
Kunming 34 D5
Kuopio 8 C11
Kuqa 34 B3
Kür → 25 E6
Kura = Kür → 25 E6
Kurdistan 46 D5
Kure 33 F3
Kurgan 29 D7
Kuril Is. = Kurilskiye Ostrova 31 E12
Kurilskiye Ostrova 31 E12
Kurnool 43 L11
Kursk 24 D4
Kuruktag 34 B3
Kurume 33 G2
Kushiro 32 B9
Kushtia 41 F7
Kuskokwim B. 69 C3
Kütahya 25 F3
Kutaisi 25 E5

Kutaraja = Banda Aceh 38 C1
Kutch, Gulf of = Kachchh, Gulf of 43 H6
Kutch, Rann of = Kachchh, Rann of 43 G6
Kuujjuaq 70 D7
Kuujjuarapik 71 D6
Kuwait = Al Kuwayt 47 E7
Kuwait ■ 47 E6
Kuybyshev = Samara 24 C7
Kuybyshevskoye Vdkhr. 24 B6
Kuzey Anadolu Dağları 25 E4
Kuznetsk 24 C6
KwaMashu 59 D6
Kwangchow = Guangzhou 35 D6
Kwango → 56 E3
Kwangsi-Chuang = Guangxi Zhuangzu Zizhiqu □ 35 D5
Kwangtung = Guangdong □ 35 D6
KwaZulu Natal □ 59 D6
Kweichow = Guizhou □ 35 D5
Kwekwe 59 B5
Kyoga, L. 57 D6
Kyōto 33 F4
Kypros = Cyprus ■ 46 D3
Kyrenia 46 D3
Kyrgyzstan ■ 29 E8
Kythira 23 F4
Kyūshū 33 G2
Kyustendil 22 C4
Kyyiv 17 C10
Kyzyl Kum 29 E7
Kyzyl-Orda = Qyzylorda 29 E7

L

La Alcarria 19 B4
La Ceiba 85 D7
La Coruña = A Coruña 18 A1
La Crosse 75 D9
La Grande → 71 D6
La Grange 82 C5
La Habana 86 B3
La Línea de la Concepción 18 D3
La Mancha 19 C4
La Palma 52 C2
La Paz Bolivia 91 G5
La Paz Mexico 84 C2
La Plata 94 D5
La Quiaca 94 A3
La Rioja 94 B3
La Rioja □ 19 A4
La Roche-sur-Yon 12 C3
La Rochelle 12 C3
La Romana 87 C6
La Serena 94 B2
La Seyne-sur-Mer 13 E6
La Spézia 13 D8
La Tortuga 87 D6
La Tuque 71 E6
La Vega 87 C5
Labe = Elbe → 14 B5
Labé 53 F3
Labrador 71 D7
Labrador City 71 D7
Labrador Sea 70 D8
Labuan, Pulau 38 C5
Lac La Biche 69 C8
Lac la Martre = Wha Ti 68 B8
Laccadive Is. = Lakshadweep Is. 26 G9
Lacombe 69 C8
Ladakh Ra. 42 B10

Ladoga, L. = Ladozhskoye Ozero 8 C12
Ladozhskoye Ozero 8 C12
Ladysmith 59 D5
Lae 61 B8
Lafayette 81 D7
Lafia 53 G7
Laghouat 52 B6
Lagos Nigeria 53 G6
Lagos Portugal 18 D1
Lahn → 14 C4
Lahore 42 D9
Lahti 8 C11
Lahtis = Lahti 8 C11
Lairg 10 B4
Laizhou 35 C6
Lake Charles 81 D7
Lake City 83 D6
Lake Harbour = Kimmirut 70 C7
Lakeland 83 E7
Lakewood 76 D5
Lakhnau = Lucknow 40 D3
Lakshadweep Is. 26 G9
Lambaréné 56 E2
Lamon B. 36 B2
Lampedusa 21 G4
Lamu 57 E8
Lancaster U.K. 11 D5
Lancaster U.S.A. 77 D7
Lancaster Sd. 70 B5
Lanchow = Lanzhou 35 C5
Landes 12 D3
Land's End 11 F4
Langreo 18 A3
Langres 13 C6
Langres, Plateau de 13 C6
Langsa 38 D1
Languedoc 13 E5
Lannion 12 B2
Lansing 76 D3
Lanzarote 52 C3
Lanzhou 35 C5
Laoag 36 A2
Laon 13 B5
Laos ■ 38 A3
Lappland 8 B10
Laptev Sea 30 B10
L'Áquila 20 C4
Laramie 74 E2
Laredo 80 F4
Larisa 23 E4
Larnaca 46 D3
Larne 11 D4
Larrimah 60 D5
Larsen Ice Shelf 96 A3
Larvik 9 D8
Las Cruces 79 D9
Las Palmas 52 C2
Las Vegas 78 B5
Lashio 41 F11
Lassen Pk. 72 F3
Lastoursville 56 E2
Latacunga 90 D3
Latakia = Al Lādhiqīyah 46 D3
Latina 20 D4
Latium = Lazio □ 20 C4
Latvia ■ 24 B1
Launceston 62 D4
Laurel 81 D9
Lausanne 14 E4
Laval 12 B3
Lawrence 75 F7
Lawton 80 B4
Lazio □ 20 C4
Le Creusot 13 C6
Le Havre 12 B4
Le Mans 12 C4
Le Mont-St-Michel 12 B3
Le Puy-en-Velay 13 D5
Le Touquet-Paris-Plage 12 A4

Leamington Spa = Royal Leamington Spa 11 E6
Leavenworth 75 F7
Lebanon ■ 46 D3
Lebu 94 D2
Lecce 21 D7
Leeds 11 E6
Leeuwarden 14 B3
Leeuwin, C. 60 G2
Leeward Is. 87 C7
Lefkada 23 E3
Leganés 18 B4
Legazpi 36 B2
Leghorn = Livorno 20 C3
Legionowo 16 B5
Legnica 16 C3
Leicester 11 E6
Leiden 14 B3
Leine → 14 B5
Leinster □ 11 E3
Leipzig 15 C7
Leitrim 11 D2
Leizhou Bandao 35 D6
Léman, L. 13 C7
Lena → 30 B10
Lens 13 A5
Leodhas = Lewis 10 B3
León Mexico 84 C4
León Nic. 85 E7
León Spain 18 A3
Lérida = Lleida 19 B6
Lerwick 10 A6
Les Cayes 86 C5
Les Sables-d'Olonne 12 C3
Lesbos 23 E6
Leskovac 22 C3
Lesotho ■ 59 D5
Lesser Antilles 87 D7
Lesser Sunda Is. 37 F2
Lésvos = Lesbos 23 E6
Leszno 16 C3
Lethbridge 69 D8
Leti, Kepulauan 37 F3
Leticia 90 D4
Letterkenny 11 D3
Leuven 14 C3
Lévis 71 E6
Levkás = Lefkada 23 E3
Levkôsia = Nicosia 46 D3
Lewis 10 B3
Lewisporte 71 E8
Lewiston Idaho, U.S.A. 72 C5
Lewiston Maine, U.S.A. 77 B10
Lexington 76 E3
Leyte 36 B2
Lhasa 34 D4
Lhazê 34 D3
L'Hospitalet de Llobregat 19 B7
Liancourt Rocks 33 E2
Lianyungang 35 C6
Liaoning □ 35 B7
Liaoyuan 35 B7
Liard → 68 B7
Libau = Liepāja 24 B1
Liberal 80 A3
Liberec 16 C2
Liberia ■ 53 G4
Lībiya, Sahrā' 54 C4
Libourne 12 D3
Libreville 56 D1
Libya ■ 54 C2
Libyan Desert = Lībiya, Sahrā' 54 C4
Liechtenstein ■ 14 E5
Liège 14 C3
Liegnitz = Legnica 16 C3
Lienyünchiangshih = Lianyungang 35 C6
Liepāja 24 B1
Lietuva = Lithuania ■ 24 B1
Liffey → 11 E3
Lifford 11 D3
Liguria □ 13 D8

Ligurian Sea 20 C2
Lijiang 34 D5
Likasi 57 G5
Lille 13 A5
Lillehammer 8 C8
Lillongwe 59 A6
Lima Peru 91 F3
Lima U.S.A. 76 D3
Limassol 46 D3
Limbe 53 H7
Limeira 93 G4
Limerick 11 E2
Limfjorden 9 D7
Límnos 23 E5
Limoges 12 D4
Limón 86 E3
Limousin □ 12 D4
Limoux 12 E5
Limpopo → 59 D6
Linares Chile 94 D2
Linares Mexico 84 C5
Linares Spain 18 C4
Lincoln U.K. 11 E6
Lincoln U.S.A. 75 E6
Lindesnes 9 D7
Lingga, Kepulauan 39 E2
Linhai 35 D7
Linhares 93 F5
Linköping 9 D9
Linxia 34 C5
Linz 15 D8
Lion, G. du 13 E6
Lipa 36 B2
Lípari 21 E5
Lipetsk 24 C4
Lippe → 14 C4
Lisboa 18 C1
Lisbon = Lisboa 18 C1
Lisburn 11 D3
Lisichansk = Lysychansk 25 D4
Lisieux 12 B4
Liski 24 C4
Lismore 63 A5
Listowel 11 E2
Litani → 46 D3
Lithuania ■ 24 B1
Little Khingan Mts. = Xiao Hinggan Ling 35 B7
Little Missouri → 74 B3
Little Rock 81 B7
Little Zab = Zāb aş Şaghīr → 46 D5
Liuwa Plain 58 A4
Liuzhou 35 D5
Liverpool Canada 71 E7
Liverpool U.K. 11 E5
Livingstone 59 B5
Livorno 20 C3
Ljubljana 20 A5
Llanelli 11 F4
Llano Estacado 80 C2
Llanos 90 C4
Lleida 19 B6
Llobregat → 19 B7
Lloret de Mar 19 B7
Llullaillaco, Volcán 94 A3
Lobatse 59 D5
Lobito 58 A2
Locarno 13 C8
Loch Garman = Wexford 11 E3
Loches 12 C4
Lodwar 57 D7
Łódź 16 C4
Lofoten 8 B9
Logan 73 F8
Logan, Mt. 68 B5
Logroño 19 A4
Lohardaga 40 F5
Loir → 12 C3
Loire → 12 C2
Loja 90 D3
Lomami → 56 D4
Lombárdia □ 13 D8
Lomblen 37 F2
Lombok 39 F5
Lomé 53 G6

Lomela → 56 E4
Lomond, L. 10 C4
Łomża 16 B6
London Canada 71 E5
London U.K. 11 F6
Londonderry 11 D3
Londonderry, C. 60 C4
Londrina 94 A6
Long Beach 78 D3
Long I. Bahamas 86 B4
Long I. U.S.A. 77 D9
Long Xuyen 38 B3
Longford 11 E3
Longreach 61 E7
Longview Tex., U.S.A. 81 C6
Longview Wash., U.S.A. 72 C2
Lons-le-Saunier 13 C6
Lop Nur 34 B4
Lopez, C. 56 E1
Lorain 76 D4
Loralai 42 D6
Lorca 19 D5
Lord Howe I. 64 N10
Lord Howe Rise 64 N11
Lorestān □ 46 D6
Lorient 12 C2
Lorraine □ 13 B7
Los Alamos 79 C9
Los Andes 94 C2
Los Angeles Chile 94 D2
Los Angeles U.S.A. 78 C3
Los Mochis 84 B3
Los Roques Is. 90 A5
Lošinj 20 B5
Lot → 12 D4
Loubomo 56 E2
Lougheed I. 70 B3
Louis Trichardt 59 C5
Louis XIV, Pte. 71 D6
Louisiade Arch. 61 C9
Louisiana □ 81 D8
Louisville 76 E3
Lourdes 12 E3
Louth 11 E6
Louvain = Leuven 14 C3
Lovech 22 C5
Lowell 77 C10
Lower California = Baja California 84 A1
Lower Hutt 65 D6
Lower Saxony = Niedersachsen □ 14 B5
Lower Tunguska = Tunguska, Nizhnyaya → 30 C6
Lowestoft 11 E7
Loyalty Is. = Loyauté, Îs. 64 M11
Loyang = Luoyang 35 C6
Loyauté, Îs. 64 M11
Lualaba → 57 D5
Luanda 56 F2
Luangwa → 59 A6
Luanshya 59 A5
Luapula → 57 F5
Lubango 58 A2
Lubbock 80 C3
Lübeck 15 B6
Lubero = Luofu 57 E5
Lublin 17 C6
Lubnān = Lebanon ■ 46 D3
Lubumbashi 59 A5
Lucca 20 C3
Lucena 36 B2
Lucerne = Luzern 13 C8
Lucknow 40 D3
Lüda = Dalian 35 C7
Lüderitz 58 D3
Ludhiana 42 D9
Ludwigsburg 14 D5
Ludwigshafen 14 D5
Lufkin 81 D6
Luga 24 B2

Lugano 13 C8
Lugansk = Luhansk 25 D4
Lugo 18 A2
Luhansk 25 D4
Luichow Pen. = Leizhou Bandao 35 D6
Luimneach = Limerick 11 E2
Luleå 8 B10
Luleälven → 8 B10
Lüneburger Heide 14 B6
Lunéville 13 B7
Luni → 43 G7
Luofu 57 E5
Luoyang 35 C6
Lurgan 11 D3
Lusaka 59 B5
Luta = Dalian 35 C7
Lutherstadt Wittenberg 15 C7
Luton 11 F6
Łutselk'e 68 B8
Lutsk 17 C7
Luxembourg 13 B7
Luxembourg ■ 14 D4
Luxor = El Uqsur 54 C5
Luzern 13 C8
Luzhou 35 D5
Luziânia 93 F4
Luzon 36 A2
Lviv 17 D7
Lvov = Lviv 17 D7
Lyakhovskiye, Ostrova 31 B12
Lynchburg 77 F6
Lynn Lake 69 C9
Lyon 13 D6
Lyonnais 13 D6
Lysychansk 25 D4
Lyubertsy 24 B4

M

Ma'ān 47 E3
Ma'anshan 35 C6
Maas → 14 C3
Maastricht 13 A6
McAllen 80 F4
Macao = Macau 35 D6
Macapá 92 B3
Macau Brazil 92 D6
Macau China 35 D6
M'Clintock Chan. 68 A9
M'Clure Str. 70 B2
McComb 81 D8
MacDonnell Ranges 60 E5
Macedonia □ 23 D4
Macedonia ■ 22 D3
Maceió 93 D6
Macgillycuddy's Reeks 11 F2
Mach 42 E5
Machakos 57 E7
Machala 90 D3
Machilipatnam 40 J3
Machu Picchu 91 F4
Mackay 61 E8
Mackay, L. 60 E4
Mackenzie → 68 B6
Mackenzie King I. 70 B2
Mackenzie Mts. 68 B6
McKinley, Mt. = Denali 69 B4
McMurdo Sd. 96 B15
Mâcon France 13 C6
Macon U.S.A. 83 C6
Madagascar ■ 59 C9
Madang 61 B8
Madeira 52 B2
Madeira → 90 D7
Madeleine, Îs. de la 71 E7
Madhya Pradesh □ 43 H10
Madison 75 D10
Madiun 39 F4

Madras = Chennai
  43 N12
Madras = Tamil Nadu □
  43 P10
Madre de Dios ➤ 91 F5
Madre de Dios, I. 95 G1
Madre Occidental, Sierra
  84 B3
Madrid 18 B4
Madurai 43 Q11
Maebashi 33 E6
Mafia I. 57 F7
Magadan 31 D13
Magallanes, Estrecho de
  95 G2
Magangué 90 B4
Magdalen Is. = Madeleine,
  Îs. de la 71 E7
Magdalena ➤ 90 A4
Magdeburg 15 B6
Magelang 39 F4
Magellan's Str. =
  Magallanes, Estrecho
  de 95 G2
Maggiore, Lago 13 D8
Magnetic Pole (North)
  70 A2
Magnetic Pole (South)
  96 A13
Magnitogorsk 29 D6
Magosa = Famagusta
  46 D3
Magwe 41 G10
Magyarország =
  Hungary ■ 16 E4
Mahábád 46 C5
Mahajanga 59 B9
Makham ➤ 39 E5
Mahalapye 59 C5
Mahallát 44 C2
Mahanadi ➤ 40 G6
Maharashtra □ 43 J9
Mahdia 54 A1
Mahesana 43 H8
Mahilyow 17 B10
Mahón = Maó 19 C8
Mai-Ndombe, L. 56 E3
Maidstone 11 F7
Maiduguri 55 F1
Maijdi 41 F8
Main ➤ 14 D5
Maine 12 C3
Mainland Orkney, U.K.
  10 B5
Mainland Shet., U.K.
  10 A6
Mainz 14 C5
Maiquetía 90 A5
Majorca = Mallorca 19 C7
Majuro 64 J12
Makale 37 E1
Makarikari =
  Makgadikgadi Salt
  Pans 59 C5
Makassar 37 F1
Makassar, Selat 37 E1
Makassar, Str. of =
  Makassar, Selat 37 E1
Makedonija =
  Macedonia ■ 22 D3
Makgadikgadi Salt Pans
  59 C5
Makhachkala 25 E6
Makhado = Louis
  Trichardt 59 C5
Makkah 47 G4
Makran Coast Range
  42 G4
Makurdi 53 G7
Malabar Coast 43 P9
Malacca, Straits of 38 D1
Málaga 18 D3
Malagasy Rep. =
  Madagascar ■ 59 C9
Malakal 55 G5
Malang 39 F4
Malanje 56 F3
Mälaren 9 D9

Malatya 46 C4
Malawi ■ 59 A6
Malawi, L. 59 A6
Malåyer 46 D7
Malaysia ■ 38 D4
Malden I. 65 K15
Maldives ■ 26 H9
Maldonado 94 C6
Malegaon 43 J9
Mali ■ 53 E5
Malin Hd. 10 D3
Malindi 57 E8
Malines = Mechelen
  14 C3
Mallaig 10 C4
Mallawi 54 C5
Mallorca 19 C7
Mallow 11 E2
Malmö 9 D8
Malpelo, I. de 90 C2
Malta ■ 21 G5
Maluku 37 E3
Maluku □ 37 E3
Maluku Sea = Molucca
  Sea 37 E2
Malvinas, Is. = Falkland
  Is. ☑ 95 G5
Mamoré ➤ 91 F5
Man 53 G4
Man, I. of 11 D4
Manado 37 D2
Managua 85 E7
Manama = Al Manāmah
  44 E2
Manaos = Manaus 90 D7
Manas 34 B3
Manaus 90 D7
Manchester U.K. 11 E5
Manchester U.S.A.
  77 C10
Mandal 9 D7
Mandalay 41 F11
Mandla 40 F3
Mandsaur 43 G9
Mandvi 43 H6
Manfalût 54 C5
Manfredónia 20 D5
Mangaluru 43 N9
Mangnai 34 C4
Mangole 37 E3
Manica 59 B6
Manicoré 91 E6
Manicouagan ➤ 71 E7
Manicouagan, Rés. 71 D7
Manihiki 65 L14
Manila 36 B2
Manipur □ 41 E9
Manisa 23 E6
Manitoba □ 69 C10
Manitoba, L. 69 C10
Manitoulin I. 71 E5
Manitowoc 76 B2
Manizales 90 B3
Mannar 43 Q11
Mannar, G. of 43 Q11
Mannheim 14 D5
Manokwari 37 E4
Manosque 13 E6
Manresa 19 B6
Mansel I. 70 C5
Mansfield U.K. 11 E6
Mansfield U.S.A. 76 D4
Manta 90 D2
Mantes-la-Jolie 12 B4
Mántova 20 B3
Manuel Alves ➤ 93 E4
Manzai 42 C7
Manzanillo Cuba 86 B4
Manzanillo Mexico 84 D4
Manzhouli 35 B6
Maó 19 C8
Maoming 35 D6
Mapam Yumco 40 B3
Maputo 59 D6
Maquan He =
  Brahmaputra ➤ 41 F7
Maquinchao 95 E3

Mar Chiquita, L. 94 C4
Mar del Plata 94 D5
Marabá 92 D4
Maracá, I. de 92 B3
Maracaibo 90 A4
Maracaibo, L. de 90 B4
Maracay 90 A5
Maradi 53 F7
Marajó, I. de 92 C4
Maranguape 92 C6
Maranhão = São Luís
  92 C5
Maranhão □ 92 D4
Marañón ➤ 90 D4
Maraş = Kahramanmaraş
  46 C4
Marbella 18 D3
Marche 12 C4
Mardan 42 B8
Mardin 46 C5
Margarita, I. de 90 A6
Margate 11 F7
Marghilon 29 E8
Mârgow, Dasht-e 42 D3
Mari El □ 24 B6
Mariana Trench 64 H9
Maribor 20 A5
Marie Byrd Land 96 B18
Mariecourt =
  Kangiqsujuaq 70 C6
Mariental 58 C3
Marília 93 G3
Marion 81 A9
Maritimes, Alpes 13 D7
Maritsa ➤ Evros ➤ 22 D6
Mariupol 25 D4
Marka 49 G3
Markham, Mt. 96 C15
Marmara Denizi 22 D7
Marmaris 23 F7
Marne ➤ 12 B5
Maroua 55 F1
Marquises, Îs. 65 K17
Marrakech 52 B4
Marree 62 A2
Marsá Matrûh 54 B4
Marsabit 57 D7
Marsala 21 F4
Marseille 13 E6
Marshall 81 C6
Marshall Is. ■ 64 J12
Martaban 41 J11
Martaban, G. of 41 J11
Martapura 39 E4
Martigues 13 E6
Martinique ☑ 87 D7
Marwar 42 G8
Mary 29 F7
Maryborough = Portlaoise
  11 E3
Maryborough 63 A5
Maryland □ 77 E7
Marystown 71 E8
Marzūq 54 C1
Masan 35 C7
Masandam, Ra's 44 E4
Masaya 85 E7
Masbate 36 B2
Mascara 52 A6
Maseru 59 D5
Mashhad 44 B4
Mashonaland 59 B6
Masjed Soleyman 47 E7
Mask, L. 11 E2
Mason City 75 D8
Masqat 45 F4
Massa 13 D9
Massachusetts □ 77 C9
Massena 77 B8
Massif Central 13 D5
Masvingo 59 C6
Matabeleland 59 B5
Matadi 56 F2
Matagalpa 85 E7
Matagami 71 E6
Matagami, L. 71 E6
Matamoros Coahuila,
  Mexico 84 B4

Matamoros Tamaulipas,
  Mexico 84 B5
Matane 71 E7
Matanzas 86 B3
Mataró 19 B7
Matehuala 84 C4
Matera 21 D6
Mathura 42 F10
Mati 36 C3
Mato Grosso □ 93 E3
Mato Grosso, Planalto do
  93 F3
Mato Grosso do Sul □
  93 F3
Maţruḩ 45 F4
Matsue 33 F3
Matsumoto 33 E6
Matsusaka 33 F5
Matsuyama 33 G3
Mattagami ➤ 71 D5
Mattancheri 43 Q10
Maturín 90 B6
Maubeuge 13 A5
Maudin Sun 41 K10
Maui 78 H12
Maulamyaing = Moulmein
  41 J11
Maun 58 B4
Mauritania ■ 53 E3
Mauritius ■ 51 H9
Mawlamyine = Moulmein
  41 J11
Mayaguana 87 B5
Mayagüez 87 C6
Maykop 25 E5
Mayo 68 B6
Mayon Volcano 36 B2
Mayotte ☑ 59 A9
Mazagán = El Jadida
  52 B4
Māzandarān □ 44 B3
Mazār-e Sharīf 45 B6
Mazaruni ➤ 90 B7
Mazatlán 84 C3
Mazurski, Pojezierze
  16 B5
Mazyr 17 C9
Mbabane 59 D6
Mbaïki 56 D3
Mbala 57 F6
Mbale 57 D6
Mbandaka 56 D3
Mbanza Ngungu 56 F2
Mbeya 57 F6
Mbini = Río Muni □
  56 D2
Mbour 53 F2
Mbuji-Mayi 56 F4
Mdantsane 59 E5
Mead, L. 78 B5
Meaux 13 B5
Mecca = Makkah 47 G4
Mechelen 14 C3
Mecklenburg 15 B6
Mecklenburger Bucht
  15 A6
Medan 39 D1
Médéa 52 A6
Medellín 90 B3
Medford 72 E2
Medicine Bow Mts.
  73 F10
Medicine Hat 69 C8
Medina = Al Madīnah
  47 F4
Mediterranean Sea 50 C5
Médoc 12 D3
Medvezhyegorsk 28 C4
Meekatharra 60 F2
Meerut 42 E10
Meghalaya □ 41 E8
Meharry, Mt. 60 E2
Meighen I. 70 B4
Meiktila 41 G10
Meizhou 35 D6
Mejillones 94 A2
Mekhtar 42 D6
Meknès 52 B4

Mekong ➤ 38 C3
Mekvari = Kür ➤ 25 E6
Melaka 39 D2
Melanesia 64 K10
Melbourne 63 C3
Mèlèzes ➤ 70 D6
Melfort 69 C9
Melilla 19 E4
Melitopol 25 D4
Melun 13 B5
Melville 69 C9
Melville I. Australia 60 C5
Melville I. Canada 70 B2
Melville Pen. 70 C5
Memel = Klaipėda 24 B1
Memphis 82 B3
Mende 13 D5
Mendocino, C. 72 F1
Mendoza 94 C3
Mengzi 34 D5
Menominee 76 B2
Menorca 19 C7
Mentawai, Kepulauan
  39 E1
Merced 78 B2
Mercedes Corrientes,
  Argentina 94 B5
Mercedes San Luis,
  Argentina 94 C3
Mercedes Uruguay 94 C5
Mercy, C. 70 C7
Mergui Arch. 38 B1
Mérida Mexico 85 C7
Mérida Spain 18 C2
Mérida Venezuela 90 B4
Meridian 82 C3
Merowe Dam 55 E5
Mersin = İçel 46 C3
Merthyr Tydfil 11 F5
Meru 57 D7
Mesa 79 D7
Meshed = Mashhad
  44 B4
Mesopotamia = Al Jazirah
  46 D5
Messina = Musina 59 C6
Messina 21 E5
Messina, Str. di 21 E5
Meta ➤ 90 B5
Meta Incognita Pen.
  70 C7
Metlakatla 69 C6
Metz 13 B7
Meuse ➤ 13 A6
Mexiana, I. 92 C4
Mexicali 84 A1
México 84 D5
México ■ 84 C4
Mexico, Ciudad de 84 D5
Mexico, G. of 85 B7
Meymaneh 42 B4
Mezen ➤ 28 C5
Miami 83 G7
Miami Beach 83 G7
Miändowäb 46 C6
Miäneh 46 C6
Mianwali 42 C7
Miass 29 D7
Michigan □ 76 C3
Michigan, L. 76 C2
Michurinsk 24 C5
Micronesia 64 H11
Micronesia, Federated
  States of ■ 64 J10
Middelburg 58 E5
Middlesbrough 11 D6
Midi, Canal du ➤ 12 E4
Midland 80 D3
Mieres 18 A3
Mikhaylovgrad = Montana
  22 C4
Mikines 23 F4
Mikonos = Mykonos
  23 F5
Milan = Milano 13 D8
Milano 13 D8
Mildura 62 B3
Milford Haven 11 F4

Milford Sd. 65 F2
Milh, Baḥr al = Razāzah, Buḥayrat ar 47 D5
Millau 13 D5
Millennium I. = Caroline I. 65 K15
Millinocket 77 B11
Milos 23 F5
Milton Keynes 11 E6
Milwaukee 76 C2
Min Jiang → Fujian, China 35 D6
Min Jiang → Sichuan, China 35 D5
Minas 94 C5
Minas Gerais □ 93 F4
Mindanao 36 C2
Mindanao Sea = Bohol Sea 36 C2
Mindanao Trench 36 B3
Mindoro 36 B2
Mindoro Str. 36 B2
Minho = Miño → 18 B1
Minna 53 G7
Minneapolis 75 C8
Minnesota □ 75 B7
Miño → 18 B1
Minorca = Menorca 19 C7
Minot 74 A4
Minsk 24 C2
Minto, L. 70 D6
Miramichi 71 E7
Mirim, L. 94 C6
Mirpur Khas 42 G6
Mirzapur 40 E4
Mishan 35 B8
Miskolc 16 D5
Misool 37 E4
Mişr = Egypt ■ 54 C5
Mişrātah 54 B2
Missinaibi → 71 D5
Mississippi □ 81 C9
Mississippi → 81 E9
Mississippi River Delta 81 E9
Missoula 73 C7
Missouri □ 75 F8
Missouri → 75 F9
Mistassini, L. 71 D6
Misuratah = Mişrātah 54 B2
Mitchell 74 D5
Mitchell → 61 D7
Mito 33 E7
Mitrovica 22 C3
Mittimatalik = Pond Inlet 70 B6
Mitú 90 C4
Mitumba, Mts. 57 F5
Miyakonojō 33 H2
Miyazaki 33 H2
Miyet, Bahr el = Dead Sea 47 E3
Mizoram □ 41 F9
Mjøsa 8 C8
Mljet 20 C6
Mo i Rana 8 B8
Mobaye 56 D4
Mobile 82 D3
Moçambique = Mozambique ■ 59 B7
Moçambique 59 B8
Mochudi 59 C5
Mocoa 90 C3
Mocuba 59 B7
Módena 20 B3
Modesto 78 B2
Mogadishu = Muqdisho 49 G4
Mogador = Essaouira 52 B4
Mogi das Cruzes 94 A7
Mogilev = Mahilyow 17 B10
Moisie → 71 D7
Mojave Desert 78 C4

Moldavia = Moldova ■ 17 E9
Molde 8 C7
Moldova ■ 17 E9
Molepolole 59 C5
Mollendo 91 G4
Moloka'i 78 H12
Molopo → 58 D4
Molucca Sea 37 E2
Moluccas = Maluku 37 E3
Mombasa 57 E7
Mompós 90 B4
Mona Passage 87 C6
Monaco ■ 13 E7
Monastir = Bitola 22 D3
Mönchengladbach 14 C4
Monclova 84 B4
Moncton 71 E7
Monghyr = Munger 40 E6
Mongibello = Etna 21 F5
Mongolia ■ 35 B5
Mongu 58 B4
Monroe 81 C7
Monrovia 53 G3
Mons 14 C2
Mont-de-Marsan 12 E3
Mont-Laurier 71 E9
Mont-St-Michel, Le 12 B3
Montana 92 A4
Montana □ 73 C9
Montargis 13 C5
Montauban 12 D4
Montbéliard 13 C7
Montceau-les-Mines 13 C6
Monte Azul 93 F5
Monte-Carlo 13 E7
Monte Caseros 94 C5
Montego Bay 86 C4
Montélimar 13 D6
Montemorelos 84 B5
Montenegro ■ 22 C2
Monterey 78 B2
Montería 90 B3
Monterrey 84 B4
Montes Claros 93 F5
Montevideo 94 C5
Montgomery 82 C4
Montluçon 13 C5
Montpellier 13 E5
Montréal 71 E9
Montrose U.K. 10 C5
Montrose U.S.A. 79 A9
Montserrat ☑ 87 C7
Monywa 41 F10
Monza 13 D8
Monze, C. 43 G5
Moose Jaw 69 C9
Moosomin 69 C9
Moosonee 71 D5
Mopti 53 F5
Mora 8 C8
Moradabad 42 E11
Moratuwa 43 R11
Moravá → Serbia 22 B3
Moravá → Slovak Rep. 16 D3
Moravian Hts. = Českomoravská Vrchovina 16 D8
Moray Firth 10 D5
Morden 69 D10
Mordvinia □ 24 C5
Moree 63 A4
Morelia 84 D4
Morena, Sierra 18 C3
Morgan City 81 E8
Morioka 32 F7
Morlaix 12 B2
Morocco ■ 52 B4
Morogoro 57 F7
Morón 86 B4
Morondava 59 C8
Morotai 37 D3
Morphou 46 D3
Morrinhos 93 F4
Morvan 13 C6

Moscos Is. 41 L11
Moscow = Moskva 24 B4
Moscow 72 C5
Mosel → 13 A7
Moselle = Mosel → 13 A7
Moshi 57 E7
Mosjøen 8 B8
Moskva 24 B4
Mosselbaai 58 E4
Mossoró 92 D6
Most 16 C1
Mostaganem 52 A6
Mostar 20 C6
Motihari 40 D5
Motril 18 D4
Mouila 56 E2
Moulins 13 C5
Moulmein 41 J11
Moundou 55 G2
Mount Gambier 62 C3
Mount Isa 61 E6
Mount Lofty Ranges 62 B2
Moyen Atlas 52 B4
Mozambique ■ 59 B7
Mozambique Chan. 51 H8
Mozdok 25 E5
Mozyr = Mazyr 17 C9
Mpanda 57 F6
Mthatha 59 E5
Mu Us Shamo 35 C5
Muar 39 D2
Mubarraz = Al Mubarraz 47 F7
Mubi 55 F1
Mucuri 93 F6
Mudanjiang 35 B7
Mufulira 59 A5
Muğla 23 F7
Mujnak = Müynoq 29 E6
Mukden = Shenyang 35 B7
Muktsar 42 D9
Mulde → 15 C7
Mulhacén 18 D4
Mulhouse 13 C7
Mull 10 C4
Mullingar 11 E3
Multan 42 D7
Mumbai 43 K8
Muna 37 F2
München 15 D6
Munchen-Gladbach = Mönchengladbach 14 C4
Muncie 76 D3
Mundo Novo 93 E5
Munger 40 E6
Munich = München 15 D6
Münster 14 C4
Munster □ 11 E2
Muqdisho 49 G4
Murashi 24 B6
Murchison → 60 F1
Murcia 19 C5
Murcia □ 19 D5
Mureş → 22 A3
Murfreesboro 82 B4
Müritz 15 B7
Murmansk 8 B12
Murom 32 B7
Muroran 32 B7
Murray → 62 C2
Murrumbidgee → 62 B3
Murwara 40 F3
Muş 46 C5
Mûsa, Gebel 47 D8
Muscat = Masqaṭ 45 F4
Musgrave Ranges 60 F5
Musina 59 C5
Muskegon 81 B6
Muskogee 81 B6
Mutare 59 B6
Müynoq 29 E6
Muzaffarabad 42 B8
Muzaffarnagar 42 E10

Mwanza 57 E6
Mweru, L. 57 F5
My Tho 38 B3
Myanmar = Burma ■ 41 G11
Mycenae = Mikines 23 F4
Myingyan 41 G10
Myitkyina 41 E11
Mykolayiv 25 D3
Mykonos 23 F5
Mymensingh 41 E8
Mysore = Karnataka □ 43 N10
Mysuru 43 N10
Mytishchi 24 B4

N

Na Hearadh = Harris 10 C3
Naab → 15 D7
Naberezhnyye Chelny 29 D6
Nabeul 54 A1
Nāblus = Nābulus 46 D3
Nābulus 46 D3
Nacala 59 A8
Nacogdoches 81 D6
Nacozari de García 84 A3
Nadiad 43 H8
Nafud Desert = An Nafūd 47 E5
Naga 36 B2
Nagaland □ 41 E10
Nagano 33 E6
Nagaoka 33 E6
Nagappattinam 43 P11
Nagasaki 33 G1
Nagaur 42 F8
Nagercoil 43 Q10
Nagoya 33 F5
Nagpur 43 J11
Naha 35 D7
Nain 70 D7
Nairn 10 D5
Nairobi 57 E7
Najaf = An Najaf 47 D6
Najafābād 44 C2
Najd 47 F5
Najibabad 42 E11
Nakhichevan Rep. = Naxçıvan □ 25 F6
Nakhon Ratchasima 38 B2
Nakhon Sawan 38 A2
Nakhon Si Thammarat 38 C2
Nakina 71 D5
Nakuru 57 E7
Nalchik 25 E5
Nallamalai Hills 43 M11
Nam Co 34 C4
Nam-Phan 38 B3
Namak, Daryācheh-ye 44 C3
Namaland 58 D3
Namangan 29 E8
Namib Desert 58 C2
Namibe 58 B2
Namibia ■ 58 C3
Nampa 72 E5
Namp'o 35 C7
Nampula 59 B7
Namur 14 C3
Nanaimo 69 D7
Nanchang 35 D6
Nanchong 35 C5
Nancy 13 B7
Nanda Devi 42 D11
Nanded 43 K10
Nandurbar 43 J9
Nanga Parbat 42 B9
Nangarhār □ 42 B7
Nanjing 35 C6
Nanking = Nanjing 35 C6
Nanning 35 D5
Nanping 35 D6

Nansei-Shotō = Ryūkyū-rettō 35 D7
Nansen Sd. 70 A4
Nantes 12 C3
Nantucket I. 77 D10
Nanuque 93 F5
Nanyang 35 C6
Nanyuki 57 D7
Napa 72 G2
Napier 64 C7
Naples = Nápoli 21 D5
Naples 83 F7
Napo → 90 D4
Nápoli 21 D5
Narayanganj 41 F8
Narbonne 13 E5
Narmada → 43 J8
Narodnaya 28 C6
Narva 24 B2
Narvik 8 B9
Naryan-Mar 28 C6
Naser, Buheirat en 54 D5
Nashville 82 A4
Nasik 43 K8
Nasirabad 42 F9
Nassau 86 A4
Nasser, L. = Naser, Buheirat en 54 D5
Natal 92 D6
Natashquan 71 D7
Natashquan → 71 D7
Natchez 81 D8
Nathdwara 43 G8
Natitingou 53 F6
Natron, L. 57 E7
Natuna Besar, Kepulauan 39 D3
Naujaat = Repulse Bay 70 C5
Nauru ■ 64 K11
Navarino, I. 95 H3
Navarra □ 19 A5
Navojoa 84 B3
Navsari 43 J8
Nawabshah 42 F6
Naxçıvan □ 25 F6
Naxos 23 F5
Nazas → 84 B4
Ndjamena 55 F1
Ndola 59 A5
Neagh, Lough 11 D3
Near Is. 69 C1
Neath 11 F5
Nebitdag = Balkanabat 29 F6
Nebraska □ 74 E5
Nébrodi, Monti 21 F5
Neckar → 14 D5
Necochea 94 D5
Nederland = Netherlands ■ 14 B3
Neemuch = Nimach 43 G9
Neepawa 69 C10
Negapatam = Nagappattinam 43 P11
Negele 49 F2
Negombo 43 R11
Negrais, C. = Maudin Sun 41 K10
Negro → Argentina 95 E4
Negro → Brazil 90 D6
Negros 36 C2
Nei Mongol Zizhiqu □ 35 B6
Neijiang 35 D5
Neiva 90 C3
Nejd = Najd 47 F5
Nellore 43 M11
Nelson Canada 69 D8
Nelson N.Z. 65 D5
Nelson → 69 C10
Neman = Nemunas → 24 B1
Nemunas → 24 B1
Nemuro 32 B9
Nenagh 11 E2

Nenjiang 35 B7
Nepal ■ 40 D5
Ness, L. 10 C4
Netherlands ■ 14 B3
Netherlands Antilles =
ABC Islands ☑ 87 D6
Nettilling L. 70 C6
Neuquén 94 D3
Neva → 24 B3
Nevada □ 72 G5
Nevers 13 E5
Nevinnomyssk 25 E5
New Amsterdam 92 B2
New Britain *Papua N. G.*
64 K10
New Brunswick □ 71 E7
New Caledonia ☑ 64 M11
New Castile = Castilla-La
Mancha □ 18 C4
New Delhi 42 E10
New Forest △ 11 F6
New Glasgow 71 E7
New Hampshire □
77 C10
New Haven 77 D9
New Hebrides =
Vanuatu ■ 64 L11
New Ireland 64 K10
New Jersey □ 77 E9
New Liskeard 71 E6
New London 77 D9
New Mexico □ 79 C9
New Orleans 81 E8
New Plymouth 64 C6
New Providence 86 A4
New Siberian Is. =
Novosibirskiye Ostrova
31 B12
New South Wales □
63 B4
New York 77 D9
New York □ 77 D8
New Zealand ■ 64 D7
Newark 77 D8
Newburgh 77 D8
Newbury 11 F6
Newcastle 63 B5
Newcastle-upon-Tyne
11 D6
Newfoundland &
Labrador □ 71 D8
Newman 60 E2
Newport *I. of W., U.K.*
11 F6
Newport *Newport, U.K.*
11 F5
Newport *U.S.A.* 77 D10
Newport News 77 F7
Newquay 11 F4
Newry 11 D3
Neyshābūr 44 B4
Nezhin = Nizhyn 24 C3
Nganglong Kangri 40 A3
Ngaoundéré 56 C2
Ngoring Hu 34 C4
Nha Trang 38 B3
Niagara Falls *Canada*
71 E6
Niagara Falls *U.S.A.*
77 C6
Niamey 53 F6
Nias 39 D1
Nicaragua ■ 85 E7
Nicaragua, L. de 85 E7
Nice 13 E7
Nicobar Is. 27 H11
Nicosia 46 D3
Nicoya, Pen. de 85 F7
Niedersachsen □ 14 B5
Niemen = Nemunas →
24 B1
Nieuw Nickerie 92 A2
Niğde 46 C3
Niger ■ 53 E7
Niger → 53 G7
Nigeria ■ 53 G7

Nihon = Japan ■ 33 F5
Niigata 33 E6
Ni'ihau 78 H10
Nijmegen 14 C3
Nikolayev = Mykolayiv
25 D3
Nikopol 25 D3
Nikšić 22 C2
Nîl, Nahr en → 54 B5
Nîl el Abyad → 55 E5
Nîl el Azraq → 55 E5
Nile = Nîl, Nahr en →
54 B5
Nimach 43 G9
Nîmes 13 E6
Nimrūz □ 45 D5
Ninawá 46 C5
Nineveh = Nīnawá 46 C5
Ningbo 35 B7
Ningxia Huizu Zizhiqu □
35 C5
Niobrara → 74 D5
Niort 12 C3
Nipawin 69 C9
Nipigon, L. 71 E6
Nipissing, L. 71 E6
Nippon = Japan ■ 33 F5
Niquelândia 93 E4
Niš 22 C3
Nistru = Dnister →
17 E10
Niterói 93 G5
Niue 65 L14
Nivernais 13 C5
Nizamabad 43 K11
Nizhnevartovsk 29 C8
Nizhniy Novgorod 24 B5
Nizhniy Tagil 29 D6
Nizhyn 24 C3
Nkongsamba 53 H7
Noakhali = Majidi 41 F8
Nobeoka 33 G2
Nogales *Mexico* 84 A2
Nogales *U.S.A.* 79 E7
Noirmoutier, Î. de 12 C2
Nola 56 D3
Nome 69 B3
Noranda =
Rouyn-Noranda 71 E6
Nord-Ostsee-Kanal 14 A5
Norderstedt 14 B5
Nordfriesische Inseln
14 A5
Nordkapp 8 A11
Norfolk 77 F7
Norfolk I. 64 M11
Norge = Norway ■ 8 C8
Norilsk 30 C6
Norman 80 B5
Norman Wells 68 B7
Normandie 12 B4
Normanton 61 D7
Norrköping 9 D9
Norrland 8 C9
Norseman 60 G3
North, C. 71 E7
North Battleford 69 C9
North Bay 71 E6
North C. 64 A5
North Cape = Nordkapp
8 A11
North Carolina □ 83 B7
North Channel 11 D4
North Dakota □ 74 B4
North East Frontier
Agency = Arunachal
Pradesh □ 41 C10
North Frisian Is. =
Nordfriesische Inseln
14 A5
North I. 64 B5
North Korea ■ 35 C7
North Magnetic Pole
70 A2
North Minch 10 B4

North Ossetia-Alaniya □
25 E5
North Platte 74 E4
North Platte → 74 E4
North Rhine Westphalia =
Nordrhein-Westfalen □
14 C4
North Saskatchewan →
69 C8
North Sea 10 D8
North Thompson →
69 C7
North Uist 10 C3
North West C. 60 E1
North West Frontier =
Khyber Pakhtunkhwa □
42 B8
North West Highlands
10 C4
North West River 71 D7
Northampton 11 E6
Northern Circars 40 J4
Northern Ireland □ 11 D3
Northern Marianas ☑
64 H9
Northern Sporades 23 E4
Northern Territory □
60 D5
Northumberland Str.
71 E7
Northwest Territories □
68 B9
Norton Sd. 69 B3
Norway ■ 8 C8
Norway House 69 C10
Norwegian B. 70 B5
Norwegian Sea 6 B5
Norwich 11 E7
Nossob → 58 D4
Notre Dame B. 71 E8
Notre-Dame-de-Koartac =
Quaqtaq 70 C7
Notre-Dame-d'Ivugivic =
Ivujivik 70 C6
Nottaway → 71 D6
Nottingham 11 E6
Nottingham I. 70 C6
Nouâdhibou 52 D2
Nouâdhibou, Râs 52 D2
Nouakchott 53 E2
Nouméa 64 M11
Nouveau Comptoir =
Wemindji 71 D6
Nouvelle-Calédonie =
New Caledonia ☑
64 M11
Nova Casa Nova 93 D5
Nova Friburgo 93 G5
Nova Iguaçu 93 G5
Nova Lima 93 F5
Nova Scotia □ 71 E7
Nova Venécia 93 F5
Novara 13 D8
Novaya Zemlya 28 B6
Novgorod 24 B3
Novi Pazar 22 C3
Novi Sad 22 B2
Novo Remanso 93 D5
Novocherkassk 25 D5
Novokuybyshevsk 24 C6
Novokuznetsk 29 D9
Novomoskovsk 24 C4
Novorossiysk 25 E4
Novoshakhtinsk 25 D5
Novosibirsk 29 D9
Novosibirskiye Ostrova
31 B12
Novotroitsk 29 D6
Nowra 63 B5
Nubian Desert = Nûbîya,
Es Sahrâ en 54 D5
Nûbîya, Es Sahrâ en
54 D5
Nueltin L. 68 B10
Nueva Rosita 84 B4
Nuevitas 86 B4
Nuevo Laredo 84 B5
Nuku'alofa 65 M13
Nukus 29 E6

Nullarbor Plain 60 G4
Numan 55 G1
Numazu 33 F6
Nunavut □ 70 C5
Nuneaton 11 E6
Nunivak I. 69 B3
Núoro 21 D2
Nuremberg = Nürnberg
15 D6
Nürnberg 15 D6
Nuuk 66 C14
Nuweveldberge 58 E4
Nyahururu 57 D7
Nyaingêntanglha Shan
34 C4
Nyâlâ 55 F3
Nyasa, L. = Malawi, L.
59 A6
Nyíregyháza 17 E9
Nyoman = Nemunas →
24 B1
Nysa 16 C3
Nysa → 16 B2
Nystad = Uusikaupunki
9 C10
Nzérékoré 53 G4

O

Oahe, L. 74 C4
O'ahu 78 H12
Oak Ridge 83 A5
Oakland 78 B1
Oamaru 64 F4
Oates Land 96 A15
Oaxaca 84 D5
Ob → 28 C7
Oba 71 E5
Oban 10 C4
Oberhausen 14 C4
Obi, Kepulauan 37 E3
Óbidos 92 C2
Obihiro 32 B8
Obozerskiy 28 C5
Obskaya Guba 28 C8
Ocala 83 E6
Occidental, Cordillera
90 C3
Ocean I. = Banaba
64 K11
Oceanside 78 D4
Odawara 33 F6
Odense 9 D8
Oder → 15 B8
Odesa 25 D3
Odessa 80 D2
Odintsovo 24 B4
Odisha □ 40 G5
Odra = Oder → 15 B8
Odzi 59 B6
Offa 53 G6
Offenbach 14 C5
Ōgaki 33 F5
Ogbomosho 53 G6
Ogden 73 F7
Ogdensburg 77 B8
Ogooué → 56 E1
Ohio □ 76 D4
Ohio → 76 F1
Ohře → 16 C2
Ohridsko Jezero 23 D3
Oise → 12 B5
Ōita 33 G2
Ojos del Salado, Cerro
94 B3
Oka → 28 D5
Okanogan → 72 B4
Okara 42 D8
Okavango Delta 58 B4
Okayama 33 F3
Okazaki 33 F5
Okeechobee, L. 83 F7
Okefenokee Swamp
83 D6
Okhotsk, Sea of 31 D12
Oki-Shotō 33 E3
Okinawa-Jima 35 D7

Oklahoma □ 80 B5
Oklahoma City 80 B5
Öland 9 D9
Olavarría 94 D4
Ölbia 20 D2
Old Castile = Castilla y
Leon □ 18 A3
Old Crow 68 B6
Oldenburg 14 B5
Oldham 11 E5
Olekminsk 31 C10
Olenek → 30 B10
Oléron, Î. d' 12 D3
Olifants = Elefantes →
59 C6
Ólimbos, Óros = Olymbos
Oros 23 D4
Ollagüe 91 H5
Olmaliq 29 E7
Olomouc 16 D3
Olsztyn 16 B5
Olt → 22 C5
Olymbos Oros 23 D4
Olympia *Greece* 23 F3
Olympia *U.S.A.* 72 C2
Olympic Mts. 72 C2
Olympus, Mt. = Olymbos
Oros 23 D4
Omagh 11 D3
Omaha 75 E7
Oman ■ 48 C6
Oman, G. of 45 E4
Omdurmân 55 E5
Ometepec 84 D5
Omsk 29 D8
Ōmuta 33 G2
Ondangwa 58 B3
Onega → 28 C4
Onega, L. = Onezhskoye
Ozero 8 C13
Onezhskoye Ozero 8 C13
Onitsha 53 G7
Ontario □ 71 E5
Ontario, L. 77 C7
Oostende 14 C2
Ootacamund =
Udagamandalam
43 P10
Opava 16 D3
Opole 16 C3
Oporto = Porto 18 B1
Oradea 17 E5
Öræfajökull 8 C2
Oral = Zhayyq → 29 E6
Oran 52 A5
Orange *Australia* 63 B4
Orange *France* 13 D6
Orange → 58 D3
Orange, C. 92 B3
Orange Free State = Free
State □ 59 D5
Orangeburg 83 C7
Orange = Orange →
58 D3
Ordos = Mu Us Shamo
35 C5
Ordu 46 B4
Ore Mts. = Erzgebirge
15 C7
Örebro 9 D9
Oregon □ 72 E3
Orekhovo-Zuyevo 24 B4
Orel 24 C4
Orenburg 29 D6
Orense = Ourense 18 A2
Orhon Gol → 35 A5
Oriental, Cordillera 90 B4
Orihuela 19 C5
Orinoco → 90 B6
Orissa = Odisha □ 40 G5
Oristano 21 E2
Orizaba 84 D5
Orizaba, Pico de 84 D5
Orkney Is. 10 B5
Orlando 83 E7
Orléanais 12 C5
Orléans 12 C4

Ormara 42 G4
Ormoc 36 B2
Örnsköldsvik 8 C9
Orol Dengizi = Aral Sea 29 E6
Orsha 24 C3
Orsk 29 D6
Ortegal, C. 18 A2
Orümïyeh 46 C6
Orümïyeh, Daryācheh-ye 46 C6
Oruro 91 G5
Oruzgān □ 42 C5
Ōsaka 33 F4
Ösel = Saaremaa 24 B1
Oshakati 58 B2
Oshawa 71 E6
Oshogbo 53 G6
Osijek 20 B7
Osizweni 59 D6
Oskarshamn 9 D9
Öskemen 29 E9
Oslo 9 D8
Oslofjorden 9 D8
Osmaniye 46 C4
Osnabrück 14 B5
Osorno 95 E2
Ossa, Mt. 62 D4
Ostend = Oostende 14 C2
Österdalälven 8 C8
Österreich = Austria ■ 15 E8
Östersund 8 C8
Ostfriesische Inseln 14 B4
Ostrava 16 D4
Ostrołęka 16 B5
Ostrów Wielkopolski 16 C3
Ostrowiec-Świętokrzyski 16 C5
Oswego 77 C7
Otago □ 65 F3
Otaru 32 B7
Otjiwarongo 58 C3
Otranto 21 D7
Otranto, Str. of 21 D7
Ōtsu 33 F4
Ottawa = Outaouais → 71 E6
Ottawa 71 E6
Ottawa Is. 70 D5
Ottumwa 75 E8
Ouachita Mts. 81 B6
Ouagadougou 53 F5
Ouahran = Oran 52 A5
Oubangi → 56 E3
Oudtshoorn 58 E4
Ouessant, Î. d' 12 B1
Ouezzane 52 B4
Oujda 52 B5
Oulu 8 C11
Oulujärvi 8 C11
Oulujoki → 8 B11
Ourense 18 A2
Ouro Prêto 93 G5
Outaouais → 71 E6
Outer Hebrides 10 C3
Outjo 58 C3
Ovalle 94 C2
Ovamboland 58 B3
Oviedo 18 A3
Owambo = Ovamboland 58 B3
Owen Sound 71 E5
Owen Stanley Ra. 61 B8
Owo 53 G7
Owyhee → 74 E5
Oxford 11 F6
Oxnard 78 C3
Oxus = Amudarya → 29 E6
Oyama 33 E6
Oyem 56 D2
Oyo 53 G6
Ozark Plateau 81 A8

P
Paarl 58 E3
Pab Hills 42 F5
Pabna 41 E7
Pacaraima, Sa. 90 C6
Pacasmayo 91 E3
Pachuca 84 C5
Padang 39 E2
Padangsidempuan 39 D1
Paderborn 14 C5
Pádova 20 B3
Padua = Pádova 20 B3
Paducah 76 F1
Pag 20 B5
Pagadian 36 C2
Pagalu = Annobón 51 G4
Paint Hills = Wemindji 71 D6
Painted Desert 79 C7
País Vasco □ 19 A4
Paita 90 E2
Pakistan ■ 42 E7
Paktīā □ 42 C6
Pakxe 38 A3
Palagruža 20 C6
Palani Hills 43 P10
Palanpur 43 G8
Palapye 59 C5
Palau ■ 36 C4
Palawan 38 C5
Palembang 39 E2
Palencia 18 A3
Palermo 21 E4
Palestine 81 D6
Palghat 43 P10
Pali 42 G8
Palikir 64 J10
Palk Strait 43 Q11
Palm Springs 78 D4
Palma de Mallorca 19 C7
Palmares 92 D6
Palmas, C. 53 H4
Palmeira dos Índios 93 D6
Palmer 69 B5
Palmer Land 96 B3
Palmira 90 C3
Palmyra = Tudmur 46 D4
Palopo 37 E2
Palu Indonesia 37 E1
Palu Turkey 46 C5
Pamiers 12 E4
Pamir 29 F8
Pamlico Sd. 83 B10
Pampa 80 B3
Pampas 94 D4
Pamplona-Iruña 19 A5
Panaji 43 M8
Panamá 85 F9
Panama ■ 86 E4
Panamá Canal 86 E4
Panamá City 82 D5
Panay 36 B2
Pančevo 22 B3
Panevėžys 24 B1
Pangani 57 F7
Pangfou = Bengbu 35 C6
Pangkalpinang 39 E3
Pangnirtung 70 C7
Panjim = Panaji 43 M8
Pannirtuuq = Pangnirtung 70 C7
Pantar 37 F2
Pante Macassar 37 F2
Pantelleria 21 F3
Paoting = Baoding 35 C6
Paot'ou = Baotou 35 B6
Papantla 84 C5
Papeete 65 L16
Papua □ 37 E5
Papua New Guinea ■ 64 K9
Pará = Belém 92 C4

Pará □ 92 C3
Paracatu 93 F4
Paracel Is. 38 A4
Paraguaçu → 93 E6
Paraguaná, Pen. de 90 A4
Paraguari 94 B5
Paraguay ■ 94 A5
Paraguay → 94 B5
Paraíba = João Pessoa 92 D7
Paraíba □ 92 D6
Parakou 53 G6
Paramaribo 92 A2
Paraná Argentina 94 C4
Paraná Brazil 93 E4
Paraná □ 94 A6
Paraná → 94 C4
Paranaguá 94 B7
Paranaíba → 93 G3
Paranapanema → 94 A6
Parbhani 43 K10
Pardo → 93 F6
Pardubice 16 C2
Parecis, Serra dos 91 F7
Parepare 37 E1
Parima, Serra 90 C6
Parintins 92 C7
Paripiriri Kyun 12 K9
Paris France 12 B5
Paris U.S.A. 81 C6
Park Range 73 G10
Parkersburg 76 E5
Parla 18 B4
Parma 13 D9
Parnaguá 93 E5
Parnaíba 92 C5
Parnaíba → 92 C5
Parnassós 23 E4
Pärnu 24 B1
Paros 23 F5
Parry Is. 70 B3
Parry Sound 71 E6
Paru → 92 C3
Pas, The 69 C9
Pasadena Calif., U.S.A. 78 C3
Pasadena Tex., U.S.A. 81 E6
Paschimbanga □ 40 F7
Pasco, Cerro de 91 F3
Passau 15 D7
Passo Fundo 94 B6
Passos 93 G4
Pastaza → 90 D3
Pasto 90 C3
Patagonia 95 F3
Patan 43 H8
Paterson 77 D8
Pathankot 42 C9
Patkai Bum 41 D10
Patmos 23 F6
Patna 40 E5
Patos, L. dos 94 C5
Patos de Minas 93 F4
Patra 23 E3
Patras = Patra 23 E3
Patrocínio 93 F4
Pau 12 E3
Paulistana 92 D5
Paulo Afonso 93 D6
Pavia 13 D8
Pavlodar 29 D8
Pavlohrad 25 D6
Pavlovo 24 B5
Pawtucket 77 D10
Payakumbuh 39 E2
Payne Bay = Kangirsuk 70 D7
Payne L. 70 D6
Paysandú 94 C5
Paz, B. de la 84 C2
Pazardzhik 22 C5
Peace → 68 C8
Peawanuck 71 D5
Peć = Peje 22 C3

Pechora → 28 C6
Pechorskaya Guba 28 C6
Pecos → 80 E3
Pécs 16 E4
Pedra Azul 93 F5
Pedro Afonso 93 D4
Peel → 68 B6
Pegu 41 J11
Pegu Yoma 41 H10
Peip'ing = Beijing 35 C6
Peipus, L. = Chudskoye, Ozero 24 B2
Peixe 93 E4
Peje 22 C3
Pekalongan 39 F3
Pekanbaru 39 D2
Pekin 75 E10
Peking = Beijing 35 C6
Pelagie, Is. 21 G4
Peleng 37 E2
Pelješac 20 C6
Pelly → 68 B6
Pelly Bay 70 C14
Peloponnese □ 23 F4
Pelotas 94 C5
Pelvoux, Massif du 13 D7
Pematangsiantar 39 D1
Pemba 59 A8
Pemba I. 57 F7
Pembroke Canada 71 E6
Pembroke U.K. 11 F3
Penang = Pinang 38 C2
Peñas, G. de 95 F2
Pench'i = Benxi 35 B7
Pend Oreille, L. 72 C5
Pendleton 72 D4
Penedo 93 E6
Peninsular Malaysia □ 39 D2
Penmarch, Pte. de 12 C1
Pennines 11 D5
Pennsylvania □ 77 D7
Penong 60 G5
Penrhyn 65 K15
Pensacola 82 D4
Pensacola Mts. 96 C4
Penticton 69 D8
Pentland Firth 10 B5
Penza 24 C6
Penzance 11 F4
Peoria 75 E10
Perabumulih 39 E2
Perdido, Mte. 19 A6
Perdu, Mt. = Perdido, Mte. 19 A6
Pereira 90 C3
Pergamino 94 C4
Péribonka → 71 E6
Périgueux 12 D4
Perm 29 D6
Pernambuco = Recife 92 D7
Pernik 22 C4
Perpignan 13 E5
Persepolis 44 D3
Persia = Iran ■ 44 C3
Persian Gulf 44 E2
Perth Australia 60 G2
Perth U.K. 10 C5
Peru ■ 90 C3
Perúgia 20 C4
Pervomaysk 25 D8
Pervouralsk 29 D6
Pésaro 20 C4
Pescara 20 C5
Peshawar 42 B7
Pesqueira 92 D6
Petah Tiqwa 46 D3
Peterborough Canada 71 E6
Peterborough U.K. 11 E6
Peterhead 10 C6
Petersburg Alaska, U.S.A. 69 C6
Petersburg Va., U.S.A. 77 F7
Petitsikapau L. 71 D7
Peto 85 C7

Petrolândia 93 D6
Petrolina 93 D5
Petropavl 29 D7
Petropavlovsk-Kamchatskiy 31 D13
Petrópolis 93 G5
Petrozavodsk 8 C12
Pforzheim 14 D5
Phalodi 42 F8
Phan Rang 38 B3
Philadelphia 77 E8
Philippine Trench = Mindanao Trench 36 B3
Philippines ■ 36 B2
Philippopolis = Plovdiv 22 C5
Phitsanulok 38 A2
Phnom Penh 38 B2
Phoenix 79 D6
Phra Nakhon Si Ayutthaya 38 B2
Phuket 38 C1
Piacenza 13 D8
Piatra Neamţ 17 E8
Piauí □ 92 D5
Piave → 20 B4
Picardie □ 13 B5
Pichilemu 94 C1
Picton 65 D6
Piedmont = Piemonte □ 13 D7
Piedras Negras 84 B4
Piemonte □ 13 D7
Pietermaritzburg 59 D6
Pietersburg = Polokwane 59 C5
Pilar 94 B5
Pilcomayo → 94 B5
Pilibhit 42 E11
Pílica → 16 C5
Pilipinas = Philippines ■ 36 B2
Pimentel 91 E3
Pinang 38 C2
Pinar del Río 86 B3
Pindos Oros 23 E3
Pindus Mts. = Pindos Oros 23 E3
Pine Bluff 81 B7
Pine Point 68 B8
Pinega → 28 C5
Pingliang 35 C5
Pingxiang 35 D5
Pinsk 17 B8
Piombino 20 C3
Piopiotaki = Milford Sd. 65 F2
Piotrków Trybunalski 16 C4
Piracicaba 94 A7
Piraeus = Pireas 23 F4
Praiévs = Pireas 23 F4
Pirapora 93 F5
Pireas 23 F4
Pirineos = Pyrénées 12 E4
Pirmasens 14 D4
Pisa 20 C3
Pisagua 91 G4
Pishan 34 C3
Pistóia 20 C3
Pitcairn I. 65 M17
Piteå 8 B10
Piteşti 22 B5
Pittsburg 81 A6
Pittsburgh 77 D5
Piura 90 E2
Placentia 71 E8
Placentia B. 71 E8
Plainview 80 B3
Plata, Río de la → 94 C5
Platte → 75 F7
Plauen 15 C7
Plenty, B. of 64 B7
Pleven 22 C5
Płock 16 B4
Ploieşti 22 B6

Plovdiv 22 C5
Plymouth 11 F4
Plzeň 16 D1
Po → 20 B4
Po Hai = Bo Hai 35 C6
Pobedy, Pik 29 E8
Pocatello 73 E7
Poços de Caldas 93 G4
Podgorica 22 C2
Podolsk 24 B4
Pohnpei 64 J10
Pointe-à-Pitre 87 C7
Pointe-Noire 56 E2
Poitiers 12 C4
Poitou 12 C3
Pola = Pula 20 B4
Poland ■ 16 B5
Polatsk 24 B2
Polesye = Pripet Marshes 17 B9
Polokwane 59 C5
Poltava 24 D3
Polynesia 65 L15
Polynésie française = French Polynesia ☑ 65 M16
Ponape = Pohnpei 64 J10
Ponca City 80 A5
Ponce 87 C6
Pond Inlet 70 B6
Pondicherry = Puducherry 43 P11
Ponferrada 18 A2
Ponta Grossa 94 B6
Pontarlier 13 C7
Pontchartrain, L. 81 D8
Ponte Nova 93 G5
Pontevedra 18 A1
Pontiac 76 C4
Pontianak 39 E3
Pontine Is. = Ponziane, Ísole 21 D4
Pontine Mts. = Kuzey Anadolu Dağları 25 E4
Pontivy 12 B2
Ponziane, Ísole 21 D4
Poole 11 F6
Poona = Pune 43 K8
Poopó, L. de 91 G5
Popayán 90 C3
Poplar Bluff 81 A8
Popocatépetl, Volcán 84 D5
Porbandar 43 J6
Porcupine → 69 B5
Pori 8 C10
Port Alberni 69 D7
Port Arthur 81 E7
Port Augusta 62 B2
Port Elizabeth 59 E5
Port-Gentil 56 E1
Port Harcourt 53 H7
Port Harrison = Inukjuak 70 D6
Port Hawkesbury 71 E7
Port Hedland 60 E2
Port Hope Simpson 71 D8
Port Huron 76 C4
Port Laoise = Waterford 11 E3
Port Lincoln 62 B2
Port Louis 51 J9
Port Macquarie 63 B5
Port Moresby 61 B8
Port Nolloth 58 D3
Port Nouveau-Québec = Kangiqsualujjuaq 70 D7
Port of Spain 87 D7
Port Pirie 62 B2
Port Safaga = Bûr Safâga 54 C5
Port Said = Bûr Sa'îd 54 B5

Port Shepstone 59 E6
Port Stanley = Stanley 95 G5
Port Sudan = Bûr Sûdân 55 E6
Port Talbot 11 F5
Port Vila 64 L11
Portadown 11 D3
Portage la Prairie 69 D10
Portile de Fier 22 B4
Portland Maine, U.S.A. 77 C10
Portland Oreg., U.S.A. 72 D2
Portlaoise 11 E3
Pôrto 18 B1
Pôrto Alegre 94 C6
Pôrto Esperança 91 G7
Pôrto Nacional 93 E4
Porto-Novo 53 G6
Pôrto Seguro 93 F6
Pôrto Tôrres 20 D2
Porto-Vecchio 13 F8
Pôrto Velho 91 E6
Portree 10 C3
Portsmouth U.K. 11 F6
Portsmouth U.S.A. 77 F7
Porttipahdan tekojärvi 8 B11
Portugal ■ 18 C1
Posadas 94 B5
Posse 93 E4
Poste-de-la-Baleine = Kuujjuarapik 71 D6
Postmasburg 58 D4
Potchefstroom 59 D5
Potenza 21 D5
Poti 25 E5
Potomac → 77 E7
Potosí 91 G5
Potsdam 15 B7
Poughkeepsie 77 D9
Povungnituk = Puvirnituq 70 C6
Powder → 74 B2
Powell, L. 79 B7
Poyang Hu 35 D6
Poznań 16 B3
Pozzuoli 21 D5
Prado 93 F6
Prague = Praha 16 C2
Praia 16 C2
Prata 93 F4
Prato 20 C3
Praya 39 F5
Presidencia Roque Saenz Peña 94 B4
Presidente Prudente 93 G3
Prespansko Jezero 23 D3
Presque Isle 77 A11
Preston 11 E5
Pretoria 59 D5
Prieska 58 D4
Prilep 22 D3
Priluki = Pryluky 24 C3
Prince Albert 69 C9
Prince Albert Pen. 68 A8
Prince Albert Sd. 68 A8
Prince Albert, C. 70 B1
Prince Charles I. 70 C6
Prince Charles Mts. 96 B10
Prince Edward I. ☑ 71 E7
Prince of Wales I. 68 A10
Prince Patrick I. 70 B2
Pripet = Prypyat → 17 C10
Pripet Marshes 17 B9
Priština 22 C3
Privas 13 D6
Privolzhskaya Vozvyshennost 24 C6
Prizren 22 C3
Progreso 85 C7
Prome 41 H10
Propriá 93 E6
Provence 13 E6

Providence 77 D10
Providencia, I. de 86 D3
Provins 13 B5
Provo 73 F8
Pruszków 16 B5
Prut → 17 F9
Prypyat → 17 C10
Pskov 24 B2
Puducherry 43 P11
Puebla 84 D5
Pueblo 74 F2
Puerto Aisén 95 F2
Puerto Barrios 85 D7
Puerto Cabello 90 A5
Puerto Cabezas 86 D3
Puerto Carreño 90 B5
Puerto Cortés 85 D7
Puerto Deseado 95 F3
Puerto La Cruz 90 A6
Puerto Madryn 95 E3
Puerto Maldonado 91 F5
Puerto Montt 95 E2
Puerto Plata 87 C5
Puerto Princesa 36 C1
Puerto Rico ☑ 87 C6
Puerto Suárez 91 G7
Puerto Wilches 90 B4
Puertollano 18 C3
Puget Sound 72 C2
Pukapuka 65 L14
Pula 20 B4
Pullman 72 C5
Puncak Jaya 39 E5
Pune 43 K8
Punjab □ India 42 D9
Punjab □ Pakistan 42 D8
Puno 91 G4
Punta Arenas 95 G2
Puntland 49 F4
Puralia = Puruliya 40 F6
Puri 40 H5
Purnia 40 E6
Puruliya 40 F6
Purus → 90 D6
Pusan = Busan 35 C7
Putorana, Gory 30 C7
Puttalam 43 Q11
Putumayo → 90 D5
Puvirnituq 70 C6
Puy-de-Dôme 13 D5
Pwllheli 11 E4
Pyatigorsk 25 E5
Pyè = Prome 41 H10
Pyinmana 41 H11
P'yŏngyang 35 C7
Pyrénées 13 E4

Q

Qā'emshahr 44 B3
Qahremānshahr = Kermānshāh 46 D6
Qaidam Pendi 34 C4
Qamani'tuaq = Baker Lake 68 B10
Qandahār = Kandahār 42 D4
Qandyaghash 29 E6
Qaraghandy 29 E8
Qarqan He → 34 C3
Qarshi 29 F7
Qatar ■ 44 E2
Qattâra, Munkhafed el 54 C4
Qattâra Depression = Qattâra, Munkhafed el 54 C4
Qausuittuq = Resolute 70 B4
Qazaqstan = Kazakhstan ■ 29 E7
Qazvin 46 C7
Qena 54 C5
Qeshm 44 E4
Qikiqtarjuaq 70 C7
Qilian Shan 34 C5
Qingdao 35 C7

Qinghai □ 34 C4
Qinghai Hu 34 C5
Qinhuangdao 35 C6
Qinzhou 35 D5
Qiqihar 35 B7
Qitai 34 B3
Qom 44 C2
Qomolangma Feng = Everest, Mt. 40 C6
Qondūz = Kondoz 45 B7
Qo'qon 29 E8
Qoraqalpog'iston □ 29 E6
Quan Long = Ca Mau 38 C3
Quang Ngai 38 A3
Quanzhou 35 D6
Quaqtaq 70 C7
Quartu Sant'Élena 21 E2
Québec 71 E6
Québec □ 71 E6
Queen Charlotte Is. = Haida Gwaii 69 C6
Queen Charlotte Sd. 69 C7
Queen Elizabeth Is. 66 B9
Queen Elizabeth Land 96 C3
Queen Maud G. 68 B9
Queen Maud Land = Dronning Maud Land 96 B7
Queensland □ 61 E7
Queenstown N.Z. 65 F3
Queenstown S. Africa 59 E5
Queimadas 93 E6
Quelimane 59 B7
Quelpart = Jeju-do 35 C7
Querétaro 84 C4
Quetta 42 D5
Quezon City 36 B2
Qui Nhon 38 B3
Quibdo 90 B3
Quiberon 12 C2
Quilán, C. 95 E2
Quilon = Kollam 43 Q10
Quilpie 63 A4
Quimper 12 B1
Quincy 75 F9
Quito 90 D3
Qulsary 29 E6
Quseir 54 C5
Quzhou 35 D6
Qyzylorda 29 E7

R

Raahe 8 C10
Raba 37 F1
Rabat 52 B4
Rābigh 47 G4
Race, C. 71 E8
Rach Gia 38 B3
Racine 76 C2
Radom 16 C5
Rae 68 B8
Rae Bareli 40 D3
Rae Isthmus 70 C5
Rafaela 94 C4
Rafsanjān 44 D4
Ragusa 21 F5
Rahimyar Khan 42 E7
Raichur 43 L10
Raigarh 40 G4
Rainier, Mt. 72 C3
Raipur 40 G3
Raj Nandgaon 40 G3
Rajahmundry 40 J3
Rajapalaiyam 43 Q10
Rajasthan □ 42 F8
Rajasthan Canal = Indira Gandhi Canal 42 F8
Rajkot 43 H7
Rajshahi 41 E7
Rakata, Pulau 39 F3

Raleigh 83 B8
Ramgarh 40 F5
Râmnicu Vâlcea 17 F7
Rampur 42 E11
Ramree I. 41 H9
Rancagua 94 C2
Ranchi 40 F5
Randers 9 D8
Rangoon = Yangôn 41 J11
Rangpur 41 E7
Rankin Inlet 68 B10
Rapa 65 M13
Rapallo 13 D8
Raper, C. 70 C7
Rapid City 74 C3
Rarotonga 65 M14
Ra's al Khaymah 44 E4
Rasht 46 C7
Rat Islands 69 C1
Ratangarh 42 E9
Ratlam 43 H9
Ratnagiri 43 L8
Rauma 8 C10
Raumo = Rauma 8 C10
Raurkela 40 F5
Ravenna 20 B4
Ravi → 42 D7
Rawalpindi 42 C8
Rawlins 73 F10
Rawson 95 E3
Ray, C. 71 E8
Raz, Pte. du 12 B1
Razāzah, Buḩayrat ar 47 D5
Razazah, L. = Razāzah, Buḩayrat ar 47 D5
Rē, Î. de 12 C3
Reading U.K. 11 F6
Reading U.S.A. 77 D8
Recife 92 D7
Reconquista 94 B5
Red → 81 D8
Red Deer 69 C8
Red River of the North → 74 A6
Red Sea 48 C2
Redcar 11 D6
Redding 72 F2
Redditch 11 E6
Redon 12 C2
Ree, L. 11 E3
Regensburg 15 D7
Reggâne = Zaouiet Reggâne 52 C6
Réggio di Calábria 21 E5
Réggio nell'Emilia 20 B3
Regina 69 C9
Reichenbach 15 C7
Reigate 11 F6
Reims 13 B6
Reina Adelaida, Arch. 95 G2
Reindeer L. 69 C9
Rennes 12 B3
Reno 72 G4
Republican → 74 F6
Repulse Bay 70 C5
Resht = Rasht 46 C7
Resistencia 94 B5
Resolute 70 B4
Resolution I. 70 C7
Rethimno 23 G5
Réunion ☑ 51 J9
Reus 19 B6
Reutlingen 14 D5
Revelstoke 69 C8
Revillagigedo, Is. de 84 D2
Rewa 40 G3
Rey Malabo 53 H7
Reykjavík 8 C1
Reynosa 84 B5
Rhein → 14 C4
Rheine 14 B4
Rheinland-Pfalz □ 14 C4
Rhine = Rhein → 14 C4

Rhineland-Palatinate = Rheinland-Pfalz □ 14 C4
Rhode Island □ 77 D10
Rhodes 23 F7
Rhodope Mts. = Rhodopi Planina 22 D5
Rhodopi Planina 22 D5
Rhön 14 C5
Rhondda 11 F5
Rhône → 13 E6
Rhum 10 C3
Riau, Kepulauan 39 D2
Ribeirão Prêto 93 G4
Riberalta 91 F5
Richards Bay 59 D6
Richland 72 C4
Richmond 77 F7
Riga 24 B1
Riga, G. of 24 B1
Rigestān 42 D4
Rigolet 70 D8
Rijeka 20 B5
Rimini 20 B4
Rimouski 71 E7
Rio Branco 91 E5
Rio Cuarto 94 C4
Rio de Janeiro 93 G5
Rio de Janeiro □ 93 G5
Rio Gallegos 95 G3
Rio Grande 94 C6
Rio Grande → 84 B5
Rio Grande de Santiago → 84 C3
Rio Grande do Norte □ 92 D6
Rio Grande do Sul □ 94 B6
Rio Largo 93 D6
Rio Muni □ 56 D2
Riobamba 90 D3
Riohacha 90 A4
Rivera 94 C5
Riverside 78 D4
Rivière-du-Loup 71 E7
Rivne 17 C8
Riyadh = Ar Riyāḍ 47 F6
Rize 25 E5
Roanne 13 D6
Roanoke 77 F6
Roberval 71 E6
Robson, Mt. 69 C8
Roca, C. da 18 C1
Rocha 94 C6
Rochefort 12 D3
Rochester Minn., U.S.A. 75 C8
Rochester N.Y., U.S.A. 77 C7
Rock Hill 83 B7
Rock Island 75 E9
Rock Springs 73 F9
Rockford 75 D10
Rockhampton 61 E9
Rocky Mount 83 B9
Rocky Mts. 68 C7
Rodez 13 E5
Ródhos = Rhodes 23 F7
Roes Welcome Sd. 70 C5
Rohri 42 F6
Rojo, C. 84 C5
Roma Australia 63 A4
Roma Italy 20 D4
Romaine → 71 D7
Romania ■ 22 B5
Romans-sur-Isère 13 D6
Rome = Roma 20 D4
Rome 82 B5
Romorantin-Lanthenay 12 C4
Roncador, Serra do 93 E3
Rondônia □ 91 F6
Rondonópolis 93 F3
Ronge, L. la 69 C9
Ronne Ice Shelf 96 B3
Roosevelt → 91 E6
Roosevelt I. 96 B16

Roquetas de Mar 19 D4
Roraima □ 90 C6
Roraima, Mt. 90 B6
Rosario Argentina 94 C4
Rosario Mexico 84 C3
Rosario de la Frontera 94 B3
Roscommon 11 E2
Roseau 87 C7
Roseburg 72 E2
Rosenheim 15 E7
Rosetown 69 C9
Roseville 72 G3
Roslavl 24 C3
Ross Ice Shelf 96 C16
Ross Sea 96 B15
Rossiya = Russia ■ 26 C10
Rosslare 11 E3
Rossosh 24 C4
Rostock 15 A7
Rostov 25 D4
Roswell 80 C1
Rotherham 11 E6
Rotorua 64 C7
Rotterdam 14 C3
Rotuma 64 L12
Roubaix 13 A5
Round Mt. 63 B5
Rousse = Ruse 22 C5
Roussillon 13 E5
Rouyn-Noranda 71 E6
Rovaniemi 8 B11
Rovigo 20 B3
Rovno = Rivne 17 C8
Rovuma = Ruvuma → 57 G8
Roxas 36 B2
Royal Leamington Spa 11 E6
Royan 12 D3
Rub' al Khālī 48 D4
Rufiji → 57 F7
Rugby 11 E6
Rügen 15 A7
Ruhr → 14 C4
Rukwa, L. 57 F6
Rum = Rhum 10 C3
Rumania = Romania ■ 22 B5
Rundu 58 B3
Ruoqiang 34 C3
Rupert → 71 D6
Rupert House = Waskaganish 71 D6
Ruse 22 C5
Rustavi 25 E6
Rustenburg 59 D5
Ruvuma → 57 G8
Ruwenzori 57 D6
Rwanda ■ 57 E6
Ryazan 24 C4
Rybinsk 24 B4
Rybinskoye Vdkhr. 24 B4
Ryōtsu 35 D7
Ryukyu Is. = Ryūkyū-rettō 35 D7
Ryūkyū-rettō 35 D7
Rzeszów 16 C5
Rzhev 24 B3

S

Saale → 15 C6
Saar → 13 B7
Saarbrücken 14 D4
Saaremaa 24 B1
Sabadell 19 B7
Sabah □ 38 C5
Sabará 93 F5
Sabhā 54 C1
Sabinas 84 B4
Sabinas Hidalgo 84 B4
Sable, C. Canada 71 E7
Sable, C. U.S.A. 86 A3
Sable I. 71 E8

Sachsen □ 15 C7
Sachsen-Anhalt □ 15 C7
Sacramento 72 G3
Sacramento → 72 G3
Sacramento Mts. 79 D10
Sadd el Aali 54 D5
Sado 32 E6
Saga 33 G2
Sagarmatha = Everest, Mt. 40 C6
Saginaw 76 C4
Saglouc = Salluit 70 C6
Sagua la Grande 86 B3
Sagunt 19 C5
Sahara 52 D6
Saharanpur 42 E10
Saharien, Atlas 52 B6
Sahiwal 42 D8
Sahrawi = Western Sahara ■ 52 D3
Sa'īdābād = Sirjān 44 D3
Saidpur 41 E7
Saigon = Thanh Pho Ho Chi Minh 38 B3
St. Andrews 10 C5
St. Anthony 71 D8
St. Augustin 71 D8
St. Augustine 83 E7
St. Austell 11 F4
St-Brieuc 12 B2
St. Catharines 77 C6
St. Christopher-Nevis = St. Kitts & Nevis ■ 87 C7
St. Cloud 75 C7
St. Croix 87 C7
St-Denis 12 B5
St-Dizier 13 B6
St. Elias, Mt. 68 B5
St-Étienne 13 D6
St-Flour 13 D5
St-Gaudens 12 E4
St. George's 87 D7
St. George's Channel 11 F3
St. Gotthard P. = San Gottardo, P. del 13 C8
St. Helena 51 H3
St. Helier 11 G5
St-Hyacinthe 71 E6
St-Jean, L. 71 E6
St. John 71 E7
St. John's Antigua & B. 87 C7
St. John's Canada 71 E8
St. Johns → 83 D7
St. Joseph 75 F7
St. Joseph, L. 71 D4
St. Kilda 10 C2
St. Kitts & Nevis ■ 87 C7
St. Lawrence → 71 E7
St. Lawrence, Gulf of 71 E7
St. Lawrence I. 69 B2
St-Lô 12 B3
St. Louis Senegal 53 E2
St. Louis U.S.A. 75 F9
St. Lucia ■ 87 D7
St-Malo 12 B2
St-Marc 87 C5
St-Nazaire 12 C2
St-Omer 12 A5
St. Paul 75 C8
St. Peter Port 11 G5
St. Petersburg = Sankt-Peterburg 24 B3
St. Petersburg 83 F6
St-Pierre-et-Miquelon ☑ 71 E8
St-Quentin 13 B5
St-Tropez 13 E7
St. Vincent, G. 62 C2
St. Vincent & the Grenadines ■ 87 D7
Saintes 12 D3
Saintonge 12 D3
Saipan 64 H9

Saitama 33 F6
Sajama 91 G5
Sakakawea, L. 74 B4
Sakartvelo = Georgia ■ 25 E5
Sakarya 25 E3
Sakata 32 D6
Sakhalin 31 D12
Sala 9 D9
Salado → La Pampa, Argentina 94 D3
Salado → Santa Fe, Argentina 94 C3
Salālah 49 D5
Salamanca 18 B3
Salar de Uyuni 91 H5
Salaverry 91 E3
Salayar 37 F2
Saldanha 58 E3
Sale Australia 63 C4
Salé Morocco 52 B4
Salekhard 28 C7
Salem India 43 P11
Salem U.S.A. 72 D2
Salerno 21 D5
Salina 74 F6
Salina Cruz 85 D5
Salinas Ecuador 90 D2
Salinas U.S.A. 78 B2
Salinas Grandes 94 C3
Salisbury 11 F6
Salisbury I. 70 C6
Salliq = Coral Harbour 70 C5
Salluit 70 C6
Salmon → 72 D5
Salmon River Mts. 73 D6
Salon-de-Provence 13 E6
Salonica = Thessaloniki 23 D4
Salsk 25 D5
Salt Lake City 73 F8
Salta 94 A3
Saltillo 84 B4
Salton Sea 78 D5
Salvador 93 E6
Salvador, El ■ 85 E7
Salween → 41 J11
Salyan 25 F6
Salzburg 15 E7
Salzgitter 14 B6
Sama de Langreo = Langreo 18 A3
Samangān □ 45 B7
Samar 36 B3
Samara 24 C7
Samarinda 39 E5
Samarkand = Samarqand 29 F7
Samarqand 29 F7
Sambalpur 40 G5
Sambhal 42 E11
Sambhar 42 F9
Samoa ■ 65 L13
Samos 23 F6
Samothraki 23 D5
Samsun 25 E4
Samui, Ko 38 C2
San Andrés, I. de 86 D3
San Andrés Tuxtla 85 D5
San Angelo 80 D4
San Antonio Chile 94 C2
San Antonio U.S.A. 80 E4
San Antonio Oeste 95 E4
San Bernardino 78 C4
San Bernardino Str. 36 B2
San Bernardo 94 C2
San Carlos 36 B2
San Carlos de Bariloche 95 E2
San Cristóbal Argentina 94 C4
San Cristóbal Venezuela 90 B4
San Cristóbal de las Casas 85 D6
San Diego 78 D4

San Felipe 90 A5
San Fernando Chile 94 C2
San Fernando Spain 18 D2
San Fernando Trin. & Tob. 87 D7
San Fernando U.S.A. 78 C3
San Fernando de Apure 90 B5
San Francisco 78 B1
San Francisco de Macorís 87 C5
San Gottardo, P. del 13 C8
San Ignacio 91 G6
San Joaquin → 78 A2
San Jorge, G. 95 F3
San José Costa Rica 86 E3
San Jose Phil. 36 B2
San Jose U.S.A. 78 B2
San José de Chiquitos 91 G6
San José de Jáchal 94 C3
San José de Mayo 94 C5
San Juan Argentina 94 C3
San Juan Puerto Rico 87 C6
San Juan → 86 D3
San Juan de los Morros 90 B5
San Juan Mts. 79 B9
San Lorenzo, Mte. 95 F2
San Lucas, C. 84 C2
San Luis 94 C3
San Luis Obispo 78 C2
San Luis Potosí 84 C4
San Marino ■ 20 C4
San Matías, G. 95 E4
San Miguel 85 E7
San Miguel de Tucumán 94 B3
San Nicolás de los Arroyas 94 C4
San Pedro 53 H4
San Pedro de las Colonias 84 B4
San Pedro de Macorís 87 C6
San Pedro Sula 85 D7
San Pietro 21 E2
San Rafael 94 C3
San Remo 13 E7
San Salvador 85 E7
San Salvador de Jujuy 94 A4
San Salvador I. 86 B5
San Sebastián = Donostia-San Sebastián 19 A5
San Severo 20 D5
San Valentin, Mte. 95 F2
Sana' 49 D3
Sanaga → 56 D1
Sanandaj 46 D6
Sancti Spiritus 86 B4
Sancy, Puy de 13 D5
Sandakan 38 C5
Sanday 10 B5
Sandusky 76 D4
Sandy, L. 69 C10
Sanford 83 E7
Sanford, Mt. 69 B5
Sangihe, Pulau 37 D3
Sangli 43 L9
Sangre de Cristo Mts. 80 A1
Sanikiluaq 71 D6
Sanirajak 70 C5
Sankt Gallen 13 C8
Sankt Moritz 13 C8
Sankt-Petersburg 24 B3
Sankt Pölten 15 D8
Sankuru → 56 E4

Sanliurfa 46 C4
Sanlúcar de Barrameda 18 D2
Sanmenxia 35 C6
Sant Feliu de Guíxols 19 B7
Santa Ana El Salv. 85 E7
Santa Ana U.S.A. 78 D4
Sant' Antioco 21 E2
Santa Barbara 78 D3
Santa Catarina □ 94 B7
Santa Clara 86 B4
Santa Coloma de Gramenet 19 B7
Santa Cruz Bolivia 91 G6
Santa Cruz U.S.A. 78 B1
Santa Cruz de Tenerife 52 C2
Santa Cruz Is. 64 L11
Santa Fe Argentina 94 C4
Santa Fe U.S.A. 79 C10
Santa Inés, I. 95 G2
Santa María Brazil 94 B6
Santa María U.S.A. 78 C2
Santa María → 84 A3
Santa Marta 90 A4
Santa Marta, Sierra Nevada de 90 A4
Santa Maura = Lefkada 23 E3
Santa Rosa Argentina 94 D4
Santa Rosa U.S.A. 72 G2
Santai 35 C5
Santana do Livramento 94 C5
Santander 18 A4
Santarém Brazil 92 C3
Santarém Portugal 18 C1
Santiago = Rio Grande de Santiago → 84 C3
Santiago 94 C2
Santiago de Compostela 18 A1
Santiago de Cuba 86 C4
Santiago de los Caballeros 87 C5
Santiago del Estero 94 B4
Santo Amaro 93 E6
Santo Domingo 87 C6
Santo Tomé de Guayana = Ciudad Guayana 90 B6
Santorini 23 F5
Santos 94 A7
São Bernardo do Campo 93 G4
São Borja 94 B5
São Carlos 94 A7
São Francisco → 93 E6
São João del Rei 93 G5
São João do Piauí 92 D5
São José do Rio Prêto 93 G4
São Lourenço 93 G4
São Luís 92 C5
São Marcos → 93 F4
São Marcos, B. de 92 C5
São Mateus 93 F6
São Paulo 94 A7
São Paulo □ 94 A7
São Roque, C. de 92 D6
São Tomé & Príncipe ■ 51 F4
São Vicente, C. de 18 D1
Saône → 13 D6
Sapele 53 G4
Sapporo 32 B7
Saqqez 46 C6
Sarasota 83 F6
Saratov 24 C6
Saragossa = Zaragoza 19 B5
Sarajevo 20 C7
Saransk 24 C6
Sarapul 29 D6
Sarasota 83 F6
Saratov 24 C6

Sarawak □ 39 D4
Sarda → 40 D3
Sardegna □ 21 D2
Sardinia = Sardegna □ 21 D2
Sargodha 42 C8
Sarh 55 G2
Sārī 44 B3
Sark 11 G5
Sarlat-la-Canéda 12 D4
Sarmiento 95 F3
Sarnia 71 E5
Sarre = Saar → 13 B7
Sarreguemines 13 B7
Sarthe → 12 C3
Sasebo 33 G1
Saskatchewan □ 69 C9
Saskatchewan → 69 C9
Saskatoon 69 C9
Sássari 21 D2
Sassnitz 15 A7
Satmala Hills 43 J9
Satna 40 E3
Satpura Ra. 43 J10
Satu Mare 17 E6
Saudi Arabia ■ 47 F6
Sault Ste. Marie Canada 71 E5
Sault Ste. Marie U.S.A. 76 A3
Saumur 12 C3
Saurimo 56 F4
Sava → 22 B3
Savage I. = Niue 65 L14
Savannah 83 C7
Savannah → 83 C7
Savannakhet 38 A2
Save → 59 C6
Savoie □ 13 D7
Savona 13 D8
Savoy = Savoie □ 13 D7
Sawatch Range 79 A9
Sawu 37 F2
Sawu Sea 37 F2
Saxony = Sachsen □ 15 C7
Saxony, Lower = Niedersachsen □ 14 B5
Sayan, Zapadnyy 30 D7
Saydā 46 D3
Saynshand = Buyant-Uhaa 35 B6
Sázava → 16 D2
Scandicci 20 C3
Scandinavia 8 C8
Scarborough 11 D6
Scebeli, Wabi → 49 G3
Schaffhausen 13 C8
Schefferville = Kawawachikamach 71 D7
Schelde → 14 C3
Schenectady 77 C9
Schleswig 14 A5
Schleswig-Holstein □ 14 A5
Schwäbische Alb 14 D5
Schwarzwald 14 D5
Schweiz = Switzerland ■ 13 C8
Schwerin 15 B6
Schwyz 13 C8
Scilly, Isles of 11 G3
Scotland □ 10 C4
Scottsbluff 74 E3
Scranton 77 D8
Scunthorpe 11 E6
Scutari = Shkodër 22 C2
Seattle 72 C2
Sebastopol = Sevastopol 25 E3
Sebha = Sabhā 54 C1
Şebinkarahisar 46 B4
Sebta = Ceuta 18 E3
Sedalia 75 F8
Sedan 13 B6
Segesta 21 F4

Ségou 53 F4
Segovia = Coxo → 86 D3
Segovia 18 B3
Séguéla 53 G4
Sehore 43 H10
Seine → 12 B4
Seistan = Sīstān 45 D5
Sekondi-Takoradi 53 H5
Selebi-Pikwe 59 C5
Selenga = Selenge Mörön → 35 A5
Selenge Mörön → 35 A5
Selkirk 69 C10
Selkirk Mts. 69 C8
Selvas 91 E5
Semarang 39 F4
Semey 29 D9
Semipalatinsk = Semey 29 D9
Semnān 44 C3
Sena Madureira 91 E5
Sendai Kagoshima, Japan 33 H2
Sendai Miyagi, Japan 32 D7
Senegal ■ 53 F3
Sénégal → 53 E2
Senge Khambab = Indus → 43 G5
Senhor-do-Bonfim 93 E5
Senja 8 B9
Senlis 13 B5
Sens 13 B5
Seoul 35 C7
Sept-Îles 71 D7
Sequoia △ 78 B3
Seram 37 E3
Seram Sea 37 E3
Serbia ■ 22 B3
Serdar 29 F6
Seremban 39 D2
Sergipe □ 93 E6
Sergiyev Posad 24 B4
Serifos 23 F5
Serov 28 D7
Serowe 59 C5
Serpukhov 24 C4
Serrinha 93 E6
Sète 13 E5
Sete Lagôas 93 F5
Sétif 52 A7
Settat 52 B4
Setúbal 18 C1
Setúbal, B. de 18 C1
Sevana Lich 25 E6
Sevastopol 25 E3
Severn → Canada 71 D5
Severn → U.K. 11 F5
Severnaya Zemlya 30 B7
Severodvinsk 28 C4
Sevilla 18 D2
Seward 69 B5
Seward Peninsula 69 B3
Seychelles ■ 26 J7
Seyðisfjörður 8 B3
Sfântu Gheorghe 17 F7
Sfax 54 B1
Shaanxi □ 35 C5
Shaba = Katanga □ 57 F4
Shaballe = Scebeli, Wabi → 49 G3
Shache 34 C2
Shahjahanpur 42 F11
Shakhty 25 D5
Shaki 53 G6
Shām, Bādiyat ash 47 D4
Shamo = Gobi 35 B6
Shamo, L. 55 G6
Shan □ 41 G12
Shandong □ 35 C6
Shanghai 35 C7
Shangqiu 35 C6
Shangrao 35 D6
Shangshui 35 C6
Shannon → 11 E2
Shansi = Shanxi □ 35 C6

Shantou 35 D6
Shantung = Shandong □ 35 C6
Shanxi □ 35 C6
Shaoguan 35 D6
Shaoxing 35 C7
Shaoyang 35 D6
Shaqra' 47 F6
Sharjah = Ash Shāriqah 44 E3
Sharon 76 D5
Sharya 24 B6
Shashi 35 C6
Shasta, Mt. 72 F2
Shatt al Arab 47 E7
Shawinigan 71 E6
Shebele = Scebeli, Wabi → 49 G3
Sheboygan 76 C2
Sheffield 11 E6
Shenandoah → 77 E7
Shendi 55 E5
Shensi = Shaanxi □ 35 C5
Shenyang 35 B7
Shepparton 63 C4
Sherbrooke 71 E6
Sheridan 73 D10
Sherman 81 C5
Shetland Is. 10 A6
Shibām 49 D4
Shijiazhuang 35 C6
Shikarpur 42 F6
Shikoku □ 33 G3
Shiliguri 40 D7
Shillong 41 E8
Shimla 42 D10
Shimonoseki 33 G2
Shinyanga 57 E6
Shiquan He = Indus → 43 G5
Shīrāz 44 D3
Shire → 59 B7
Shirwa, L. = Chilwa, L. 59 B7
Shivamogga 43 N9
Shivpuri 43 G10
Shizuoka 33 F6
Shkodër 22 C2
Sholapur = Solapur 43 L9
Shoshone Mts. 72 G5
Shqipëria = Albania ■ 23 D3
Shreveport 81 C7
Shrewsbury 11 E5
Shrirampur 40 F7
Shuangyashan 35 B8
Shule 34 C2
Shumagin Is. 69 C4
Shumen 22 C6
Shuqrā' 49 E4
Shwebo 41 F10
Shymkent 29 E7
Si Kiang = Xi Jiang → 35 D6
Siahan Range 42 F4
Sialkot 42 C9
Siam = Thailand ■ 38 A2
Sian = Xi'an 35 C5
Šiauliai 24 B1
Šibenik 20 C6
Siberia 30 C8
Siberut 39 E1
Sibi 42 E5
Sibiu 17 F7
Sibolga 39 D1
Sibu 39 D4
Sibuyan Sea 36 B2
Sichuan □ 34 C5
Sicilia 21 F5
Sicily = Sicilia 21 F5
Sicuani 91 F4
Sidi-bel-Abbès 52 A5
Sidon = Saydā 46 D3
Sidra, G. of = Surt, Khalīj 54 B2
Siedlce 17 B6
Siegen 14 C5

Siena 20 C3
Sierra Leone ■ 53 G3
Sierra Madre Occidental 84 B3
Sierra Nevada Spain 18 D4
Sierra Nevada U.S.A. 72 G3
Sifnos 23 F5
Sikar 42 F9
Sikasso 53 F4
Sikhote Alin, Khrebet 32 A5
Sikkim □ 40 D7
Silesia = Śląsk 16 C3
Silifke 46 C3
Siliguri = Shiliguri 40 D7
Siling Co 34 C3
Simbirsk = Ulyanovsk 24 C6
Simeulue 39 D1
Simferopol 25 E3
Simi 23 F6
Simla = Shimla 42 D10
Simpson Desert 60 F6
Simpson Pen. 70 C5
Sinai = Es Sînâ' 54 C5
Sinai, Mt. = Mûsa, Gebel 47 E3
Sincelejo 90 B3
Sind = Sindh □ 42 F6
Sind Sagar Doab 42 D7
Sindh □ 42 F6
Sines 18 D1
Singapore ■ 39 D2
Singaraja 39 F5
Singida 57 E6
Singkawang 39 D3
Singora = Songkhla 38 C2
Sinkiang = Xinjiang Uygur Zizhiqu □ 34 B3
Sinop 25 E4
Sintra 18 C1
Sioux City 75 D6
Sioux Falls 74 D6
Sioux Lookout 69 C10
Siping 35 B7
Siracusa 21 F5
Sirajganj 41 E7
Sīrjān 44 D3
Siros = Syros 23 F5
Sirsa 42 E9
Sīstān 45 D5
Sīstān, Daryācheh-ye 45 D5
Sitapur 40 D3
Sitges 19 B6
Sitka 69 C6
Sittwe 41 G9
Sivas 25 F4
Sivrihisar 25 F3
Sīwa 54 C4
Siwalik Range 40 D4
Siwan 40 D5
Sjælland 9 D8
Sjumen = Shumen 22 C6
Skagerrak 9 D7
Skagway 69 C6
Skeena → 68 C6
Skegness 11 E7
Skeleton Coast 58 C2
Skellefteå 8 C10
Skellefteälven → 8 C10
Skiathos 23 E4
Skien 9 D7
Skikda 52 A7
Skiros 23 E5
Skopelos 23 E4
Skopje 22 C3
Skye 10 C3
Skyros = Skiros 23 E5
Śląsk 16 C3
Slatina 22 B5
Slave → 68 B8
Slavyansk = Slovyansk 25 D4
Sleeper Is. 70 D5

Sligeach = Sligo 11 D2
Sligo 11 D2
Sliven 22 C6
Slough 11 F6
Slovak Rep. ■ 16 D4
Slovakian Ore Mts. = Slovenské Rudohorie 16 D4
Slovenia ■ 20 B5
Slovenska = Slovak Rep. ■ 16 D4
Slovenské Rudohorie 16 D4
Slovyansk 25 D4
Słupsk 16 A3
Slutsk 17 B8
Smallwood Res. 71 D7
Smederevo 22 B3
Smolensk 24 C3
Smyrna = İzmir 23 E6
Snake → 72 C4
Snake River Plain 73 E7
Snøhetta 8 C7
Snowdon 11 E4
Snowdrift = Łutselk'e 68 B8
Snowy → 63 C4
Snowy Mts. 63 C4
Sobat, Nahr → 55 G5
Sobral 92 C5
Soc Trang 38 C3
Sochi 25 E4
Soch'e = Shache 34 C2
Société, Îs. de la 65 L15
Society Is. = Société, Îs. de la 65 L15
Socotra 49 E5
Söderhamn 8 C9
Sofia = Sofiya 22 C4
Sofiya 22 C4
Sognefjorden 8 C7
Sohâg 54 C5
Soissons 13 B5
Sokhumi 25 E5
Sokodé 53 G6
Sokoto 53 F7
Solapur 43 L9
Solikamsk 28 D6
Solimões = Amazonas → 92 C3
Solingen 14 C4
Sóller 19 C7
Sologne 12 C4
Solomon Is. ■ 64 K10
Solomon Sea 61 B9
Solon 35 B7
Somalia ■ 49 F4
Somaliland □ 49 E4
Sombrerete 84 C4
Somerset I. 68 A10
Somme → 12 A4
Songhua Jiang → 35 B8
Songkhla 38 C2
Songpan 34 C5
Sonora → 84 B2
Sonsonate 85 E7
Soochow = Suzhou 35 C7
Soomaaliya = Somali Rep. ■ 49 F4
Sopot 16 A4
Sorel-Tracy 71 E6
Soria 19 B4
Sorocaba 94 A7
Sørøya 8 A10
Sosnowiec 16 C4
Sŏul = Seoul 35 C7
Souris → 69 D10
Sousse 54 A1
South Africa ■ 58 E4
South Australia □ 62 B2
South Bend 76 D2
South Carolina □ 83 C7
South China Sea 38 C4
South Dakota □ 74 C4
South East C. 62 D4
South I. 65 E3
South Korea ■ 35 C7

South Magnetic Pole 96 A13
South Nahanni → 68 B7
South Orkney Is. 96 A4
South Platte → 74 E4
South Pole 96 C
South Ronaldsay 10 B5
South Saskatchewan → 69 C9
South Shetland Is. 96 A4
South Shields 11 D6
South Sudan ■ 55 G4
South Uist 10 C3
Southampton 11 F6
Southampton I. 70 C5
Southend-on-Sea 11 F7
Southern Alps 65 E4
Southern Indian L. 69 C10
Southern Ocean 96 A9
Southern Uplands 10 D5
Sovetsk 24 B1
Soweto 59 D5
Spain ■ 18 C4
Spanish Town 86 C4
Sparta = Sparti 23 F4
Spartanburg 83 B7
Sparti 23 F4
Spartivento, C. 21 F6
Spence Bay = Taloyoak 68 B10
Spencer G. 62 B2
Spey → 10 C5
Split 20 C6
Spokane 72 C5
Spratly Is. 38 C4
Spree → 15 B7
Springs 59 D5
Srbija = Serbia ■ 22 B3
Srebrenica 20 B7
Sredinnyy Khrebet 31 D14
Sri Lanka ■ 43 R12
Srikakulam 40 H4
Srinagar 42 B9
Stafford 11 E5
Stakhanov 25 D4
Stamford 77 D9
Stanley 95 G5
Stanovoy Khrebet 31 D10
Stara Planina 22 C4
Stara Zagora 22 C5
Staraya Russa 24 B3
Starbuck I. 65 K15
Staryy Oskol 24 C4
State College 77 D7
Staten, I. = Estados, I. de Los 95 G4
Stavanger 9 D7
Stavropol 25 D5
Stefanie L. = Chew Bahir 55 H6
Steiermark □ 15 E8
Steinkjer 8 C8
Steornabhagh = Stornoway 10 B3
Stepanakert = Xankändi 25 F6
Stephenville 71 E8
Sterlitamak 29 D6
Stettin = Szczecin 16 B2
Stettiner Haff 15 B8
Stettler 69 C8
Steubenville 76 D5
Stevenage 11 F6
Stewart → 68 B6
Stewart I. 65 G2
Steyr 15 D8

Stillwater 80 A5
Stirling 10 C5
Stockerau 16 D9
Stockport 11 E5
Stockton 88 B2
Stockton-on-Tees 11 D6
Stoke-on-Trent 11 E5
Stonehaven 10 C5
Stony Tunguska = Tunguska, Podkamennaya → 30 C7
Stora Lulevatten 8 B9
Storavan 8 B9
Store Bælt 9 D8
Stormberge 59 E5
Stornoway 10 B3
Storsjön 8 C8
Storuman 8 B9
Stralsund 15 A7
Stranraer 11 D4
Strasbourg 13 B7
Stratford 76 C5
Strómboli 21 E5
Stronsay 10 B5
Stuttgart 14 D5
Styria = Steiermark □ 15 E8
Suakin 55 E6
Subotica 16 E8
Suceava 17 E8
Suchou = Suzhou 35 C7
Süchow = Xuzhou 35 C6
Sucre 91 G5
Sudan ■ 55 E4
Sudbury 71 E5
Sudd 55 G4
Sudeten Mts. = Sudety 16 C3
Sudety 16 C3
Suez = El Suweis 54 C5
Suez, G. of = Suweis, Khalîg el 54 C5
Sugluk = Salluit 70 C6
Şuhār 44 E4
Suihua 35 B7
Sukhona → 28 C5
Sukhumi = Sokhumi 25 E5
Sukkur 42 F6
Sulaiman Range 42 D6
Sulawesi 37 E2
Sulawesi Sea = Celebes Sea 37 D2
Sullana 90 D2
Sulu Arch. 36 C2
Sulu Sea 36 C2
Sumatera 39 D2
Sumatra = Sumatera 39 D2
Sumba 37 F1
Sumbawa 39 F5
Sumen = Shumen 22 C6
Sumgait = Sumqayit 25 E6
Summerside 71 E7
Sumqayit 25 E6
Sumter 83 C7
Sumy 24 C3
Sunda, Selat 39 F3
Sunda Str. = Sunda, Selat 39 F3
Sundarbans 41 G7
Sunderland 11 D6
Sundsvall 8 C9
Sungaipenuh 39 E2
Sungari = Songhua Jiang → 35 B8
Suomi = Finland ■ 8 C11
Superior 75 B8
Superior, L. 71 E5
Suquţra = Socotra 49 E5
Sūr 46 D3
Sura → 24 B6
Surabaya 39 F4
Surakarta 39 F4

Surat 43 J8
Surgut 29 C8
Surigao 36 C3
Suriname ■ 92 B2
Surt 54 B2
Surt, Khalîj 54 B2
Surtsey 8 C1
Susquehanna → 77 E7
Sutherland Falls 65 F2
Sutlej → 42 E7
Suva 64 L12
Suvorov Is. = Suwarrow Is. 65 L14
Suwałki 17 A6
Suwarrow Is. 65 L14
Suweis, Khalîg el 54 C5
Suzhou 35 C7
Svealand □ 9 D9
Sverdrup Chan. 70 B4
Sverdrup I. 70 B4
Sverige = Sweden ■ 9 D9
Svizzera = Switzerland ■ 13 C8
Swabian Alps = Schwäbische Alb 14 D5
Swakopmund 58 C2
Swan Hill 62 C3
Swansea 11 F5
Swatow = Shantou 35 D6
Swaziland ■ 59 D6
Sweden ■ 9 D9
Sweetwater 80 C3
Swellendam 58 E4
Swift Current 69 C9
Swindon 11 F6
Switzerland ■ 13 C8
Sydney Australia 63 B5
Sydney Canada 71 E7
Sydra, G. of = Surt, Khalîj 54 B2
Syktyvkar 28 C6
Sylhet 41 E8
Syracuse 77 C7
Syrdarya → 29 E7
Syria ■ 46 D4
Syrian Desert = Shām, Bādiyat ash 47 D4
Syros 23 F5
Syzran 24 C6
Szczecin 16 B2
Szczeciński, Zalew = Stettiner Haff 15 B8
Szechwan = Sichuan □ 34 C5
Szeged 16 E5
Székesfehérvár 16 E4
Szekszárd 16 E4
Szolnok 16 E5
Szombathely 16 E3

T

Tabas 44 C4
Tablas 36 B2
Table B. 58 E3
Table Mt. 58 E3
Tabora 57 F6
Tabrīz 46 C6
Tacheng 34 B3
Tacloban 36 B2
Tacna 91 G4
Tacoma 72 C2
Tacuarembó 94 C5
Tademaït, Plateau du 52 C6
Tadzhikistan = Tajikistan ■ 29 F8
Taegu = Daegu 35 C7
Taejŏn = Daejeon 35 C7
Tafelbaai = Table B. 58 E3
Taganrog 25 D4
Taguatinga 93 E5
Tagus = Tejo → 18 C1
Tahiti 65 L16

Tahoe, L. 72 G3
Tahoua 53 F7
Tahta 54 C5
Taibei = T'aipei 35 D7
T'aichung 35 D7
Taimyr Peninsula = Taymyr, Poluostrov 30 B7
Tain 10 C4
T'ainan 35 D7
T'aipei 35 D7
Taiping 38 D2
Taitao, Pen. de 95 F1
Taiwan ■ 35 D7
Taiyuan 35 C6
Taizhong = T'aichung 35 D7
Ta'izz 49 E3
Tajikistan ■ 29 F8
Tajo = Tejo → 18 C1
Tak 38 A1
Takamatsu 33 F4
Takaoka 33 E5
Takapuna 64 B6
Takasaki 33 E6
Takeshima = Liancourt Rocks 33 E2
Takhār □ 45 B7
Takla Makan 34 C3
Taklamakan Shamo = Takla Makan 34 C3
Talara 90 D2
Talaud, Kepulauan 36 D3
Talavera de la Reina 18 C3
Talca 94 D2
Talcahuano 94 D2
Taldyqorghan 29 E8
Tallahassee 83 D5
Tallinn 24 B1
Taloyoak 68 B10
Taltal 94 B2
Tamale 53 G5
Tamanrasset 52 D7
Tamatave = Toamasina 59 B9
Tambov 24 C5
Tamil Nadu □ 43 P10
Tammerfors = Tampere 8 C10
Tampa 83 F6
Tampere 8 C10
Tampico 84 C5
Tamworth 63 B5
Tana → Kenya 57 E8
Tana → Norway 8 A11
Tana, L. 55 F6
Tanami Desert 60 D5
Tananarive = Antananarivo 59 B9
Tandil 94 D5
Tanen Tong Dan = Dawna Ra. 41 J12
Tanezrouft 52 D6
Tanga 57 F7
Tanganyika, L. 57 F5
Tanger 52 A4
Tanggula Shan 34 C4
Tanghla Range = Tanggula Shan 34 C4
Tangier = Tanger 52 A4
Tangshan 35 C6
Tanimbar, Kepulauan 37 F4
Tanjore = Thanjavur 43 P11
Tanjungbalai 39 D1
Tanjungkarang Telukbetung = Bandar Lampung 39 F3
Tanjungpandan 39 E3
Tanjungredeb 39 D5
Tanta 54 B5
Tantung = Dandong 35 B7
Tanzania ■ 57 F6
Taolanaro 59 D9

Tapa Shan = Daba Shan 35 C5
Tapajós → 92 C3
Tapti → 43 J8
Tarābulus *Lebanon* 46 D3
Tarābulus *Libya* 54 B1
Tarakan 39 D5
Taranaki □ 64 C6
Taranaki, Mt. 64 C6
Táranto 21 D6
Táranto, G. di 21 D6
Tarawa 64 J12
Taraz 29 E8
Tarbagatay, Khrebet 29 E9
Tarbes 12 E4
Tarcoola 62 B1
Taree 63 B5
Tarfaya 52 C2
Târgoviște 22 B5
Târgu Jiu 17 F6
Târgu Mureș 17 E7
Tarija 94 A3
Tarim Basin = Tarim Pendi 34 C3
Tarim He → 34 C3
Tarim Pendi 34 C3
Tarn → 12 D4
Tarnów 16 C5
Taroudannt 52 B4
Tarragona 19 B6
Tarrasa = Terrassa 19 B7
Tarsus 46 C3
Tartu 24 B2
Țarțūs 46 D3
Tashauz = Daşoguz 29 E6
Tashi Chho Dzong = Thimphu 41 D7
Tashkent = Toshkent 29 E7
Tasman Mts. 65 D5
Tasmania □ 62 D4
Tatarstan □ 29 D6
Tatnam, C. 71 D4
Tatra = Tatry 16 D4
Tatry 16 D4
Tatta 43 G5
Tat'ung = Datong 35 B6
Tatvan 46 C5
Taubaté 94 A7
Tauern 15 E7
Taunggyi 41 G11
Taunton 11 F5
Taupo, L. 64 C6
Taurus Mts. = Toros Dağları 46 C3
Tavastehus = Hämeenlinna 8 C10
Tawau 38 D5
Tay → 10 C5
Taymyr, Oz. 30 B8
Taymyr, Poluostrov 30 B7
Taz → 28 C8
Taza 52 B5
Tbilisi 25 E5
Tchad = Chad ■ 55 E2
Tchad, L. 55 F1
Te Ika a Maui = North I. 64 B5
Te Wai Pounamu = South I. 65 E3
Tébessa 52 A7
Tedzhen = Tejen 29 F7
Tegal 39 F3
Tegucigalpa 85 E7
Teheran = Tehrān 44 C2
Tehrān 44 C2
Tehuantepec 85 D5
Tehuantepec, G. de 85 D5
Tehuantepec, Istmo de 85 D6
Tejen 29 F7
Tejo → 18 C1
Tekirdağ 22 D6
Tel Aviv-Yafo 46 D3

Tela 85 D7
Telanaipura = Jambi 39 E2
Telangana □ 40 J2
Teles Pires → 91 E7
Telford 11 E5
Tellicherry 43 P9
Teluk Anson = Teluk Intan 39 D2
Teluk Betung = Bandar Lampung 39 F3
Teluk Intan 39 D2
Tema 53 H5
Tempe 79 D7
Temple 80 D5
Temuco 94 D2
Tenali 40 J3
Tenerife 52 C2
Tengchong 34 D4
Tennessee □ 82 B4
Tennessee → 76 F1
Teófilo Otoni 93 F5
Tepic 84 C4
Téramo 20 C4
Teresina 92 D5
Termiz 29 F7
Ternate 39 D3
Terni 20 C4
Ternopil 17 D7
Terrassa 19 B7
Terre Haute 76 E2
Teruel 19 B5
Tesiyn Gol → 34 A4
Teslin 68 B6
Tete 59 B6
Tétouan 52 A4
Tetovo 22 C3
Teuco → 94 B4
Teutoburger Wald 14 B5
Tevere → 20 D4
Texarkana 81 C6
Texas □ 80 D4
Texel 14 B5
Tezpur 41 D9
Thabana Ntlenyana 59 D5
Thabazimbi 59 C5
Thailand ■ 38 A2
Thailand, G. of 38 B2
Thala La = Hkakabo Razi 41 C11
Thames → 11 F7
Thane 43 K8
Thanh Pho Ho Chi Minh 38 B3
Thanjavur 43 P11
Thar Desert 42 F7
Thargomindah 63 A3
Thasos 23 D5
The Bahamas ■ 86 A4
The Gambia ■ 53 F2
The Gulf = Persian Gulf 44 E2
The Hague = 's-Gravenhage 14 B3
The Pas 69 C9
The Wash 11 E7
Thermopylae 23 E4
Thessaloniki 23 D4
Thetford 11 E7
Thetford Mines 71 E6
Thiers 12 D5
Thiès 53 F2
Thika 57 E7
Thimphu 41 D7
Thionville 13 B7
Thira = Santorini 23 F5
Thiruvananthapuram 43 Q10
Thomasville 83 D6
Thompson 69 C10
Thrace 22 D6
Thunder Bay 71 E5
Thüringer Wald 14 C6
Thurles 11 E3
Thurso 10 B5
Thurston I. 96 B2
Tian Shan 34 B3

Tianjin 35 C6
Tianshui 35 C5
Tiaret 52 A6
Tiber = Tevere → 20 D4
Tiberias, L. = Yam Kinneret 46 D3
Tibesti 54 D2
Tibet = Xizang Zizhiqu □ 34 C3
Tiburón, I. 84 B2
Ticino → 13 D8
Tien Shan = Tian Shan 34 B3
Tientsin = Tianjin 35 C6
Tierra de Campos 18 A3
Tierra del Fuego, I. Gr. de 95 G3
Tighina 17 E9
Tigris = Dijlah, Nahr → 47 E6
Tijuana 84 A1
Tikhoretsk 25 D5
Tikiraqjuaq = Whale Cove 68 B10
Tikrit 46 D5
Tiksi 30 B10
Tilburg 14 C3
Timaru 65 F4
Timbuktu = Tombouctou 53 E5
Timișoara 16 F5
Timmins 71 E5
Timor 37 F2
Timor Leste = East Timor ■ 37 F3
Tinnevelly = Tirunelveli 43 Q10
Tinogasta 94 B3
Tinos 23 F5
Tipperary 11 E2
Tīranë 22 D2
Tiraspol 17 E9
Tirebolu 25 E4
Tiree 10 C3
Tîrgoviște = Târgoviște 22 B5
Tîrgu Jiu = Târgu Jiu 17 F6
Tîrgu Mureș = Târgu Mureș 17 E7
Tirich Mir 42 A7
Tiritiri o te Moana = Southern Alps 65 E4
Tirol □ 14 E6
Tiruchchirappalli 43 P11
Tirunelveli 43 Q10
Tiruppur 43 P10
Tisa → 22 B3
Tisdale 69 C9
Tisza = Tisa → 22 B3
Titicaca, L. 91 G5
Tivoli 20 D4
Tizi-Ouzou 52 A6
Tjirebon = Cirebon 39 F3
Tlaxiaco 84 D5
Tlemcen 52 B5
Toamasina 59 B9
Toba Kakar 42 D6
Tobago 87 D7
Tobermory 10 C3
Tobruk = Tubruq 54 B3
Tocantins □ 93 E4
Tocantins → 92 C4
Todos os Santos, B. de 93 E6
Togliatti 24 C6
Togo ■ 53 G6
Tojikiston = Tajikistan ■ 29 F8
Tokat 46 B4
Tokelau Is. ☑ 65 K13
Tokushima 33 F4
Tokuyama 33 F2
Tōkyō 33 F6
Tolbukhin = Dobrich 22 C6
Toledo *Spain* 18 C3
Toledo *U.S.A.* 76 D4

Toledo, Montes de 18 C3
Toliara 59 C8
Tolima 90 C3
Toluca 84 D5
Tomakomai 32 B7
Tomaszów Mazowiecki 16 C4
Tombouctou 53 E5
Tomini, Teluk 37 E2
Tomsk 29 D9
Tonga ■ 65 L13
Tonga Trench 65 L13
Tongareva = Penrhyn 65 K15
Tongchuan 35 C5
Tonghua 35 B7
Tongking, G. of = Tonkin, G. of 35 D5
Tongue → 74 B2
Tonk 42 F9
Tonkin, G. of 35 D5
Tonle Sap 38 B2
Toowoomba 63 A5
Topeka 75 F7
Topolobampo 84 B3
Torbay □ 11 F5
Torino 13 D7
Torneå = Tornio 8 E12
Torneälven → 8 B10
Torneträsk 8 B9
Tornio 8 E12
Tornionjoki = Torneälven → 8 B10
Toro, Cerro del 94 B3
Toronto 71 E6
Toros Dağları 46 C3
Torre del Greco 21 D5
Torrejón de Ardoz 18 B4
Torrelavega 18 A3
Torremolinos 18 D3
Torrens, L. 62 B2
Torrent 19 C5
Torreón 84 B4
Tórshavn 8 E20
Toruń 16 B4
Toscana □ 20 C3
Toshkent 29 E7
Tottori 33 F4
Toubkal, Djebel 52 B4
Tougourt 52 B7
Toul 13 B6
Toulon 13 E6
Toulouse 12 E4
Touraine 12 C4
Tournai 14 C2
Tournon-sur-Rhône 13 D6
Tours 12 C4
Townsville 61 D8
Toyama 33 E5
Toyohashi 33 F5
Toyota 33 F5
Trá Li = Tralee 11 E2
Trabzon 25 E4
Trafalgar, C. 18 D2
Trail 69 D8
Tralee 11 E2
Trang 38 C1
Transantarctic Mts. 96 C3
Transilvania 17 F7
Transilvanian Alps = Carpații Meridionali 17 F7
Transnistria □ 17 E9
Trápani 21 E4
Trasimeno, L. 20 C4
Treinta y Tres 94 C6
Trelew 95 E3
Trent → 11 E6
Trento 20 A3
Trenton 77 D8
Tres Arroyos 94 D4
Três Lagoas 93 G3
Tres Puntas, C. 95 F3
Três Ríos 93 G5
Treviso 20 B4
Tribal Areas □ 45 C7

Trichinopoly = Tiruchchirappalli 43 P11
Trichur 43 P10
Trier 14 D4
Trieste 20 B4
Trinidad *Bolivia* 91 F6
Trinidad *Cuba* 86 B3
Trinidad *U.S.A.* 80 A1
Trinidad & Tobago ■ 87 D7
Trinity → 81 E6
Trinity B. 71 E8
Tripoli = Tarābulus *Lebanon* 46 D3
Tripoli = Tarābulus *Libya* 54 B1
Tripura □ 41 F8
Trivandrum = Thiruvananthapuram 43 Q10
Trois-Rivières 71 E6
Trollhättan 9 D8
Tromsø 8 B9
Tronador, Mte. 95 E2
Trondheim 8 C8
Trondheimsfjorden 8 C8
Trout L. 68 B7
Troy *Turkey* 23 E6
Troy *Ala., U.S.A.* 82 D5
Troy *N.Y., U.S.A.* 77 C9
Troyes 13 B6
Trujillo *Honduras* 85 D7
Trujillo *Peru* 91 E3
Trujillo *Venezuela* 90 B4
Truk 64 J10
Truro *Canada* 71 E7
Truro *U.K.* 11 F4
Tsetserleg 34 B5
Tshikapa 56 F4
Tshwane = Pretoria 59 D5
Tsiigehtchic 68 B6
Tsimlyanskoye Vdkhr. 25 D5
Tsinan = Jinan 35 C6
Tsinghai = Qinghai □ 34 C4
Tsingtao = Qingdao 35 C7
Tsirigo = Kythira 23 F4
Tskhinvali 25 E5
Tsuchiura 33 E7
Tsugaru Str. 32 C7
Tsumeb 58 B3
Tsuruoka 32 D6
Tsushima 33 F1
Tuamotu, Is. 65 L16
Tuamotu Ridge 65 M17
Tuapse 25 E4
Tubarão 94 B7
Tübingen 14 D5
Tubruq 54 B3
Tubuai, Is. 65 M16
Tucson 79 D7
Tucumcari 80 B2
Tucupita 90 B6
Tucuruí 92 C4
Tucuruí, Reprêsa de 92 C4
Tudmur 46 D4
Tuguegarao 36 A2
Tuktoyaktuk 68 B6
Tula 24 C4
Tulare 78 B3
Tulcán 90 C3
Tulcea 17 F9
Tulita 68 B7
Tullamore 11 E3
Tulle 12 D4
Tulsa 81 A6
Tumaco 90 C3
Tumbes 90 D2
Tumucumaque, Serra 92 B3
Tunguska, Nizhnyaya → 30 C6

Tunguska,
  Podkamennaya ➔
  30 C7
Tunis 50 A1
Tunisia ■ 50 B1
Tunja 90 B4
Tupelo 82 B3
Tupiza 94 A3
Turfan = Turpan 34 B3
Turfan Basin = Turpan
  Pendi 34 B3
Turgutlu 23 E6
Turin = Torino 13 D7
Turkana, L. 57 D7
Turkestan = Türkistan
  29 E7
Turkey ■ 25 F4
Türkistan 29 E7
Türkmenabat 29 F7
Türkmenbashi 29 E6
Turkmenistan ■ 29 F6
Turks & Caicos Is. ☑
  87 B5
Turku 9 C10
Turneffe Is. 85 D7
Túrnovo = Veliko Tŭrnovo
  22 C5
Turpan 34 B3
Turpan Pendi 34 B3
Tuscaloosa 82 C4
Tuscany = Toscana □
  20 C3
Tuticorin 43 Q11
Tutuila 65 L13
Tutume 59 C5
Tuvalu ■ 64 K12
Tuxpan 84 C5
Tuxtla Gutiérrez 85 D6
Tuz Gölü 46 C3
Tuzla 20 B7
Tver 24 B4
Twin Falls 73 E6
Tychy 16 C4
Tyler 81 C6
Tyre = Sūr 46 D3
Tyrol = Tirol □ 14 E6
Tyrrhenian Sea 21 E4
Tyumen 29 D7
Tzaneen 59 C6
Tzukong = Zigong 35 D5

U

U.S.A. = United States of
  America ■ 67 F10
Uaupés ➔ 90 C5
Ubá 93 G5
Ubaitaba 93 E6
Ubangi = Oubangi ➔
  56 E3
Ube 33 G2
Uberaba 93 F4
Uberlândia 93 F4
Ubon Ratchathani 38 A2
Ucayali ➔ 90 D4
Udagamandalam 43 P10
Udaipur 43 G8
Údine 20 A4
Udmurtia □ 28 D6
Udon Thani 38 A2
Udupi 43 N9
Uele ➔ 57 D4
Ufa 29 D6
Uganda ■ 57 D6
Uíbhist a Deas = South
  Uist 10 C3
Uíbhist a Tuath = North
  Uist 10 C3
Uinta Mts. 73 F8
Uitenhage 59 E5
Ujjain 43 H9
Ujung Pandang =
  Makassar 37 F1
Ukhta 28 C6
Ukraine ■ 25 D3
Ulaanbaatar 35 B5

Ulaangom 34 A4
Ulaanjirem 35 B5
Ulan Bator = Ulaanbaatar
  35 B5
Ulan Ude 30 D8
Ule älv = Oulujoki ➔
  8 C11
Uleåborg = Oulu 8 B11
Ulhasnagar 43 K8
Uliastay 34 B4
Ullapool 10 C4
Ulleungdo 33 E2
Ulm 14 D5
Ulster □ 11 D3
Ulungur He ➔ 34 B3
Uluru 60 F5
Ulyanovsk 24 C6
Ulyasutay = Uliastay
  34 B4
'Umān = Oman ■ 48 C6
Uman 17 D10
Umeå 8 C10
Umeälven ➔ 8 C10
Umlazi 59 E6
Umm al Qaywayn 44 E3
Umm Durman =
  Omdurman 55 E5
Umnak I. 69 C3
Umtata = Mthatha 59 E5
Umuarama 93 G3
Unalaska 69 C3
Uncía 91 G5
Ungava, Pén. d' 70 C6
Ungava B. 70 D7
Unimak I. 69 C3
United Arab Emirates ■
  44 F3
United Kingdom ■ 11 D5
United States of
  America ■ 67 F10
Unst 10 A6
Upington 58 D4
Uppsala 9 D9
Uqsuqtuuq = Gjoa Haven
  68 B10
Ur 47 E6
Ural = Zhayyq ➔ 29 E6
Ural Mts. = Uralskie Gory
  28 D6
Uralsk = Oral 24 C7
Uralskie Gory 28 D6
Urania 76 D1
Urfa = Şanlıurfa 46 C4
Urganch 29 E7
Urmia = Orūmīyeh 46 C6
Uruapan 84 D4
Uruguai ➔ 94 B6
Uruguaiana 94 B5
Uruguay ■ 94 C5
Uruguay ➔ 94 C5
Ürümqi 29 E9
Usakos 58 C3
Usedom 15 B8
Ushant = Ouessant, Î. d'
  12 B1
Ushuaia 95 G3
Uspallata, P. de 94 C3
Ussuriysk 32 B2
Ust-Kamenogorsk =
  Öskemen 29 E9
Ust-Urt = Ustyurt Plateau
  29 E6
Ústí nad Labem 16 C2
Ústica 21 E4
Ustinov = Izhevsk 28 D6
Ustyurt Plateau 29 E6
Usu 34 B3
Usumacinta ➔ 85 D6
Usumbura = Bujumbura
  57 E5
Utah □ 73 G8
Utica 77 C8
Utrecht 14 B3
Utsunomiya 33 E6
Uttar Pradesh □ 42 F11

Uttaradit 38 A2
Uttarakhand □ 40 B2
Uusikaupunki 9 C10
Uvira 57 E5
Uvs Nuur 34 A4
Uyuni 91 H5
Uzbekistan ■ 29 E7
Uzhgorod = Uzhhorod
  17 D6
Uzhhorod 17 D6

V

Vaal ➔ 58 D4
Vaasa 8 C10
Vadodara 43 H8
Vadsø 8 D13
Vaduz 13 C8
Váhtjer = Gällivare 8 B10
Valahia 22 B5
Valai Hills = Valdayskaya
  Vozvyshennost 24 B3
Valdayskaya
  Vozvyshennost 24 B3
Valdés, Pen. 95 E4
Valdez 69 B5
Valdivia 95 D2
Valdosta 83 D6
Valença 93 E6
Valence 13 D6
Valencia Spain 19 C5
Valencia Venezuela 90 A5
Valencia □ 19 C5
Valencia, G. de 19 C6
Valencia I. 11 F1
Valenciennes 13 A5
Valera 90 B4
Valladolid Mexico 85 C7
Valladolid Spain 18 B3
Valledupar 90 A4
Vallejo 72 G2
Vallenar 94 B2
Valletta 21 G5
Valona = Vlorë 23 D2
Valparaíso 94 C2
Van 46 C5
Van, L. = Van Gölü 46 C5
Van Gölü 46 C5
Vanadzor 25 E5
Vancouver Canada 69 D7
Vancouver U.S.A. 72 D2
Vancouver I. 69 D7
Vänern 9 D8
Vännäs 8 C9
Vannes 12 C2
Vanrhynsdorp 58 E3
Vanua Levu 64 L12
Vanuatu ■ 64 L11
Varanasi 40 E4
Varangerfjorden 8 A11
Varberg 9 D8
Vardak □ 45 C7
Vardar = Axios ➔ 23 D4
Varese 13 D8
Varna 22 C6
Vasa = Vaasa 8 C10
Vasa Barris ➔ 93 E6
Vascongadas = País
  Vasco □ 19 A4
Västerås 9 D9
Västervik 9 D9
Vatican City ■ 20 D4
Vatnajökull 8 C2
Vättern 9 D8
Vaupés = Uaupés ➔
  90 C5
Vega 8 B8
Vegreville 69 C8
Vélez-Málaga 18 D3
Velhas ➔ 93 F5
Velikiye Luki 24 B3
Velikonda Range 43 M11
Vellore 43 N11
Vendée □ 12 C3

Vendôme 12 C4
Venézia 20 B4
Venézia, G. di 20 B4
Venezuela ■ 90 B5
Venezuela, G. de 90 A4
Vengurla 43 M8
Venice = Venézia 20 B4
Ventspils 24 B1
Veracruz 84 D5
Veraval 43 J7
Vercelli 13 D8
Verdun 13 B6
Vereeniging 59 D5
Verkhoyansk 31 C11
Verkhoyanskiy Khrebet
  31 C10
Vermont □ 77 C9
Vernon Canada 69 C8
Vernon U.S.A. 80 B4
Verona 20 B3
Versailles 12 B5
Verviers 14 C3
Vesoul 13 C7
Vesterålen 8 B9
Vestfjorden 8 B8
Vesuvio 21 D5
Vesuvius, Mt. = Vesuvio
  21 D5
Veszprém 16 E3
Viangchan = Vientiane
  38 A2
Vianópolis 93 F4
Viaréggio 20 B3
Vicenza 20 B3
Vichy 13 C5
Vicksburg 81 C8
Victoria □ 62 C3
Victoria, L. 57 E6
Victoria de Durango =
  Durango 84 C4
Victoria Falls 59 B5
Victoria Ld. 96 B14
Vidin 22 C4
Viedma, L. 95 F2
Vienna = Wien 15 D9
Vienne 13 C6
Vienne ➔ 12 C4
Vientiane 38 A2
Vierzon 12 C5
Vietnam ■ 38 A3
Vigévano 13 D8
Vigo 18 A1
Vijayawada 40 J3
Vikna 8 C8
Vila Nova de Gaia 18 B1
Vila Velha 93 G5
Vilaine ➔ 12 C2
Vilhelmina 8 C9
Vilhena 91 F6
Vilkitskogo, Proliv 30 B8
Villa Bella 91 F5
Villa Maria 94 C4
Villach 15 E7
Villahermosa 85 D6
Villajoyosa 19 C5
Villarrica 94 B5
Villavicencio 90 C4
Villeneuve-sur-Lot 12 D4
Vilnius 24 C2
Vilyuy ➔ 31 C10
Vilyuysk 31 C10
Viña del Mar 94 C2
Vindhya Ra. 43 H10
Vineland 77 E8
Vinnitsa = Vinnytsya
  17 D9
Vinnytsya 17 D9
Virden 69 D9
Vire 12 B3
Vírgenes, C. 95 G3
Virgin Is. 87 C7
Virginia 59 D5
Virginia □ 77 F6

Virginia Beach 77 F8
Vis 20 C6
Visalia 78 B3
Visby 9 D9
Viscount Melville Sd.
  70 B3
Vishakhapatnam 40 J4
Vistula = Wisła ➔ 16 A4
Vitebsk = Vitsyebsk
  24 B3
Viterbo 20 C4
Viti Levu 64 L12
Vitória 93 G5
Vitória da Conquista
  93 E5
Vitoria-Gasteiz 19 A4
Vitsyebsk 24 B3
Vittória 21 F5
Vizianagaram 40 H4
Vladikavkaz 25 E5
Vladimir 24 B5
Vladivostok 32 B2
Vlissingen 14 C2
Vlorë 23 D2
Vltava ➔ 16 C2
Vogelkop = Doberai,
  Jazirah 37 E8
Vogelsberg 14 C5
Vohimena, Tanjon' i
  59 D9
Voi 57 E7
Vojvodina □ 22 B2
Volga ➔ 25 D6
Volga Hts. =
  Privolzhskaya
  Vozvyshennost 24 C6
Volgodonsk 25 D5
Volgograd 25 D5
Volgogradskoye Vdkhr.
  24 C6
Vologda 24 B4
Volos 23 E4
Volsk 24 C6
Volta, L. 53 G6
Volta Redonda 93 G5
Volzhskiy 25 D5
Vorkuta 28 C7
Voronezh 24 C4
Vosges 13 B7
Vostok I. 65 L15
Vrangelya, Ostrov 31 B15
Vratsa 22 C4
Vryburg 58 D4
Vryheid 59 D6
Vulcano 21 E5
Vung Tau 38 B3
Vyatka = Kirov 28 D5
Vyazma 24 B3
Vyborg 28 C3
Vychegda ➔ 28 C5
Východné Beskydy 17 D5
Vyshniy Volochek 24 B3

W

Waal ➔ 14 C3
Wabash ➔ 76 F1
Waco 80 D5
Wad Medanî 55 F5
Waddington, Mt. 69 C7
Wadi Halfa 54 D5
Wager B. 70 C5
Wagga Wagga 63 C4
Wah 42 C8
Waigeo 37 E4
Wakayama 33 F4
Wakkanai 32 A7
Wałbrzych 16 C3
Wales □ 11 E4
Walgett 63 A4
Walla Walla 72 C4
Wallachia = Valahia
  22 B5
Wallis & Futuna, Is. ☑
  64 L13
Walvis Bay 58 C2
Wamba 57 D5

Wanganui 64 C6
Warangal 43 L11
Wardha 43 J11
Warrego ➤ 63 B4
Warren 76 C4
Warri 53 G7
Warrington 11 E5
Warrnambool 62 C3
Warsaw = Warszawa 16 B5
Warszawa 16 B5
Warta ➤ 16 B2
Wasatch Ra. 73 F8
Wash, The 11 E7
Washington 77 E7
Washington □ 72 C3
Washington, Mt. 77 B10
Waskaganish 71 D8
Watampone 37 E2
Waterbury 77 D9
Waterford 11 E3
Waterloo 75 D8
Watertown 77 C8
Waterville 77 B11
Watford 11 F6
Watling I. = San Salvador I. 86 B5
Watrous 69 C9
Watsa 57 D5
Watson Lake 68 B7
Wau 55 G4
Waukegan 76 C2
Waukesha 76 C1
Wausau 75 C10
Wauwatosa 76 C2
Waycross 83 D6
Wazirabad 42 C9
Weddell Sea 96 A4
Weifang 35 C6
Weipa 61 C7
Welkom 59 D5
Wellesley Is. 60 D6
Wellington 65 D6
Wellington, I. 95 F1
Wellington Chan. 70 B4
Wels 15 D8
Welshpool 11 E5
Wemindji 71 D6
Wenatchee 72 C3
Wenchow = Wenzhou 35 D7
Wensu 34 B3
Wenzhou 35 D7
Weser ➤ 14 B5
West Bank ■ 46 D3
West Bengal = Paschimbanga □ 40 F7
West Beskids = Západné Beskydy 16 D4
West Falkland 95 G4
West Fjord = Vestfjorden 8 B8
West Palm Beach 83 F7
West Virginia □ 76 E5
Western Australia □ 60 F3
Western Dvina = Daugava ➤ 24 B1
Western Ghats 43 N9
Western Sahara ■ 52 D3
Western Samoa = Samoa ■ 65 L13
Western Sierra Madre = Madre Occidental, Sierra 84 B3
Westerwald 14 C4
Westland Bight 65 E4
Weston-super-Mare 11 F5
Westport Ireland 11 E2
Westport N.Z. 65 D4
Westray 10 B5
Wetar 37 F3
Wetaskiwin 69 C6
Wexford 11 E3
Weyburn 69 D9
Weymouth 11 F5
Wha Ti 68 B8

Whale ➤ 70 D7
Whale Cove 68 B10
Whales, B. of 96 B16
Whangarei 64 A6
Wheeling 76 D5
White = Ark., U.S.A. 81 C8
White = Ind., U.S.A. 76 E2
White Nile = Nîl el Abyad ➤ 55 E5
White Russia = Belarus ■ 24 C2
White Sea = Beloye More 8 B13
Whitehaven 11 D5
Whitehorse 68 B6
Whitney, Mt. 78 B3
Whyalla 62 B2
Wichita 80 A5
Wichita Falls 80 C4
Wick 10 B5
Wicklow Mts. 11 E3
Wien 15 D9
Wiener Neustadt 15 E9
Wiesbaden 14 C5
Wight, I. of 11 F6
Wilhelm, Mt. 61 B8
Wilhelmshaven 14 B5
Wilkes-Barre 77 D8
Willemstad 87 D6
Williams Lake 69 C7
Williamsburg 77 F7
Williamsport 77 D7
Williston 74 A3
Wilmington Del., U.S.A. 77 E8
Wilmington N.C., U.S.A. 83 B9
Winchester 11 F6
Wind River Range 73 E9
Windau = Ventspils 24 B1
Windhoek 58 C3
Windsor 71 D5
Winisk ➤ 71 D5
Winnipeg 69 D10
Winnipeg, L. 69 C10
Winnipegosis L. 69 C9
Winona 75 C8
Winston-Salem 83 A7
Winterthur 13 C8
Winton 61 E7
Wisconsin □ 75 C10
Wisła ➤ 16 A4
Witbank = eMalahleni 59 D5
Wkra ➤ 16 B5
Włocławek 16 B4
Wolfsburg 15 B6
Wolin 16 B2
Wollaston Pen. 68 B8
Wollongong 63 B5
Wolverhampton 11 E5
Wonsan 35 C7
Woodroffe, Mt. 60 F5
Woods, L. of the 69 D10
Woodstock 71 E7
Worcester S. Africa 58 E3
Worcester U.K. 11 E5
Worcester U.S.A. 77 C10
Workington 11 D5
Worms 14 D5
Worthing 11 F6
Wrangel I. = Vrangelya, Ostrov 31 B15
Wrangell 69 C6
Wrangell Mts. 69 B5
Wrath, C. 10 B4
Wrexham 11 E5
Wrigley 68 B7
Wrocław 16 C3
Wu Jiang ➤ 35 D5
Wuhan 35 C6
Wuhsi = Wuxi 35 C7
Wuhu 35 C6
Wulumuchi = Ürümqi 29 E9

Wuppertal 14 C4
Würzburg 14 D5
Wutongqiao 34 D5
Wuwei 34 C5
Wuxi 35 C7
Wuyi Shan 35 D6
Wuzhong 35 C5
Wuzhou 35 D6
Wyndham 60 D4
Wyoming □ 73 E10

X

Xainza 34 C3
Xalapa 84 D5
Xankändi 25 F6
Xi Jiang ➤ 35 D6
Xiaguan 34 D5
Xiamen 35 D6
Xi'an 35 C5
Xiang Jiang ➤ 35 D6
Xiangfan 35 C6
Xianggang = Hong Kong □ 35 D6
Xiangquan He = Sutlej ➤ 42 E7
Xiangtan 35 D6
Xiao Hinggan Ling 35 B7
Xichang 34 D5
Xigazê 34 D3
Xing'an 35 D6
Xingu ➤ 92 C3
Xining 34 C5
Xinjiang Uygur Zizhiqu □ 34 B3
Xinxiang 35 C6
Xinyang 35 C6
Xique-Xique 93 E5
Xisha Qundao = Paracel Is. 34 A4
Xixón = Gijón 18 A3
Xizang Zizhiqu □ 34 C3
Xuanhua 35 B6
Xuzhou 35 C6

Y

Yablonovyy Khrebet 30 D9
Yablonovyy Ra. = Yablonovyy Khrebet 30 D9
Yacuiba 94 A4
Yakima 72 C3
Yakutat 69 C6
Yakutsk 31 C10
Yala 38 C2
Yalong Jiang ➤ 34 D5
Yalta 25 E3
Yam Ha Melah = Dead Sea 47 E3
Yam Kinneret 46 D3
Yamagata 32 D7
Yamaguchi 33 F2
Yamal, Poluostrov 28 B8
Yambol 22 C6
Yamethin 41 G11
Yamoussoukro 53 G4
Yamuna ➤ 40 E3
Yamzho Yumco 34 D4
Yanbu 'al Bahr 47 F4
Yangambi 56 D4
Yangjiang 35 D6
Yangôn 41 J11
Yangquan 35 C6
Yangtse = Chang Jiang ➤ 35 C7
Yangtze Kiang = Chang Jiang ➤ 35 C7
Yanji 35 B7
Yanqi 34 B3
Yantai 35 C7
Yaoundé 56 D2
Yapen 37 E5
Yaqui ➤ 84 B2
Yaraka 61 E7

Yarkand = Shache 34 C2
Yarkhun ➤ 42 A8
Yarlung Zangbo Jiang = Brahmaputra ➤ 41 F7
Yarmouth 71 E7
Yaroslavl 24 B4
Yathkyed L. 68 B10
Yatsushiro 33 G2
Yavari ➤ 90 D4
Yazd 44 D3
Yazoo ➤ 81 C8
Yekaterinburg 29 D7
Yelets 24 C4
Yelizavetgrad = Kirovohrad 25 D3
Yell 10 A6
Yellow = Huang He ➤ 35 C6
Yellow Sea 35 C7
Yellowhead Pass 69 C8
Yellowknife 68 B8
Yellowstone ➤ 74 B3
Yellowstone △ 73 D9
Yemen ■ 49 D4
Yenbo = Yanbu 'al Bahr 47 F4
Yenisey ➤ 28 B9
Yeola 43 J9
Yeovil 11 F5
Yerevan 25 E5
Yerushalayim = Jerusalem 47 E3
Yeu, Î. d' 12 C2
Yevpatoriya 25 D3
Yeysk 25 D4
Yezd = Yazd 44 D3
Yibin 35 D5
Yichang 35 C6
Yichun 35 B7
Yinchuan 35 C5
Yingkou 35 B7
Yining 29 E9
Yishan 35 D5
Yiyang 35 D6
Yogyakarta 39 F4
Yokkaichi 33 F5
Yokohama 33 F6
Yonago 33 F3
Yonkers 77 D9
Yonne ➤ 13 B5
York U.K. 11 E6
York U.S.A. 77 E7
York, C. 61 C7
Yorkton 69 C9
Yosemite △ 78 B3
Yoshkar Ola 24 B6
Youghal 11 F3
Youngstown 76 D5
Yozgat 25 F3
Ysyk-Köl 29 E8
Yu Jiang ➤ 35 D6
Yuan Jiang ➤ 35 D6
Yuba City 72 G3
Yucatán □ 85 C7
Yucatán, Canal de 85 C7
Yucatán, Península de 85 D7
Yuci 35 C6
Yugoslavia = Serbia ■ 22 B3
Yukon ➤ 69 B3
Yukon Territory □ 68 B6
Yuma 78 D5
Yumen 34 C4
Yungas 91 G5
Yunnan □ 34 D5
Yurimaguas 91 E3
Yushu 34 C4
Yuzhno-Sakhalinsk 31 E12
Yvetot 12 B4

Z

Zäb al Kabir ➤ 46 C5
Zäb aş Şaghir ➤ 46 D5

Zäbol □ 45 D6
Zabrze 16 C4
Zacatecas 84 C4
Zadar 20 B5
Zagazig 54 B5
Zagreb 20 B6
Zagros, Kühhä-ye 44 C2
Zagros Mts. = Zagros, Kühhä-ye 44 C2
Zähedän 45 D5
Zahlah 46 D3
Zaïre = Congo ➤ 56 F2
Zakhodnaya Dzvina = Daugava ➤ 24 B1
Zakinthos = Zakynthos 23 F3
Zakynthos 23 F3
Zambeze ➤ 59 B7
Zambezi = Zambeze ➤ 59 B7
Zambia ■ 59 B5
Zamboanga 36 C2
Zamora Mexico 84 D4
Zamora Spain 18 B3
Zamość 17 C6
Zanesville 76 E4
Zanjän 46 C7
Zante = Zakynthos 23 F3
Zanzibar 57 F7
Zaouiet Reggâne 52 C6
Zap Suyu = Zäb al Kabir ➤ 46 C5
Zapadnaya Dvina = Daugava ➤ 24 B1
Západné Beskydy 16 D4
Zaporizhzhya 25 D4
Zaragoza 19 B5
Zaranj 42 D2
Zaria 53 F7
Zarzis 54 B1
Zaskar Mts. 42 C10
Zäwiyat al Bayḍä = Al Bayḍä 54 B3
Zeebrugge 14 C2
Zelenograd 24 B4
Zenica 20 B6
Zhambyl = Taraz 29 E8
Zhangjiakou 35 B6
Zhangye 34 C5
Zhangzhou 35 D6
Zhanjiang 35 D6
Zhanyi 34 D5
Zhaotong 34 D5
Zhayyq ➤ 29 E6
Zhdanov = Mariupol 25 D4
Zhejiang □ 35 D7
Zhengzhou 35 C6
Zhezqazghan 29 E7
Zhigansk 30 C10
Zhitomir = Zhytomyr 17 C9
Zhlobin 17 B10
Zhob 42 D6
Zhongdian 34 D4
Zhumadian 35 C6
Zhytomyr 17 C9
Zibo 35 C6
Zielona Góra 16 C2
Zigong 35 D5
Ziguinchor 53 F2
Zimbabwe ■ 59 B5
Zinder 53 F7
Zion △ 79 B6
Zlatoust 29 D6
Zlín 16 D3
Zonguldak 25 E3
Zrenjanin 22 B3
Zug 13 C8
Zugspitze 14 E6
Zunyi 35 D5
Zürich 13 C8
Zuwärah 54 B1
Zvishavane 59 C6
Zwelitsha 59 E5
Zwickau 15 C7